MUSIC IN TRANSITION

A study of tonal expansion
and atonality, 1900–1920

Jim Samson

J M Dent, London

To my Mother and Father

First published 1977
Reprinted 1979
First paperback edition 1993

Printed and bound in Great Britain by
Butler & Tanner Ltd, Frome and London
for J. M. Dent
The Orion Publishing Group
Orion House, 5 Upper St Martin's Lane
London WC2H 9EA

British Library Cataloguing-in-Publication Data
A catalogue record for this book is available
from The British Library

ISBN: 0 460 86150 6

Preface

My purpose in this study is to examine the radical changes in the language of music which took place during the first two decades of the present century. The central development of these years was the breakdown of traditional tonal functions and the subsequent rejection, by some composers at least, of the principle underlying those functions. This indeed is the main theme of the book. I am sensible of the dangers in attempting to draw tidy conclusions about such a phenomenon; witness the remarkable confusion in existing theoretical literature concerning the meaning of 'tonality' in the first place. My aim is no more ambitious than to untangle some of the threads which run through the complex processes of change involved in declining tonality and early atonality, investigating in particular the interaction of traditional and innovatory features.

The book is emphatically not intended as a comprehensive survey of early twentieth-century music. In selecting a small number of composers for detailed analytical study I was guided less by considerations of quality, which would have been uppermost in such a survey, than by the light these composers shed upon the central development. Each of them—major and minor figures alike—presents a unique and distinctive aspect of declining tonality.

In addition to straightforward quotations I have often found it useful to present harmonic abstracts which attempt to summarize the harmonic content of a work or part of a work. In these abstracts, accidentals apply *only* to the notes which they precede.

I am indebted to Mr Ronald Stevenson, Mr Leslie East and Dr Robert Orledge for information concerning, respectively, Busoni, Van Dieren and Koechlin. I also wish to express my gratitude to Dr Arnold Whittall, whose teaching helped to shape many of my ideas about twentieth-century music, and to the staff and students of Exeter University Music Department for their tolerance and interest.

Jim Samson   Exeter, 1975

Preface to the 1993 edition

This book grew out of postgraduate studies undertaken in the late 1960s and early 1970s, more than twenty years ago. At that time music analysis in Britain was not quite the formal discipline it later became. Even as the book was in preparation, British analysts were beginning to respond to the achievements of North American colleagues by bringing their analytical assessments into a closer relationship with underlying theory. Above all, they followed the Americans in their approach to Schenker, stripping his work of its philosophical content, and transforming it into a neat and efficient method for the analysis of tonal repertories. At the same time the set-theoretic approaches developed by Allen Forte were adopted no less widely in Britain for the analysis of post-tonal music.

Without exception, the composers examined in my book have since been subjected to rigorous analysis of Schenkerian or set-theoretic persuasion, or both. Much has been learnt in the process. Yet I am less embarassed by the comparison than perhaps I should be. In recent years there have been significant realignments within musicology, such that a whole-hearted subscription to certain analytical orthodoxies begins to appear no less limited than the relatively informal approach offered here. By exposing some of the philosophical roots of music analysis, we have enabled it to transcend formalism, to meet once again with history, and to enter a dialogue with critical theory and the cognitive sciences. The result has been a broadening of the nature of analytical enquiry, and a growing reluctance to separate it cleanly (as though it might offer some sort of straightforward, modern, scientific truth) from the metaphysical issues in which it is embedded.

This is not to denigrate those analytical studies of early-twentieth-century music which followed mine—some of an admirably rigorous and detailed kind. Or to argue that my book succeeds where they fail. It goes without saying that if I were to tackle this subject today, I would write a quite different book. I suggest only that scholarly fashion should not be a leading criterion of value in these matters. The least of this book's problems is that its analysis is a product of its time.

J.S.   Exeter, 1993

Acknowledgments

Music examples are reproduced by kind permission of the copyright owners:

Edition M. P. Belaieff (Ex. 22)

Breitkopf and Härtel (London) Ltd on behalf of the copyright owners (Exx. 7–9)

Boosey & Hawkes Music Publishers Ltd (Ex. 14)

Verlag Dreililien (Exx. 23, 25)

Rob. Forberg-P. Jurgenson Musikverlag, Germany (Ex. 13)

Editions Max Eschig (Ex. 61)

Editio Musica Budapest (Ex. 12)

P.W.M. (Cracow) (Ex. 38)

G. Ricordi & Co. (London) Ltd (Ex. 16)

Universal Edition (Alfred A. Kalmus) Ltd (Exx. 24, 26–37, 39, 43–60, 65–72)

Example 15 appears by permission of Universal Edition (London) Ltd (British market) and Boosey & Hawkes (U.S.A. market)

Contents

Part One

Tonality: its Expansion and Reinterpretation

I

The nineteenth-century background

TONAL EXPANSION IN THE NINETEENTH CENTURY

> 'The overwhelming multitude of dissonances cannot be counter-
> balanced any longer by occasional returns to such tonic triads as
> represent a key. It seemed inadequate to force a movement into the
> Procrustean bed of a tonality without supporting it by harmonic
> progressions that pertain to it. This dilemma was my concern, and
> it should have occupied the minds of all my contemporaries also.' [1]

The implication of Schoenberg's final sentence is unmistakable and it
hardly does justice to his contemporaries. He was referring to the composition in 1907–8 of his Second String Quartet, the work which
immediately preceded his development of a consistently 'atonal'
musical language.[2] Clearly Schoenberg's was not the only music to be
straining towards atonality in those early years of the present century.
The period 1907–8 also saw the completion of Strauss's *Elektra*, of
Skryabin's Fifth Piano Sonata and of Busoni's *Elegies* for piano. In
these, and in other works, there were indications that the relaxation of
traditional tonal functions might very soon culminate in their disintegration.

Yet many of Schoenberg's contemporaries, no less 'progressive',
drew quite different conclusions from the decline of traditional tonality.
A lack of sympathy with Austro-German late-Romantic music directed
several French and East European composers to alternative sources of
inspiration—to folk music and pre-nineteenth-century styles—which
could enrich and renovate their musical language while safeguarding its
tonality, though not its adherence to major-minor keys. There were
distinguished precedents. Already in the nineteenth century Russian
composers had developed unorthodox harmonic techniques which

preserve tonality as an organizing principle while modifying significantly the classical tonality of Western European traditions.

The 'expanded' or 'extended' tonality of Schoenberg's early compositions, on the other hand, evolved quite naturally from those traditions and specifically from the long and distinguished line of succession within Austro-German music. With an Hegelian sense of historical continuity he regarded his musical language as part of a collective inheritance whose evolution should follow a specific course, in a gradual acquisition and consolidation of resources. The 'secret programme' of the Second String Quartet, suggested not only by Stefan George's poetry but by the quotation from a Viennese street song *O du Lieber Augustin, alles ist hin*, gives some indication of the acute creative crisis engendered by the tonal suppression of the quartet's final movement. Schoenberg was well aware that any further expansion of tonality could lead only to an unequivocal rejection of the tonal principle.

That principle may be expressed as the requirement that all the events in a musical group (usually a complete work) should be co-ordinated by, and experienced in relation to, a central point of reference.[3] The language of classical tonality, a specific expression of the principle, emerged in popular sixteenth-century homophony before permeating and eventually superseding the modal-polyphonic styles. Although it was given its most complete realization in Viennese Classical music of the late eighteenth and early nineteenth centuries, it remained in a state of constant flux and motion, both geographical and chronological. In its most fully realized form classical tonality may be distinguished by its use of two modes only, each of them transposable to any pitch level, and by its total clarification of the relationships existing between pitches grouped around a single tonic, relationships which are only partially clarified in modal music and in most twentieth-century tonal languages. The central harmonic unit of classical tonality is the major triad, its fundamental tonal-harmonic progression I—V—I.[4] However widely ranging the harmonic movement within this fundamental progression, it takes place against a background of hierarchical relationships between diatonic triads grouped around a tonic triad and between secondary tonal regions grouped around a central tonality. A description of harmonic functions will not of course account for many of the salient characteristics of classical tonality. In most tonal compositions the gravitational leaning of harmonies towards their tonic is further supported by strongly directional, tonally focused melodic and bass motions.[5] There is, moreover, a close relationship between harmonic and rhythmic organization and between tonal and phrase structures, the latter expressed through the cadence.

The expansion of classical tonality in the nineteenth century was a result of several related developments, the most important of which were an increasing emphasis on chromatic elements, extending the range of classical tonal functions, and a decreasing structural dependence on tonal regions which would support the central tonality. The nature of these developments was unsystematic, varying substantially from composer to composer and even within the work of a single composer, so that a 'background' study must be content merely to outline the more important general trends.

During the first half of the nineteenth century diatonicism remained the foundation of musical structure. Chromatic elements, however elaborate, tended to function as expressive or decorative enrichments of fundamentally diatonic progressions or as temporary deviations from such progressions. Even the wealth of chromatic detail in Chopin, much of it closely linked to his exploration of new keyboard textures, has usually been conceived in this way. There are, of course, no firm dividing lines, but already in some works by Chopin chromatic harmony has been developed as a more thoroughgoing *alternative* to diatonic progressions, establishing an equilibrium of chromatic and diatonic material which anticipates procedures in Wagner and other late-Romantic composers. In his Mazurka in F minor, Op. 68, No. 4 (1849), the complementary relationship between the chromatic evasion of tonality and its diatonic affirmation is a basic structural feature. The harmony of the opening five bars is dominated by the chromatic scale, its semitonal part movement giving rise to a chain of chromatically descending seventh chords which have no clear tonal direction after the initial F minor triad (Ex. 1). In bar six, however, the diminished seventh chord functions diatonically, resolving onto the subdominant triad of F minor, and the final three bars are diatonic to the central tonality. The opening chromatic harmonies are therefore non-modulatory, serving to 'extend' the range of harmonic functions within a single F minor region. The term 'extended tonality', applicable here, has been used by Schoenberg to describe music (from Bach to his own early compositions) in which the most remote harmonic relationships and transformations have been incorporated within a single tonal region.[6]

This balanced relationship between chromatic and diatonic material functions on a broader scale in the piece as a whole in that the later

3

Ex. 1

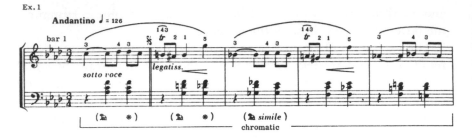

sections in mediant and dominant regions are characterized by the simplest diatonic progressions, complementing the chromatic harmonies of the opening section and of bars 32–9. The F major middle section[7] similarly balances chromatic and diatonic material. It must be emphasized, moreover, that however tonally disruptive the chromatic harmonies of the piece may appear *if removed from their context*, they are experienced in relation to a clearly defined tonal-cadential structure which ensures that the overall tonal direction of the music is clear and convincing.

The opening seventh chords of Chopin's mazurka draw attention to a widespread tendency in nineteenth-century harmony for higher numbered dissonant notes—the seventh, ninth, eleventh and thirteenth —gradually to assume harmonic rather than contrapuntal status. This 'emancipation of the dissonance', to use Schoenberg's phrase,[8] should not of course be confused with increasing chromaticism. It is a law of the evolution of harmony that notes which had originally functioned as dissonant passing-notes or suspensions should eventually discover new contexts as self-sufficient harmonic resources.[9]

In Wagner's *Tristan und Isolde* (completed 1859) the expressive quality of both chromatic and dissonant elements has been immeasurably heightened, largely through an accentuation and prolongation of the 'unessential' notes in the harmony. Yet the structural relationship between chromatic and diatonic material remains similar to that in the

4

Chopin mazurka, albeit on a greatly expanded scale. In the opera this relationship has an added dramatic symbolism, underlining as it does the contrast between 'passion' as a disruptive force and the order and stability of 'civilization'. This is already suggested at the close of the first act when the chromaticism induced by the love potion is challenged by the triadic fanfares glorifying King Mark. It is even more explicit in the second act where the tonally disruptive love duet is pitted against the tonal stability of King Mark's monologue.

Much of the harmony of *Tristan*, if removed from its context, would suggest no firm underlying tonal foundation. Harmonic combinations often result from the melodic leaning of polyphonic strands, semitonally directed, while the enharmonic evasions of orthodox diatonic progressions and the extensive use of the uni-intervallic augmented triad and diminished seventh further threaten tonal stability. As in the Chopin mazurka, however, an underlying tonal-cadential framework supports chromatic and dissonant elements and plays a crucial role in the articulation of the musical and dramatic structure. In the Prelude to the opera, for example, the overall tonal progression is from A minor to C minor, and the music strongly suggests C as a secondary area of harmonic emphasis within the prevailing A minor tonality. The initial A minor progression is immediately followed by a dominant preparation of C major, though this is part of a much larger structural motion which culminates with the cadence at bar 17; there are similar preparations of C towards the end of the prelude. More dramatically, the dominant preparation of A minor at bar 63 shifts abruptly to a dominant preparation of C major (bar 71) before returning to an interrupted cadence in A minor. (As Wagner frequently uses deceptive cadences in the prelude and throughout the opera, tonality is often established through dominant rather than tonic harmony.) These basic structural considerations— the complementary relationship between chromatic and diatonic material and a cadential framework emphasizing regions of A and C— are neatly linked in the prelude by the so-called 'Tristan chord'. This appears initially as a *chromatic* harmony in A minor but at the end as a linear progression *diatonic* to the approaching C minor of the sailor's song.

Although diatonicism has been weakened in *Tristan* by chromatic part-movement, enharmonic exchanges and unexpected discord resolution, the tonal tendencies of the harmony, confirmed at the cadence, are strong enough to withstand the impact of disruptive elements. The work's chromatically shifting textures could only have been taken

5

significantly further, however, at the risk of undermining the structural weight of the cadence and therefore the tonal foundations. Yet it was only at the turn of the century, some forty years after the completion of *Tristan*, that such radical conclusions were drawn from expanding tonality. The intervening period was characterized by a seemingly inexhaustible richness and variety of chromatic harmony in which the influence of Wagner played an important, though by no means an exclusive, role. Wagner's immediate successors in France and Germany continued to explore the widening range of harmonic relationships which could be included within a tonality and they frequently went further than Wagner himself in their contribution to 'the emancipation of the dissonance'. But their music, while readily permitting the most unorthodox harmonic progressions, seldom posed an effective challenge to the tonal cadence as the chief means of articulating a structure.

Tonal stability was more seriously threatened in some of the music of Max Reger, a composer whose harmonic practice owed as much to Brahms as to Wagner.[10] Reger's renovation of the contrapuntal forms and procedures of eighteenth-century music as a means of creating a 'bone-structure' for chromaticism itself owed something to the example of Brahms and it was to have a telling impact on Hindemith and a later generation of German composers. Yet for all his contrapuntal prowess, Reger's originality rested above all in his personal treatment of harmony and specifically of harmonic rhythm.[11] Unlike Wagner and other late-Romantics Reger was not unduly interested in the expressive potentialities of dissonance, prolongations of which often have the effect of slowing down the rate of fundamental harmonic change; indeed his repertory of chords is distinctly modest. His music inclines rather towards a compression of chromatic, but for the most part *triadic* harmonies within a short time-span and a single tonal region. In Ex. 2, an extract from his *Fantasy and Fugue on the name BACH* for organ (1900), Reger has incorporated within a B flat region triads built upon almost every note of the chromatic scale.

Throughout the *Fantasy*, as in many works from Reger's Munich period (1901–7), chromatic harmonies have been emphasized to the extent that diatonic triads are given little opportunity to assert themselves and to affirm the tonality. Moreover the coherence of the *Fantasy* depends as much on its thoroughgoing motivic integration of material as on traditional tonal-harmonic relationships. In such a context the intermittent and fleeting cadential references to a B flat tonic are only just sufficient to establish clearly the underlying tonality. Certainly

Reger remains tonal, but the expansion of tonality has here come dangerously close to its disruption.

The chromatic expansion of tonality was accompanied by a gradual weakening of the centralizing attraction of the tonic in many nineteenth-century compositions. From Beethoven onwards it was by no means uncommon for the opening harmonies of a work to avoid a clear statement of the central tonality; in Chopin's A minor Prelude, for example, explicit reference to the tonic triad is postponed until the final bar of the piece. It is of course perfectly possible to establish a tonality without referring to its tonic triad and the 'foreign opening' usually demonstrates clearly enough its allegiance to a central tonality. But in some late-nineteenth-century pieces, including several songs by Wolf, consistent cadential evasions and unexpected tonal directions do result in tonal ambiguity. In 'Wie soll ich frohlich sein' from the *Italienische Liederbuch*, the music begins and ends outside its central tonality of G minor (Ex. 3), while in the second 'Mignon' setting from the *Goethelieder* the tonality which has been established throughout is

7

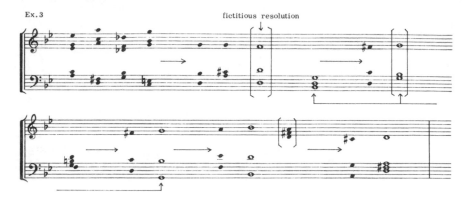

Ex.3

fictitious resolution

abandoned in the final bars in favour of an unexpected, unprepared alternative.

In more extended compositions the weakening of the tonic cannot realistically be separated from fundamental structural considerations. There was an increasing tendency in the nineteenth century for contrasting tonal regions to be chosen for their expressive rather than their structural potentialities, undermining the strength of the central tonality. Moreover, in dramatic or programmatic works—notably in the music-dramas of Wagner—specific tonal regions were often associated with particular characters or ideas, so that programmatic considerations played at least a part in determining the overall tonal scheme of a work. The natural outcome of these developments would be a structure in which coherence depended upon the association of tonal regions with each other rather than with a central region. This concept would require a wider understanding of 'tonality', by which the fundamental, as distinct from the temporary or secondary, tonic would itself change from one musical group to the next. *Tristan* is an important work in this respect in that its 'progressive' tonal scheme—A minor/ B major—is required to support a discourse of symphonic continuity.[12] This distinguishes it from most earlier instances of 'progressive tonality' in dramatic works where the overall structure is usually broken down into successive set numbers, each with an 'enclosed' rather than a 'progressive' tonal scheme.

In sonata-symphonic works the traditional role of the tonic and dominant regions as chief agents of formal articulation and as bearers of the principal thematic material of a work was similarly usurped in the nineteenth century by more remote regions, undermining a central aspect of sonata thinking (very often this widening tonal spectrum continued the classical propensity to alternate and oppose 'dark' and 'bright' tonal regions). This development culminated in the symphonies of Mahler where the tonal argument, often involving as in Wagner a programmatic key symbolism,[13] may be so widely ranging that its ultimate resolution will be in a region remote from the tonal starting place. In the Seventh Symphony, for example, there is an overall tonal 'progression' from the B minor/E minor of the first movement to the C major of the *finale*. The long-range tonal planning of the work is evident not only in major structural points, such as the highlighting of C major and B major at important stages of the thematic process in the first movement (bars 118 and 317), but in details such as the E minor tinge to the opening of the *finale*. It is of course necessary to distinguish in extended works between such 'progressive tonality', in which the fundamental tonic itself changes in the course of the work, and more straightforward 'foreign openings' such as that of Liszt's B minor Sonata.[14] Mahler's 'progressive' tonal structures are not disruptive of tonality in that they depend upon a clear statement of contrasting tonal regions. But, like *Tristan*, they offer a more flexible view of the relationship between tonality and structure than that of the Classical and early Romantic masters, a view which was to have some influence upon the development of twentieth-century tonalities.

SOURCES OF NEW METHODS

If the disruption of tonality was an extension of its nineteenth-century chromatic expansion, the emergence of 'new' constructive methods can similarly be traced to sources in the Romantic era. The nationalist styles of Janáček and Bartók, for example, with their rejection of many of the forms and procedures of Austro-German music in favour of a language moulded from the essential characteristics of authentic folk music, have their origins in the infiltration of Eastern European folkloristic elements into the music of the nineteenth century. Even where this amounted to little more than a colourful dialect of a 'mainstream' musical language it often resulted in prophetic modifications of diatonic harmony. There is, moreover, a distinction of kind between the *expansion* of classical tonality from within and its *modification* from without.

In the music of the Russian nationalist composers the modification of tonality was particularly thoroughgoing. Nor is this surprising in view of the virtual isolation of Russia from the mainstream of European cultural development, an isolation not only from technical achievements within the arts but from fundamental aesthetic changes stemming from the European Renaissance. The remarkable flowering of Russian music in the nineteenth century was characterized by a fascinating dialogue between indigenous traits—often the product of a distinctive folksong heritage—and aspects of Western traditions which were alternately embraced and rejected.[15]

From Glinka onwards Russian composers took a much freer view of harmonic and tonal relationships than their Western contemporaries. They employed unorthodox harmonic progressions and unresolving dissonance for dramatic or colouristic (less often 'expressive') purposes and they explored the Church modes and the whole-tone scale as alternatives to major-minor scales. In the music of Glinka eccentric harmonies such as the whole-tone material associated with Chernomor in *Ruslan and Lyudmila* (1842), or the tritone transpositions of unresolving seventh chords which accompany Naina in the same work, add exotic flavour to a basically Italianate harmonic idiom. His successors went much further. Like Glinka's, Balakirev's innovations were for the most part in the formal and melodic rather than the harmonic sphere, but there are strikingly prophetic harmonic procedures in Borodin, particularly in his songs. The unresolving major seconds of *The Sleeping Princess* have often provoked comment as a possible influence on Debussy, but other songs—*The Queen of the Sea* and *The Song of the Dark Forest*, for example—are hardly less adventurous in their use of colouristic dissonance.

The later music of Rimsky-Korsakov made an equally unique, if relatively minor, contribution to late-Romantic harmony. From *The Snow Maiden* (1880) onwards his music displays intriguing procedural, though seldom stylistic, parallels with Wagner. These extend beyond his fairly consistent use of *leitmotive* and of dramatic key symbolism to include a carefully planned musico-dramatic relationship between chromatic and diatonic material, underlining the relationship between fantasy and reality which was one of the composer's enduring preoccupations. The nature of Rimsky-Korsakov's chromaticism differs substantially from Wagner's, however. Particularly characteristic is his preference for harmonic material whose symmetrical construction avoids the hierarchies of diatonic harmony and the 'pull' of a tonal centre. Often such material is based on the augmented triad or diminished seventh chord, either as basic harmonic components or as the intervallic foundation for extended sequential repetition. In *Sadko* (1898), whose harmonic and orchestral affinities with Debussy are at times explicit, Rimsky-Korsakov went further, employing a symmetrical mode of alternating tones and semitones to depict the under-water scenes—the so-called 'octatonic scale' which was to play a prominent role in Stravinsky's music. His last opera *The Golden Cockerel* is his most consistently 'advanced' stylistically. In the cut of its thematic material, its chromatic symmetries (Ex. 4) and its spicy 'pan-diatonic' harmony[16] it is already close to the sound-world of Stravinsky's early scores.

Ex. 4

It should be remembered that *The Golden Cockerel* was composed as late as 1908, the year of Rimsky-Korsakov's death. The most far-reaching modifications of tonality in nineteenth-century Russia appear in the music of Mussorgsky. Here tonal regions tend to be established through the consistent use of a particular mode or by extended pedal points as much as through orthodox diatonic harmony. More often than not the leading-note, essential to diatonic recognition, has been flattened modally as in the orchestral introduction and opening chorus of *Boris Godunov* (aeolian mode on C sharp and F respectively). Moreover the harmonic language of Mussorgsky's songs and operas, in underlining their dramatic-psychological meanings, often achieves its most telling effects through progressions of 'unrelated' root position triads and abrupt juxtapositions of remote tonal regions. In the Revolution scene, for instance, the F minor of the vagabond monks' song is succeeded without transition by an F sharp minor chorus.

There are original harmonic procedures in the instrumental music too. In the familiar 'Promenade' from *Pictures at an Exhibition* a calculated ambiguity is apparent from the opening four bars, where a harmonic ambivalence between regions of G aeolian and F major is created within the overall B flat tonality. In the succeeding phrase the pentatonic mode of the melody has been retained for its harmonized consequent and the aural impression is of an unchanging harmonic 'area' built on F pentatonic rather than a sequence of tonally directional harmonies. This is entirely typical of the tendency in Mussorgsky's music for conventional harmonies to appear in unconventional contexts. The last inversion of a dominant seventh chord in bar 9, for instance, sheds new light on a familiar harmonic procedure. Although it does resolve to a temporary tonic, the rhythmic structure of the passage emphasizes that the seventh note, G flat, is a *foundation* of the harmony at this point, giving rise to passing resolutions on to supertonic harmony. Typically it moves without transition to an identical seventh chord a major third higher.

The independence of Russian music from Western European procedure was not confined to the tonal-harmonic sphere. Glinka's tone-poem *Kamarinskaya* (1841) was the prototype for many later Russian overtures and symphonic poems in which the motivic development of Austro-German music has been replaced by a constructive method which preserves the identity of the melodic idea (usually folk-inspired) and provides variety by means of changing orchestral and, to a lesser extent, harmonic backgrounds. Balakirev's *Overture on Three Russian Themes* (1859), Rimsky-Korsakov's *Russian Easter Festival Overture* (1877–1878) and Borodin's *In the Steppes of Central Asia* (1880) are three of many later works which make use of this method. It seems probable that similar procedures in Debussy were inspired by his enthusiasm for Russian music, just as the preference of both Debussy and Ravel for two-bar cellular construction may have a Russian ancestry.

The orchestral styles of Russian composers, characterized by textural clarity and a liking for the primary colours of solo woodwind, also differ noticeably from the blended, more homogeneous textures of Austro-German music. Glinka himself was a forerunner here as elsewhere, but the crucial influence was Berlioz, from whom indeed the Russians learnt most of their orchestral technique and a good deal more besides. Clearly any discussion of national styles in orchestration is likely to result in unacceptable generalizations, but in much of the music of Borodin and Rimsky-Korsakov at least, the orchestration is to a marked degree an essential part of the substance of their musical thought, in a manner which anticipates the 'emancipation' of *timbre* in Debussy.

Much of the freshness of nineteenth-century Russian music is due to the originality and vitality of its rhythmic language. We need only return to Mussorgsky's 'Promenade' or to Borodin's *Song of the Dark Forest* to observe the ambiguity of phrase structure and irregularity of metre which characterize much of their music and that of their compatriots; it is no mere coincidence that the greatest renovator of rhythm, Stravinsky, should have been a Russian. In Mussorgsky's vocal music a traditional phrase structure is often undermined by his faithful adherence to the rhythms and inflections of spoken Russian. In the first song 'With Nanny' from his song-cycle *The Nursery* (1868–72), for example, the continuity formerly provided by a background of rhythmic and metric regularity is achieved instead through a realistic reflection of speech continuity, a heightened recitative which mirrors to perfection the pleading intonations of the child. Mussorgsky himself spoke of his desire to 'make my characters speak on the stage exactly as people speak in everyday life; without exaggeration or distortion. And yet to write music which is thoroughly artistic'.[17] His realization of this ideal, inspired in part by the example of Dargomizhsky and influenced strongly by aesthetic precepts which were prevalent in nineteenth-century Russia, had a marked influence on the vocal styles of composers as different in other respects as Janáček and Debussy.

'With Nanny' has been largely freed from a dependence upon the four- or eight-bar phrase and upon the regular rhythmic units—multiples of two or three pulses—which are traditionally its basic components. Within the Western European traditions, where rhythm was to a greater extent required to support harmonic progression, the search for greater flexibility of phrase and rhythmic structure was given less obvious expression. In their different ways, however, Beethoven and Brahms each made important contributions to the rhythmic language of nineteenth-century music. In Beethoven the highest dramatic and structural effects are often achieved through a calculated exploitation of accentual patterns which contradict the underlying metre, creating at times explicit and prolonged metrical conflicts. In his later music, and also incidentally in much of Berlioz's work, more subtle effects are created by means of highly unorthodox relationships between rhythmic stress and harmonic progression. Brahms achieved an even more pliable rhythmic language by absorbing fully into his musical thought many of the rhythmic subtleties which had played a more discreet role in the music of earlier Austro-German masters. By further developing techniques already found in Mozart—irregular phrase lengths, irregular groupings within the phrase and the rhythmic contraction or expansion of motives against a basic metre—he created a plasticity of rhythm, a counterpoint of symmetries and asymmetries, which foreshadow the rhythmic flexibility of Reger and early Schoenberg.[18]

Brahms also played an innovatory role in the changing attitudes towards thematicism which developed during the century. Although there was clearly a wide diversity of procedure, some general trends can be distinguished. As the structural importance of tonality declined, composers tended to place greater emphasis on a closely integrated thematic process as a means of achieving unity in extended works. Traditional distinctions between exposition, development and recapitulation procedures became increasingly blurred in the nineteenth century as unvaried repetition was avoided and developmental processes were adopted at the outset of a work. In Brahms the continuous organic development of thematic material which underlies his sonata designs often results in a close interrelationship between all the thematic elements of a work, involving thematic transformations and subtle motivic connections.[19] A corollary of this development was the tendency for accompaniment voices to have a thematic as well as a harmonic function, a feature which foreshadows the total integration of thematic and harmonic material which is approached in Schoenberg's early compositions and which was later to be formalized by serialism. Writing of Schoenberg's First String Quartet, Op. 7 in 1912, Webern remarked: 'There is, one can say, not a single note in this work that does not have a thematic basis. This is unparalleled. If there is a connection with another composer then that composer is Johannes Brahms.'[20]

Equally significant for the thematic process of late nineteenth- and early twentieth-century music was the renewal of counterpoint as a major constructive force. There are already indications in some of Wagner's music that contrapuntal interplay was beginning to dictate, rather than derive from, the harmonic dimension, though for the most part the latter remains predominant. In the symphonies of Mahler, however, we very often sense a real tension between a strengthening contrapuntal independence and a weakening harmonic foundation. Although the larger movement of Mahler's symphonies depends upon the establishment of clearly defined tonal regions, its detailed working did have a bearing on the tonal crisis. The emotional complexity of his music—its ironical play on different levels of meaning—is reflected technically in the co-existence, often abrupt juxtaposition, of seemingly incompatible stylistic worlds. Very often in Mahler passages of transparently diatonic harmony will give way to highly contrapuntal textures in which the lines have been clearly differentiated by rhythm and colour and can be related only with difficulty to an underlying tonal-harmonic foundation. Indeed the part-movement approaches at times a sort of linear pan-diatonicism in which the most unorthodox dissonance may be justified by contrapuntal integrity. The important consequence of this contrapuntal independence is that the tensions and relaxations which propel the phrase are often achieved by means of dissonance/consonance relationships within a contrapuntal texture rather than through tonal-harmonic progressions which possess independent on-going properties. It is indeed in the linear freedom of Mahler's textures, particularly in the later symphonies, that we find the clearest forerunner of twentieth-century contrapuntal styles.

THE LATER MUSIC OF LISZT

To a remarkable extent the music of Liszt reflected, where it did not actually instigate, the most innovatory features of the Romantic period. His development of a richly expressive chromatic harmony, especially in his songs and symphonic poems, had considerable influence on Wagner during the composition of *Tristan*, an influence which has been well documented. He played a modest part, too, in the modification of tonality through a revival of modality in his sacred and folkloristic compositions and an exploration of whole-tone harmonies in several songs and piano pieces. His interest in the whole-tone scale was partly stimulated by his enthusiasm for Russian music (the Russians in turn learnt much from Liszt) and was partly, no doubt, an extension of his preoccupation with the augmented triad. In the melodrama *Der Traurige Mönch* (1860), whole-tone harmonic colouring has been emphasized to the extent that the final C minor cadence, closing on a first inversion chord, is inconclusive in effect.

Liszt's most successful extended composition, the Piano Sonata in B minor of 1852–3, was also one of his most prophetic. Quite apart from its tonal and harmonic subtleties, the sonata contributed notably to the efforts of the Romantics to achieve greater formal and thematic integration as tonality exerted a diminishing unifying control on musical structure. The technique of thematic transformation, already an important unifying device in Schubert's 'Wanderer' Fantasy of 1822, parallels similar procedures in Wagner (where they have a dramatic function) and complements the intensive motivic integration of material in Brahms.[21] Equally Liszt's fusion of the separate movements of the traditional sonata into a single, expanded sonata-form movement acted as a model for such later works as the First String Quartet and First Chamber Symphony of Schoenberg.

If Liszt's early and middle-period music summarizes many of the progressive trends of the Romantic era,[22] his final works point clearly to the approaching exhaustion of the language of the late-Romantics and of tonality. New paths are already suggested in several of the piano pieces composed during the sixties and seventies—notably in the third book of *Années de Pèlerinages*—and in the austerely beautiful *Via Crucis* of 1878, but it is above all in the short piano pieces written in the eighties that we are made acutely aware of Liszt's dissatisfaction with a traditional means of expression. The harmonic language of these late pieces often rejects traditional diatonic functions, responding freely and boldly to programmatic suggestion of a mystical or valedictory character. In *Schlaflos! Frage und Antwort* there is an unchanging harmonic pedal point which refuses to respond to the changing inflections of the melodic line, resulting in severely dissonant textures. In *Unstern* the harmony is centred on the augmented triad and relies heavily upon parallel chord movement as a basic means of progression. In *Preludio Funebre* constant revolutions of a symmetrically structured mode give rise to slender wisps of harmony based on the augmented triad which is outlined by the mode; the effect is of motionless, suspended harmony entirely without on-going momentum.

The rejection of diatonic harmony in several of these pieces is matched by their lack of tonal definition at the cadence, the pillar on which tonality rests. Liszt's avoidance of a conventional cadential structure is complete. *La Lugubre Gondola 2* ends inconclusively with an unaccompanied melodic line whose whole-tone characteristics weaken any suggestion of tonal attraction; the fourth station of *Via Crucis* comes to rest on the tonally ambiguous augmented triad, the *Bagatelle sans Tonalité* on a diminished seventh chord and *Nuages Gris* on a whole-tone harmony.

As tonality weakened in the later music, Liszt began tentatively to explore alternative methods of organization which at times reach forward to techniques evolved by younger composers during the first two decades of the twentieth century. The driving *ostinato* patterns of *Czárdás Obstiné*, for example, already suggest an affinity with similar devices in Bartók, while the use of semitonal movement as an independent principle of progression anticipates procedures in Busoni. The latter feature can perhaps be clarified through comparison with

Wagner. In *Tristan* the semitonal part-movement takes place against a tonal-triadic background which encourages us to interpret the semitonal step in a tonal way—as an appoggiatura or passing-note. In late Liszt, however, the semitonal step is often removed from this context and becomes in itself a principle of progression. The opening of the eighth station of *Via Crucis* (Ex. 5) is directed semitonally in this way.

Ex. 5
Station IV bar 1

It is also based on 'notes equally related among themselves'—a type of structure which appears in several of the late pieces and which may well have been suggested by Liszt's use of symmetrical passage-work in his earlier piano compositions; here the descending lines employ a constant interval pattern moving at a constant rate of descent. Such symmetrical structures, together with parallel chord movement, foreshadow Busoni and aspects of the mature style of Debussy.

A summary of the harmonic content of *Nuages Gris* (1881) will help to place these techniques within the context of a complete piece. Certainly the most distinctive features of Liszt's later style are present in this short work—the avoidance of a conventional cadential structure, the importance of semitonal movement, the use of the augmented triad as the central harmonic unit and of parallelism as a principal means of progression (Ex. 6).

The rejection of traditional harmonic functions in *Nuages Gris* and in several other late piano pieces strikingly anticipates the crisis in musical *language* in the early years of the twentieth century. Even the most tonally unstable passages in Wagner are composed against a background which retains tonal-harmonic progression to the cadence as the chief means of shaping and directing the phrase. In late Liszt, however, this conception is challenged and coherence, where there is coherence, is achieved by other means. In the early 1880s the only comparable developments were to be found in a handful of works by

Ex.6

Russian composers. In view of his earlier career it is perhaps ironical that Liszt, in his later years, should have felt such a profound disillusionment with the role of Romantic Artist-Hero, a disillusionment which coincided with his growing awareness of the exhaustion of existing resources in his art. It would be unrealistic to claim that the acute problems of progression and continuity posed by his rejection of tonal harmony in some of the late pieces were completely solved by his tentative exploration of alternative constructive methods; it was left for later composers to suggest more positive replacements for traditional tonality. Yet the late pieces remain a testament to the astonishing clarity of Liszt's creative vision in the final years, and to his honesty.

2

The significance of Busoni

Wagner's *Tristan und Isolde* and Mussorgsky's *Boris Godunov* are seminal works in the history of tonality. With the advantage of hindsight we may distinguish two complementary lines of development underlying the profusion of styles which characterized the years of tonal crisis in the early twentieth century, lines of development for which *Tristan* and *Boris* are early but tellingly persuasive advocates. The tonal expansion of *Tristan* formed a crucial stage in an evolutionary development within the Austro-German tradition which was to lead ultimately to the rejection of tonality in the music of Schoenberg, Berg and Webern. The tonal modification of *Boris*, on the other hand, represented a view from outside that tradition and was to culminate in a fundamental reinterpretation of the tonal principle in the music of non-German composers such as Debussy, Bartók and Stravinsky.

The enduring fascination of Busoni in this connection is that he formed a unique point of contact between both lines of development. In a number of short, exploratory works, Busoni developed some of the techniques and recaptured something of the spirit of the later music of Liszt,[1] forging a path to atonality which remained essentially separate from (though it may have been influenced by) that of Schoenberg. Yet far from defining stages in a consistent evolution towards an atonal musical language, these works are an expression of one aspect only of a complex musical personality. They must be viewed in relation to coeval and subsequent works in which Busoni remained faithful to tonality as a basic constructive principle while often rejecting the straitjacket of major-minor keys. His music forms a link between the incipient atonality of the later works of Liszt and the new tonal languages of Debussy, Bartók and Stravinsky. While offering no *single* solution to the tonal dilemma, it reflects in a peculiarly vivid way many of the problems confronting early twentieth-century composers with progressive sympathies as traditional tonality declined.

TOWARDS ATONALITY

With relatively few exceptions, Busoni's works reveal little evidence
of Wagner's influence. As his creative work matured he grew increasingly disenchanted with the stylistic atmosphere of German late-
Romanticism, turning, like Bartók and other non-German composers,
to the invigorating folk and popular music of his native country (he
was Italian by birth) for an alternative source of inspiration. The
second and fourth movements of his massive Piano Concerto (1903–4),
with their riotously unsophisticated rhythms and ingenuous folkloristic melodies, are an early and a particularly unrestrained expression of a preoccupation with the songs and dances of Italy
which can still be discerned in his last and greatest work, the opera
Doktor Faust.

Busoni's search for a modern Italian style went much deeper than
this, however, and it was hindered from the start by an inability to
identify creatively with the music of his Italian contemporaries and
immediate predecessors; he regarded Verdi's *Falstaff* as the only late
nineteenth-century Italian work which did justice to the glorious past of
Rossini and Donizetti. Moreover, unlike Bartók's, Busoni's early
training in the German classical tradition [2] remained rather more than
a means of acquiring *métier*. Throughout his creative life he felt a profound affinity with both Italian and German cultures, symbolized
perhaps by the libretti and indeed the music for his operas *Arlecchino*
(1916) and *Doktor Faust* (1916–24); the one a witty re-creation of the
Italian *Commedia dell' Arte* which is at the same time a biting satire on
war, the other a profoundly serious portrayal of the German folk
legend, rich in philosophical speculation. Busoni believed, moreover,
that he could only successfully revivify a dormant Italian instrumental
tradition by first coming to terms with the great achievements of
German symphonism.

His early works, composed during the 1880s and culminating in the
Konzertstücke, Op. 31a, and First Violin Sonata, both of 1890, are particularly indebted to the work of earlier German masters—Beethoven,
Schumann and, above all, Brahms. Often the debt is explicit as in the
Variations and Fugue in Free Form on Chopin's C minor Prelude (1884) which
has been closely modelled on Brahms's Handel Variations, both in
textural and harmonic patterns. The inspiration of Brahms persisted in
the music of the nineties but from the *Konzertstück* onwards it was
fertilized by a growing interest in Liszt. This was reflected most obviously in the textural configuration of piano compositions such as the

Fourth Ballet Scene, Op. 33a, and the *Piano Pieces*, Op. 33b, both of 1895–6, but Liszt's influence went deeper than this in two major compositions of the late nineties, the Violin Concerto (1896–7) and the Second Violin Sonata (1898). The formal and thematic organization of the sonata in particular reveals a close affinity to Liszt. It is a single-movement work of magnificent breadth whose thematic material, including the Bach chorale melody which forms the basis of a series of variations in the final section, comprises subtle transformations of three basic motives very much in the manner of Liszt's B minor sonata.

Although there are sections of the Second Violin Sonata which foreshadow the later Busoni (e.g. bars 28–35), the work is above all an impressive culmination of his early musical language, in which the influences of Brahms and Liszt are clearly discernible and are to some degree synthesized. Yet already in the *Comedy Overture* of the previous year there were indications that Busoni was turning away from prevailing German Romantic influences. In the Piano Concerto his orientation towards Italy, intimated in the overture, becomes entirely explicit. The fourth movement is significantly entitled 'All' Italia' and its whirling tarantella rhythm and Neapolitan folk-songs defiantly cock a snook at the German tradition. In a letter to Egon Petri Busoni wrote: 'The Latin attitude to art, with its cool serenity and its insistence on outward form is what refreshes me.' [3] In less obvious ways the work marks a break from the Teutonic spirit of earlier compositions, not least in its rejection of sonata-form and its allied developmental techniques. The opening lyrical melody might be compared on a superficial level with several openings in Brahms—the Second Symphony or the Second Piano Concerto, for example—but whereas Brahms's melodies contain within them the germs of later motivic development, Busoni's is a self-contained 'aria', to be decorated by countless piano figurations derived from Liszt, but seldom broken down and developed motivically. Liszt was in fact the main inspiration for the work. He represented for Busoni an all-important stylistic link between German music and an Italian 'bel canto' tradition, a composer in whom 'the melodic genius of the Latin race flowers above the serious mind of the Northerner'.[4]

Liszt was again the major influence in the work which Busoni himself regarded as his first to achieve a fully mature and personal voice, the *Elegies* for piano, composed three years after the concerto in 1907 when the composer was already forty-one. During these years of relative creative silence, Busoni gave much thought to new and far-reaching technical and aesthetic possibilities, giving expression to his speculations in the *Sketch of a New Aesthetic of Music*, written, like the *Elegies*, in 1907. In the *Sketch* he argues that Western music, still a young art, had achieved little compared to the great things which would develop from it in the future. He illustrates the limitless possibilities open to us when we free ourselves from the restricting laws of the past; 'What we call our Tonal System is nothing more than a set of "signs"; an ingenious device to grasp somewhat of the eternal harmony.' [5] Among the technical possibilities discussed are new scalar patterns, microtonal composition and electronic procedures. It has been remarked (by, among others, Busoni's pupil Varèse) that there is an inexplicable lack of correspondence between Busoni the theorist and Busoni the composer; that his music demonstrably failed to realize the ideals so challengingly postulated in the *Sketch*. To hold such a view is to misunderstand the intention of the treatise. The discussion of musical technique was not after all conceived for a composition handbook but as speculative support for an *aesthetic* argument; as such it has proved prophetic. Varèse's view also underestimates the very considerable innovative qualities of Busoni's music, discernible intermittently in early works, but finding their first real expression in the *Elegies*.

Considered as a whole the *Elegies* establish a pattern which was to recur in Busoni's music—the abrupt juxtaposition of seemingly incompatible old and new styles. The second elegy 'All' Italia', for instance, is based on material from the second, third and fourth movements of the Piano Concerto, while the fourth 'Turandots Frauengemach', making use of the popular 'Greensleeves' melody, has been derived from the *Turandot Suite* of 1904. Both these movements, with their lilting rhythms and innocent folkloristic melos, co-exist surprisingly happily with the sombre chromaticism of the third elegy 'Choralvorspiel' which was later to form a prelude to the *Fantasia Contrappuntistica*. They can do so because their rhythmic and melodic simplicity is constantly offset by a harmonic process of some sophistication. In 'Choralvorspiel' the chorale melody 'Meine Seele Bangt und Hofft zu Dir' is presented in a harmonic context of remarkable originality and modernity, though it does owe much to Liszt (in particular the Liszt of *Harmonies Poétiques et Religieuses*). Together with the first, fifth and sixth elegies, the piece foreshadows Busoni's most adventurous harmonic idiom.

Several of the more prophetic harmonic procedures in the elegies have been outlined in Ex. 7 The use of semitonal movement as an organic principle of progression is one of the strongest links with procedures in late Liszt; the semitonal step may function entirely without

Ex.7
(i) No.6 bars 1-5

(ii) No.6 bars 8-10

(iii) No.6 bars 10-13

(iv) No.5 bars 1-6

Rapido, fuggevole e velato

(v) No.3 bars 22-25

reference to a tonal-triadic background or it may serve simply to
obscure such a background through constant major-minor contradictions, resulting in a curiously unstable harmonic atmosphere peculiar to

23

Busoni (Ex. 7i). Also reminiscent of Liszt are those constructions in the *Elegies* based on 'notes equally related among themselves', including parallel chord movement (Ex. 7ii), whole-tone material (Ex. 7iii) and mirror structures (Ex. 7iii). Tonal stability is further undermined through the use of unfamiliar scalar patterns whose oriental-sounding interval structure at times recalls the table of modes suggested in the *Sketch* as an alternative to major-minor scales (Ex. 7iv), and by hints of the polychordal, almost bitonal procedure of Debussy and a younger generation of composers (Ex. 7v).

Although the *Elegies* retain an overall tonal framework (even the tonally evasive sixth elegy has a 'Neapolitan' tonal structure stressing regions of B flat and A), tonality has been considerably weakened by harmonic techniques whose potential as alternative, 'non-tonal' methods of progression and organization is explored without being fully realized. In the *Berceuse Elégiaque* of 1909 and in the remarkable epilogue to *An die Jugend* of the same year, tonal elements play an even less prominent role and the post-Lisztian harmonic techniques explored in the *Elegies* already function to some extent as independent methods of organization. But Busoni's most harmonically 'advanced' works are undoubtedly the Second Sonatina for piano and the orchestral *Nocturne Symphonique*, both composed in 1912 and both closely related technically.

In these works tonality has been weakened by the unrestricted semi-tonal movement of chord members, by symmetrical harmonic structures and by contrapuntally derived textures. Moreover the triad, tonality's closest ally, has been virtually eclipsed as fundamental harmonic unit by linear counterpoint and extreme vertical dissonance. Despite the avoidance of diatonic harmony, however, skeletal tonal schemes can just be discerned, centred on the pitches (not the triads) of C in the sonatina and E flat in the Nocturne. The areas of tonal clarification, in which centres are tentatively suggested by pedal points (Ex. 8), are not an inevitable outcome of the preceding musical argument as in classical tonality, however, but function primarily as a means of reinforcing cadential stability at important structural points.

In the sonatina symmetrical structures are especially prominent, though their technical conception has moved far beyond anything in Liszt to suggest parallels with several of Busoni's contemporaries. The parallel dissonant chords which accompany the main thematic idea of the opening section (Ex. 8, at fig. x) recall similar procedures in Debussy, for example, though their semitonal tensions are rather different in character to Debussy's soft, often dominant-quality dissonances. Sym-

metrical constructions based on the whole-tone scale and on cycles of perfect fourths (two interlocking whole-tone scales and a complete cycle of fourths will each exhaust the total chromatic) are equally common (Ex. 8), suggesting at times an influence from Schoenberg's First Chamber Symphony. Another strongly characterized procedure in the sonatina is the use of an accompaniment pattern based on chromatically ascending parallel major seconds, similar to passages in Debussy's *Jeux*, also of 1912.

In addition to semitonal and symmetrical structures the sonatina, at least in the second of its two principal sections, makes use of strict contrapuntal techniques which have moved beyond the triadically accommodated counterpoint of the *Fantasia Contrappuntistica* (1910) to achieve a strangely disembodied linear style which was to be given its most perfect expression in parts of *Doktor Faust*. Busoni's interest at this time in a freely dissonant contrapuntal practice was to some extent stimulated by the work of the German theorist Bernhard Ziehn (1845–1912). Indeed the quasi-bitonal textures in the *Fantasia Contrappuntistica*, the *Berceuse Elégiaque* and the Second Sonatina are often no more than an extension of 'Gothic' principles of linear counterpoint.[6] In the linking passage between the two main sections of the sonatina, for example, the vertical dissonance is 'explained' by a logical contrapuntal combination of single lines and triadic formations (Ex. 8). Similarly the three principal themes of the work's second section are brought into several different contrapuntal relationships with each other. But whereas the rhythmically vigorous counterpoint of Schoenberg's transitional works (in particular the First Chamber Symphony) serves to generate the on-going momentum which had formerly been achieved by harmonic means, the gently dissonant lines of Busoni's sonatina tend rather to dissipate such momentum, contributing to a sound-picture of seemingly motionless, crystalline atonality. It is a comparison which tells us something of the quite different spiritual worlds inhabited by the two composers, despite technical points of contact, and it will be taken up again in a later chapter.

NEO-TONALITY

In the Second Sonatina and the *Nocturne Symphonique*, Busoni was exploring 'new worlds of sound' comparable to those revealed by Schoenberg in his *Das Buch der hängenden Gärten*. His later music, while it assimilated many of the harmonic acquisitions of both works, never attempted to develop and expand them into a consistently atonal musical language. It is significant that Busoni's most 'progressive' works should have been small-scale structures such as these. The short piece can restrict itself to a relatively narrow range of expression and can explore new methods of organization unhampered by problems of structural planning on an extended scale. Both works are as limited in their range of expression as they are totally unique in character. To extend his expressive range—and Busoni was concerned that music should know no boundaries or limitations—he turned to established styles, filtering them through a highly personal and selective creative sensibility.

Busoni maintained that a performance of Verdi's *Falstaff* in 1894 marked a turning point in his creative development, for it seemed to him an isolated contemporary link with Rossini and Donizetti, and ultimately with Mozart to whom he became increasingly drawn throughout his life. It is in the *Comedy Overture* (1897) that we first hear unmistakable evidence of Mozart's influence on Busoni's music, but in later works—the operas *Turandot* and *Arlecchino*, the *Concertino* for clarinet and *Divertimento* for flute—the relationship between Busoni's music and Mozart's has become more than a simple case of influence, though less than pastiche. This close connection with the music of the past extended, moreover, to other composers and above all to Bach who, like Mozart and Liszt, represented for Busoni a point of contact between German and Italian musical cultures.

In addition to his well-known editions and transcriptions, Busoni paid homage to Bach by basing several of his own compositions on quotations from the earlier composer, including the second piece from *An die Jugend*, the *Two Contrapuntal Studies* and the Fifth Sonatina for piano. By far the most important of his compositions inspired by Bach is the *Fantasia Contrappuntistica* of 1910 which grew out of Busoni's attempt to complete the unfinished fugue from the *Art of Fugue* and which comprises (in its second, so-called 'definitive' version) a Preludio Corale (drawing upon the third of the *Elegies*); Fuga I; Fuga II; Fuga III (BACH); Intermezzo; three variations; Fuga IV; Corale; Stretto.[7]

This close relationship with the music of the past, reflecting a much wider historical consciousness in early twentieth-century art, suggests striking parallels with 'neo-classical' features in compositions such as Strauss's *Ariadne auf Naxos* (1912), Satie's *Sonatine Bureaucratique* (1917) and, of course, the middle-period *œuvre* of Stravinsky. It was in fact Busoni who first used the term 'Young Classicism', defining it in a letter to Paul Bekker: 'By "Young Classicism" I mean the mastery, the sifting and the turning to account of all the gains of previous experiments and their inclusion in strong and beautiful forms.' [8]

In a stimulating discussion of the attitudes of Busoni and Stravinsky to the music of the past,[9] Roman Vlad has drawn a useful distinction between Stravinsky's 'classicism', concerned with external forms and patterns derived from existing classical models, and Busoni's 'classicality', relating to the disposition of the artist, to his attitude towards his creative work. It may be that Vlad's reference to the 'profoundly different' conception of Busoni and Stravinsky overstates the case; that the work of both composers is informed by both 'classicism' and 'classicality' and the distinction is one of emphasis. Certainly Busoni's theoretical writings constantly reiterate his view that the creative artist must subject self-expression and moral idealism to Form, the all-important element in Art. Such a view is close to, and undoubtedly influenced, the artistic creeds of many younger composers working in the years following the First World War.

The distinctly personal character of Busoni's mature music, despite a complex fabric of influences and literal borrowings, is due above all to the transforming effect of those techniques whose purest expression is to be found in the short exploratory works discussed earlier in the chapter.[10] These techniques undermine the surface Mozartian humour of *Arlecchino*, belie the deceptive simplicity of the Indian melodies of *Gesang vom Reigen der Geister* (1915) and interrupt the serenely flowing counterpoint of Bach's *Fantasy and Fugue in D minor*, BWV 905 in the Fifth Sonatina (1919). Often, as in the latter work, there is an almost Stravinskian dialogue between a recognizably 'classical' background and a foreground distortion of that background. In the sonatina the diatonicism of Bach's fugue is disturbed by the chromatic intrusions of Busoni's original material as the following analysis indicates:

1. bars	1–3	Busoni	Introduction (with 'binding-motif')
	4–21	Bach-Busoni	Fantasia
	22–25	Busoni	Introductory material
2.	26–37	Bach-Busoni	Fugue (with new counter-subject and chromatic harmonies)
	38–40	Busoni	Introductory material
3.	41–67	Bach-Busoni	Fugue
	68–73	Busoni	Introductory material
	74–81	Bach-Busoni	Free Coda (Bachian hints), ending with
4.	82–85	Busoni	Introductory material

In the major extended works of Busoni's later years such calculated stylistic tensions—Goldbeck has used the phrase 'counterpoint of styles'—are projected onto a much larger scale. The operas in particular find it possible to accommodate both the diatonic idiom of the Flute *Divertimento* and the chromatically distorted harmonies of *Gesang vom Reigen der Geister*. The end-product is a musical language in which diatonic 'enclaves' find a place in a tonally polarized but for the most part non-diatonic context.

This musical language was given consummate expression in the work which moulds into a unified whole all the diverse elements in Busoni's earlier music, his masterpiece *Doktor Faust* (begun in 1916, the opera was left incomplete at Busoni's death in 1924). The most harmonically adventurous material in the opera consists of direct references to the music of the Second Sonatina, associated mainly with the three mysterious students who give Faust the ability 'to span the whole world, to know the works of all men and past belief enhance them'. As Wagner announces the arrival of the students, theme A2 (Ex. 8) is suggested in the orchestra before being stated in its entirety together with the parallel dissonant chords of the sonatina (Ex. 8, fig. x). The curiously distorted scale passages which precede theme A3 in the sonatina accompany Faust's 'Daydreams! Visions! The Hopes!' and reference is made to both the introductory ascending theme of the sonatina and to its final cadence. The parallel major seconds which accompany theme A2 (bar 15 of the sonatina) appear much later in the opera when Mephistopheles conjures up a vision of Helen of Troy, symbol of 'The unknowable, unattainable'.[11] But by far the most important motive taken from the sonatina is the fragment of theme A2 marked (y) which makes several appearances in the opera, the most dramatic coinciding with the return of the students at the end of the work.

The 'advanced' harmonies of the sonatina form one extreme in the musical language of *Doktor Faust*, representing Faust as seer and visionary. At the other extreme is the music of the Ducal court, the love duet between Faust and the Duchess and the riotous music of the tavern scene 'In Modo di Menuetto Rustico', reminiscent of the second and fourth movements of the Piano Concerto. The opera can accommodate both extremes because its most characteristic musical language finds an inspired midway-point between them. Throughout the work, the chromatically twisting melodies and tonally unstable harmonies are 'earthed' by an underlying tonal structure and by the omnipresent spirit of the dance, expressing perhaps the Latin aspect of Busoni's many-sided creative personality. Dance rhythms, epitomized by the instrumental *Cortège* and Sarabande, infiltrate the music of the entire work; Ex. 9 gives four short extracts which demonstrate the characteristic blend of chromatic textures and simple dance rhythms, respectively a polka, sarabande, waltz and tarantella.

Ex. 9

Despite its tonal foundations, the tonal-triadic background of *Doktor Faust* is distorted by chromatic intrusions to the extent that major-minor harmony no longer functions in the work as a whole, though there are diatonic 'enclaves'. If the Second Sonatina suggests a parallel with

Schoenberg, extending a late nineteenth-century style, albeit of limited expressive range, to the point at which tonal functions have been largely abandoned, *Doktor Faust*, with its replacement of major-minor tonality by a highly personal *tonal* language forged from the diverse harmonic vocabulary of Busoni's earlier music, is comparable rather to the new tonal languages of Debussy, Bartók and Stravinsky.

3

New tonal languages

The expanded tonality of Schoenberg's early compositions proved to be a transitional stage in the progression from classical tonality to atonality. For many of his contemporaries this progression seemed far from inevitable. Busoni's *Doktor Faust* was only one of several major works composed during the first quarter of the century in which major-minor harmony was superseded without any disrespect to the tonal principle. Even more successfully and consistently than Busoni, Debussy evolved a highly personal tonal language in which major-minor elements play a subsidiary role, taking their place beside harmonic phenomena which are disruptive of traditional tonal functions. Stravinsky was later to develop a tonal language which retains the triad as a central harmonic reference point, while radically modifying traditional concepts of harmonic rhythm and progression. It remained for Bartók to demonstrate that a tonal argument need not be dependent upon triadic harmony but can be built around pitch polarities which are established through repetition and emphasis. The most important consequences for later twentieth-century music stemmed from the fact that such major composers did not equate tonality with major-minor keys or for that matter with the triad.

DEBUSSY

The early music of Debussy reflects many of the stylistic enthusiasms of other young French composers working in the later nineteenth century. The melodic idiom of his teacher Massenet, whose music was highly fashionable in the Paris of the 1880s, left unmistakable traces on the early piano pieces and songs of Debussy and on his *Prix de Rome* cantata *L'Enfant Prodigue* (1884), and it was only partially submerged by the wave of Wagner worship which swept across French cultural life at the time. Debussy was already well acquainted with the music of Wagner during his year of study in Rome and he later visited Bayreuth in 1888 and 1889. Perhaps his closest point of stylistic contact with Wagner is in the Tristanesque chromaticism of the first of the *Five Baudelaire Songs* (1887–9); in later works such as *The Blessed Damozel* (notably in its final pages) and *Pelléas et Mélisande*, echoes of *Parsifal* are certainly discernible, but they have been more skilfully assimilated into a musical language which has already acquired a distinctive and personal character. The range of influences present in these early works extends even to César Franck, especially in the *Fantasy* for piano and orchestra (1890) and the *finale* of the Quartet, though Debussy was later to deplore Franck's 'Germanization' of French music.

It was indeed this growing hostility to prevailing German influences in French music which fostered Debussy's growing enthusiasm for developments outside the mainstreams of Western European traditions, in particular for the music of the Russian nationalists and for the world of the 'exotic'. The textural clarity and colourful scoring of Russian composers, and their preference for evocative, programmatic works, seemed to Debussy more attuned to the Gallic temperament than the blended orchestral textures and the philosophical and emotional 'profundity' of Wagner.[1] More specifically the exploration by Russian composers of a thematic process which avoids substantial motivic development, preferring to vary material through simple melodic decoration or constantly changing harmonic and orchestral backgrounds, evoked a sympathetic response from Debussy as did the colouristic dissonance in the songs of Borodin and Mussorgsky. There are especially close affinities between the music of Debussy and Mussorgsky, despite obvious differences in the externals of their musical languages.[2] Mussorgsky's creative deployment of natural Russian speech rhythms in his vocal music and his strikingly original harmonic thought influenced Debussy in his development of the flexible, unassertive rhythms which perfectly match spoken French (the influence of older French masters was perhaps even more crucial here) and of an harmonic language which radically modifies traditional tonal functions.

In his fascination with the exotic—both historical and geographical— Debussy was giving pronounced expression to a characteristic peculiarly associated with French music and one which forms yet another point of contact between French and Russian cultures. 'Exoticisms' in his work range from the stylization of Javanese gamelang sonorities in the second movement of the quartet to the pseudo-antiquity of the *Chansons de Bilitis* and *Danseuses de Delphes*, the orientalism of *Pagodes* and the many evocations of Spain. It is manifest above all in his lifelong preoccupation

34

with the legendary characters of the Italian *Commedia dell' Arte*, from the first set of *Fêtes Galantes* (1892) to the much later Cello Sonata (1915).[3]

Debussy's aesthetic commitments were informed to a marked extent by developments in the other arts; by the Symbolist and Impressionist movements in literature and painting, the writings of Poe and the work of the Pre-Raphaelites. Some commentators have gone so far as to trace parallels of a specific technical nature with such movements; between Debussy's treatment of the individual harmony and the poetic 'symbol', between orchestral and visual pointillism. Undoubtedly such literary and pictorial associations were important for Debussy, but only to the extent that they provided a focus for a personal and self-consistent musical language.[4]

French music had always remained to some extent separate from the most characteristic expressions of classical tonality in the symphonic and operatic literature of Austro-Germany and Italy. Even in the late nineteenth century when German influences were prominent, indigenous French qualities, relating, however remotely, to seventeenth- and eighteenth-century traditions, were by no means entirely submerged. Despite an obvious diversity of procedure, there has been a general tendency for French composers to avoid the strong accents of German music either by means of a metrical and rhythmic flexibility analogous to the spoken language or by evenly flowing figurations whose measured pulses avoid firm accentuation. Often, too, there is a close attention to the individual sound-moment in French music which is expressed through an elaborate and detailed decoration of the melodic idea rather than an intensive motive working, and through a tendency to savour the colouristic qualities of the individual harmony, occasionally at the expense of orthodox harmonic functions.

Despite his temporary seduction by Wagner, Debussy betrayed in his early compositions a fundamental affinity with such indigenous French traits. The use of chromatic substitute chords which stress the flattened seventh, as in the substitute dominant seventh and subdominant chords at the opening of *Beau Soir*, is certainly closer to procedures in Massenet, Fauré or even Bizet than to any German composer, though there are again connections with Russian music. This dissociation of the chord from a traditional diatonic context is taken very much further with the chains of unresolving seventh and ninth chords which appear in the *Ariettes Oubliées* and which are given increasing prominence in the works of the early nineties. Attention has often been drawn to the emphasis on the sound-moment which results from this dissociation. In a limited

35

sense the point has validity, particularly to the extent that Debussy's 'suspended' dissonances retain a close connection with tonal models which have specific expectations—above all in his frequent use of the dominant major ninth.[5] What has less often been demonstrated is the uniquely achieved on-going movement, essentially dynamic, which emerges from the macro-structure of his music. The nature of this on-going movement and of Debussy's reinterpretation of tonality can be grasped only after a close examination of individual harmonic finger-prints in his music.

The evolution of Debussy's tonal thinking during the last decade of the nineteenth century was admittedly a complex process in which remnants of traditional tonal functions blended with, and were only gradually ousted by, new concepts. By the late 1890s, however, his mature harmonic idiom was crystallizing and some of its more charac-teristic aspects may be discussed with reference to an early mature work, the *Trois Chansons de Bilitis* (1897), settings of poetry by Debussy's close friend Pierre Louÿs. The opening of the first song 'La Flûte de Pan' illustrates Debussy's frequent use of the old church modes as an alter-native to and modification of major-minor scales, a practice for which there were ample precedents in nineteenth-century Russia (Ex. 10i).

Ex. 10
(i) 'La Flute de Pan'
(ii) 'La Chevelure'
(iii) 'Le Tombeau des Naiades'

Here Debussy has employed a lydian mode built upon B. Each of the modes has its own triad properties which extend the range of tonality by accommodating such chromatic triads as the sharpened supertonic of Ex. 10i. Indeed the exploration of modal relationships between chromatic root-position triads is a favourite device of Debussy's; the opening bars of the Violin Sonata provide a further instance. As in Mussorgsky, the modally flattened sevenths in much of Debussy weaken tonal concentration and tend to obviate traditional cadential functions; the perfect cadence is used throughout his music with calculated economy. In addition to the familiar church modes, Debussy also made use of arabic, pentatonic and octatonic modes for exotic effects. Like the church modes these extend the range of tonality while at the same time permitting a dialogue with diatonic harmony based on their common properties with major-minor scales.

A much more radical alternative to major-minor scales in Debussy's music is the whole-tone scale. Whole-tone constructions were already implicit in a number of fairly orthodox Romantic harmonic procedures, most notably progressions involving the augmented triad or 'French sixth' chord, while passages of whole-tone harmony occur for illustrative effects in Russian music and in Liszt. It was in the early twentieth century, however, that composers began to exploit in a thorough way the unique properties of the scale—its uni-intervallic construction and limited transpositional potential— as a means of temporarily suspending their music's commitment to tonality. The whole-tone scale can also serve to create deliberate tonal ambiguities in that it embraces the dominant-quality 7/3 unit which may be emphasized by the omission of certain notes or by a particular chordal layout. In Ex. 10ii the whole-tone harmony acts as a bridge between a tonally ambiguous 'French sixth' harmony and the tonally evocative dominant ninth of bar 12.

Much of Debussy's music cannot of course be classified within a modal or whole-tone system. It has been remarked that even in early works he frequently neglected totally the traditional tonal obligations of the chord, whether a plain triad or dissonant combination, treating it as a vertical 'colour' chosen for its empirical sound quality. In doing so he modified the function of the chord in relation both to its immediate and its overall harmonic context. In tackling the resulting problems of progression Debussy often turned, as Liszt had done in his later works, to symmetry and, more specifically, parallelism (Ex. 10iii). Indeed parallelism, exact or inexact, is an integral feature of his harmonic language (as a so-called 'Impressionist' fingerprint it was one of the techniques worked to excess by lesser imitators of Debussy), and it is one which radically alters traditional tonal relationships, rejecting local tonal hierarchies and sacrificing the independence and polarity of melodic and bass voices.

An examination of these harmonic techniques out of their context has all too often led to misleading terminology such as 'static' or 'non-functional' as a description of Debussy's harmonic methods. Viewed as a whole, however, the tonal coherence of his music depends upon a carefully calculated and often dramatic interaction of these various harmonic 'types' with each other and with orthodox diatonic harmony. The result is a *tonal* language, but one which is fundamentally different in concept from classical tonality. The detailed classification of harmonic events is no longer possible in Debussy's music where the central tonality of a work emerges only through a constant focusing and re-focusing on harmonic types.

The process can be examined in particularly clear form in the extended piano piece *L'Isle Joyeuse* (1904). The central relationship in the work is that between material based on the whole-tone scale, the lydian mode and the diatonic scale, the lydian mode functioning as an effective mediator between the other two (Ex. 11i). The subtle interaction of these materials can be demonstrated in the microstructure of the piece with reference to bars 15–21, where the gradual intrusion of a G natural into the A lydian context of the preceding material effects a smooth transition into the whole-tone material of the new motive at bar 21. On a broader scale the tonal progression of the exposition section of the work is from the whole-tone material of the introduction by way of the lydian mode on A to the A major of the 'second subject' at bar 67, though it is as yet an A major inflected with occasional lydian D sharps. In the recapitulation section, however, the 'second subject' has been significantly modified to eliminate lydian inflections, revealing an unclouded A major as the ultimate tonal goal of the piece. (The eventual arrival at D minor, by way of various modal types, in 'Des pas sur la neige' from the *Préludes* is directly analogous.) In the middle section of *L'Isle Joyeuse* further harmonic contrast is provided by the alternative transposition of the whole-tone scale which is excluded from the outer sections. There is, moreover, some indication that Debussy has deliberately chosen to emphasize through points of triadic clarification tonal regions associated with the two whole-tone scales, as Ex. 11ii, a tonal-harmonic summary of the work, suggests.[6]

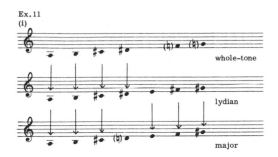

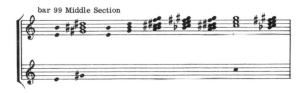

L'Isle Joyeuse presents in a particularly systematic manner the sort of interaction of harmonic types which is characteristic of Debussy's mature music, and the unambiguously tonal outcome of that interaction. It would be misleading to suggest that harmonic types are always so clearly defined in his music. Yet even in 'Gigues' from the orchestral *Images* (1912), one of his most harmonically complex works, areas of whole-tone and modal material have an important structural function and points of triadic clarification relieve the predominantly dissonant textures. These textures are stabilized, moreover, by the extended pedal points which form an independent harmonic resource in Debussy's music (as in Mussorgsky's) and by tonally centred melodic lines which often remain to some extent independent of their harmonic support, resulting in quasi-bitonal effects.[7]

In 'Voiles' from the *Préludes* (1910) the integrity of the harmonic types is much more clearly affirmed, but the outcome of their interaction is not so firmly tonal as either *L'Isle Joyeuse* or *Gigues*. Here the consistent use of a single transposition of the whole-tone scale in the outer sections of the piece's simple ternary structure does result in a suppression of both tonality and the triad. But the B flat pedal which persists throughout the piece helps to give the opening section a remote whole-tone dominant quality which finds a delayed resolution in the E flat minor of the pentatonic middle section. Part of the effectiveness of this contrasting section is due to the absence of E flat from the opening whole-tone passage, another instance of 'dramatic interaction'. Even in the middle section, however, the E flat minor tonality is discreetly veiled; cadential feeling is weakened by the anhemitonic character of the cadence and by the failure of the pedal to resolve. The final section returns to the whole-tone scale and the closing bars make no attempt to re-establish contact with an E flat tonic.

The differentiation and interaction of harmonic types—an essential part of Debussy's view of tonality—is also an integral aspect of his original attitude to musical discourse and form. Although he did not entirely eschew 'classical' methods of thematic and motivic development (they are prominent in *La Mer*), Debussy did suggest in some works a fundamentally different and prophetic approach to musical form in which the on-going movement of the music is generated by the gentle collision of differentiated materials. Contrasting harmonic types are an important element in the constitution of these materials, but often their characterization depends as much on non-pitched aspects of sound. The rejection of classical tonality made possible, indeed required, a rethinking of other parameters of music—rhythmic stress and articulation, texture and *timbre*—and these assumed in Debussy's music an unprecedented responsibility for the shaping and characterization of the musical idea.

In works such as 'Par les rues et par les chemins' from the *Images*, several of the late *Etudes* for piano and the ballet *Jeux* (1912), we find the seeds of a formal concept which was to come to fruition in the music of younger non-German composers such as Stravinsky and Messiaen. The abrupt juxtaposition of unchanging harmonic 'areas' in 'Par les rues' is already close in its detailed conception to procedures in Stravinsky. But it is in the *Etudes* and in *Jeux* (particularly in the section from fig. 27 to fig. 35) that the 'intercutting' of strongly characterized groups, each preserving its own identity and creating its own 'continuity', is given its clearest expression.

BARTÓK AND STRAVINSKY

It is at least arguable that Debussy has exerted a greater influence upon the course of twentieth-century music than any other single composer. That influence has operated in three principal spheres. The *sonority* of his music—its textural and orchestrational characteristics, together with certain harmonic fingerprints—had an impact on early twentieth-century composers which is strictly comparable to that of *Le Marteau sans Maître* on the music of the 1950s. Composers as different stylistically as Puccini, Vaughan Williams and Szymanowski each succumbed at one time or another to the allurements of 'Impressionist' harmony and orchestral style. On a rather different level of influence Debussy's emancipation of 'non-essential' parameters of sound and his unique concept of musical discourse and form has proved of considerable importance for many composers working since the Second World War, and not only in Europe. But of most immediate relevance to the present study, Debussy's rejection of traditional tonality and his development of an individual harmonic language which reinterprets the tonal principle had a crucial influence on the emerging tonal languages of Bartók and Stravinsky, an influence which both composers have acknowledged.[8]

Bartók's stylistic sympathies with German late-Romantic composers persisted long after his years of study in the German tradition at the Budapest conservatory. His earliest compositions betray their indebtedness to several of the stylistic influences present within that tradition at the turn of the century, from Wagner and Richard Strauss in the symphonic poem *Kossuth* (1903) to Brahms in the Piano Quintet (1904–5), its finale surely modelled on that of Brahms's Second Piano Concerto, and Liszt's 'Hungarian' manner in the *Rhapsody*, Op. 1, and *Scherzo*, Op. 2. German Romantic influences are still discernible, moreover, in the First Violin Concerto of 1908 and the First String Quartet of the following year; they were finally exorcised only in the expressionistic heat of the opera *Bluebeard's Castle* (1911).

Two factors helped to liberate Bartók's music from such influences: his encounter with Magyar folk music (distinct from the gypsy music which had inspired Brahms, Liszt and nineteenth-century Hungarian composers) in 1905, and his discovery of new harmonic possibilities in the music of Debussy with which he became familiar in 1907. His response to Debussy was immediate and is reflected particularly clearly in the short piano pieces written in 1908, the *Ten Easy Pieces* and the *Fourteen Bagatelles*, Op. 6, several of which Bartók himself described as 'experimental' pieces.

Several of the harmonic procedures in the bagatelles are indeed remarkable for 1908, and a number have been summarized in Ex. 12.

One obvious affinity with Debussy is the use of parallel dissonant chord colours in the outer sections of the eighth bagatelle (Ex. 12i), though the character of the dissonances in Bartók's piece is entirely different from anything in Debussy. The dissociation of the chord from a diatonic context is expressed particularly clearly in the progression marked (x) (Ex. 12i), where a V-I progression has been telescoped into a single dissonant chord which then 'resolves' onto another dissonance by means of traditional part-movement. The middle section of the bagatelle is characterized by a less severely dissonant harmonic language, but its final section returns to the parallel dissonances of the opening, combining at the semitone single pitches, minor sixths and tritones.

Ex. 12
(i) No. 8

(ii) No. 2

(iii) No. 11

(iv) No. 1

42

Ex. 12i indicates the presence of a remote tonal-triadic background centred on G minor but it is given little opportunity to assert itself firmly.

The unresolving major second pedal of the second bagatelle (Ex. 12ii) again recalls Debussy who employed the same interval 'colour' in several works—sections of *Masques*, for example, or the 'Serenade of the Doll' from *Children's Corner*—though Bartók characteristically transforms the influence by means of a rhythmic impetus which is missing in Debussy. Bartók's major second forms an accompaniment to a symmetrical melodic structure similar to those examined in Busoni (Ex. 7iii), its lack of tonal definition emphasized by its later transposition at the tritone interval. As in the eighth bagatelle Bartók relieves the dissonant tension of the opening section with a more traditionally conceived middle section before returning to the opening material. The final cadence of the piece demonstrates that already in the bagatelles, Bartók's attitude to the triad is more radical than Debussy's, for the tonal centre is the pitch D flat rather than the triad on D flat, while the quasi-dominant A flat/B flat pedal is retained until the end (cf. the eighth bagatelle where a triadic resolution on G minor is implied).

In the eleventh bagatelle any traces of tonal thinking which remain are subsidiary to the piece's close intervallic integration of material using the intervals of the perfect and augmented fourth (Ex. 12iii). Debussy's removal of the chord from a traditional tonal context undoubtedly proved a major stimulus for Bartók and other early twentieth-century composers in their experiments with new ways of building chords. In the outer sections of the eleventh bagatelle chords built of fourths are employed in parallel movement and as cadential points of relative repose, though the middle section typically introduces harmony based on the more traditional major and minor thirds. Certainly the harmonic language of this and other bagatelles in the set is far in advance of anything in the music of Bartók's contemporaries at the time,[9] but we should remember that in the same year he composed the much more traditionally conceived and firmly tonal First Violin Concerto. The informed listener in 1908 would have found it difficult indeed to predict the future stylistic direction of Bartók's music.

Stravinsky's earliest music had of course quite different stylistic roots to that of Bartók. Echoes of Tchaikovsky and Mussorgsky are obvious enough in the early pieces—the Piano Sonata, the E flat Symphony and *The Faun and the Shepherdess*—though they occasionally brush shoulders with colouristic and harmonic devices borrowed from French composers

43

from Chabrier to Debussy. But in the *Scherzo Fantasque* and the orchestral fantasy *Fireworks*, Op. 4, both composed in 1907–8, such influences are subsidiary to an orchestral glitter and harmonic pungency clearly inspired by Stravinsky's teacher Rimsky-Korsakov and evidenced again in the early sketches for *Le Rossignol*. The Korsakovian 'fantasy' of these works and of the first Diaghilev ballet *The Firebird* (1910) is expressed in technical details which are often precisely modelled on the older composer—the use of chromatic symmetries, pan-diatonic harmony and the octatonic scale; indeed many features which are often attributed to French influence have a directly Russian origin. Tonality, of course, remains secure, though it is a tonality highly spiced with chromatic and pan-diatonic elements.

Pan-diatonic harmony is even more prominent in the second of Stravinsky's ballets for Diaghilev, *Petrouchka* (1911), and above all in the popular 'Dance Russe' where all the diatonic tones of C major are presented in unorthodox harmonic combinations. A much-discussed chromatic effect in the same work is the superimposition of phrases built on the triads of C major and F sharp major, a device which, had it been extended, could have led to bitonal harmonic effects. No less prophetic of Stravinsky's later music are the hints of multi-layered textures which are a direct result of the programmatic element in the work, depicting simultaneously the diverse activities of the fairground. But more significant perhaps than such technical features is the general aesthetic atmosphere of *Petrouchka*. Its inclusion of popular carnival material and its pointed rejection of a nineteenth-century attitude to tragedy mark an important departure from the 'Romantic' character of Stravinsky's earlier work.

There is little in these early compositions which could have prepared Stravinsky's contemporaries for his next work, the cantata *Le Roi des Étoiles* (1911), dedicated, significantly, to Debussy. In the highly dissonant context of this extraordinary work there is little of the relaxation afforded by the middle sections of Bartók's bagatelles. There is admittedly some lessening of tension when the complex dissonance of structures Aii and iii gives way to the relatively simple textures of Aiv, and when the towering chords of B are answered by an elusive, Debussyan final section C which admits for the first time some rhythmic variety. But Stravinsky avoids throughout the simple consonance of major-minor triads, presenting as the most stable harmonic unit in the piece the telescoped major and minor triads of a single tonality (Ex. 13). Moreover, apart from the final section, the rhythms are static and

uniform throughout, affording little relief from the quiet tension generated by a consistently dissonant harmonic idiom.

The evenly paced wind chords of B (based on the opening 'motto' idea) are particularly interesting in this connection in that they invite comparison with similar passages in later Stravinsky, notably with the coda to the *Symphonies of Wind Instruments* (1920). Here measured dissonant chords of similar character occur but they now serve as a relaxation from the harmonic and rhythmic tension which had been generated in preceding sections. In the intervening period Stravinsky had discovered the potential of rhythm as a major constructive element, capable of providing the on-going energy, the 'drive' to the cadence, which had formerly been the responsibility of harmony.

The construction of these wind chords extends the concept which was implicit in the superimposed triadic phrases in *Petrouchka*, harmonizing the three-note 'motto' with a chain of superimposed 'unrelated' triads, each to some extent retaining an independent identity by remaining in close position (Ex. 13). These 'polychords' point to two related techniques which should be examined, the development of multi-layered textures and the separation of two or more keys usually referred to as bi- or poly-tonality.

The development of ideas on several strata simultaneously is suggested tentatively by the section marked Aii (Ex. 13), where the musical planes have been differentiated by spacing, harmony and rhythm, though such textures were to be adopted in a more thorough-going manner in *The Rite of Spring* and the *Symphonies of Wind Instruments*. Multi-layered textures of this kind are clearly only possible when the notion of root harmonic progression has been abandoned. They are intimately associated in Stravinsky's music with an attitude to form and progression which rejects evolutionary procedures in favour of a juxtaposition and superimposition of sharply differentiated and strongly characterized materials in a manner which is often analogous to cinematic 'intercutting' techniques.[10] This formal concept, central to Stravinsky's work from every period of his creative life, had a precedent, as we have noted, in some aspects of Debussy's work and it was to play an important role in the music of younger composers such as Elliott Carter and Michael Tippett.

The hints of bitonality in *Petrouchka* and *Le Roi des Étoiles* appeared several years after Bartók's much more systematic experiment in bimodal procedure in the first of his *Bagatelles*, Op. 6 (Ex. 12iv). Here a melody in C sharp aeolian is accompanied by an *ostinato* descending phrase in C phrygian. Although both modes are employed consistently to the final cadence, the effect of bimodality is blurred by Bartók's exploitation of their common notes to form a stable figure (x) on C. Consistent bitonality is a severe limitation, and even when carefully controlled so that the tonal 'split' is always audible, it is more suitable for short pieces than as the basis for an extended structure. The first of Stravinsky's *Three Pieces for String Quartet* effectively separates centres of G and F sharp by restricting each to four notes, avoiding common pitches (Virgil Thomson calls these 'leaks') and employing a minor ninth 'dominants' drone to emphasize the duality. Despite attempts by Milhaud and others to apply bitonal procedures to large-scale forms, they have most often and most effectively been used as a means of heightening contrapuntal differentiation or of temporarily suspending the music's commitment to a single key.[11] One technical feature which the Bartók bagatelle and the Stravinsky piece share with many 'bitonal' works is the use of *ostinato* accompaniment patterns. These are a useful way of establishing or asserting a tonal region when it no longer emerges naturally from the harmonic syntax of the music as in classical tonality.

A further characteristic of Stravinsky's harmonic language in *Le Roi des Étoiles* and one which was to prove particularly important in his neo-classical music is the distortion of orthodox triadic harmonies by means of 'tonal interferences'.[12] Unlike that of Debussy and Bartók, Stravinsky's chromaticism is often substitute-triadic in character, suggesting a triadic background which is subject to foreground distortion. Section Aiv of *Le Roi des Étoiles* is interesting from this point of view, though the technique is already present in the opening three chords of the work, the second of which might be regarded as a 'distorted' diminished seventh chord on B flat.

In these early, exploratory works the attitudes of Bartók and Stravinsky towards tonality were already more radical than that of Debussy. In several of the Bartók bagatelles tonality has been almost completely suppressed, while the C major-minor of Stravinsky's cantata, like the C of Busoni's Second Sonatina, acts as a cadential point of reference rather than an inevitable outcome of the foregoing harmonic argument. For both composers it was the discovery of unexplored potential in their native folk cultures which prevented them from taking the short step into a consistently atonal language. While their music was based on, or inspired by, folkloristic materials a *tonal* language, albeit not of an orthodox kind, remained the most appropriate means of expression. Yet it was some time before Bartók succeeded in integrating folkloristic

47

elements with his 'advanced' harmonic vocabulary. Although the experimental harmonies of the *Fourteen Bagatelles* were developed concurrently with his early researches into Magyar folk music, they were not a direct outcome of those researches; both lines of development only came together satisfactorily in later works such as the Second String Quartet of 1917. The fourth and fifth of the bagatelles do, however, represent an interesting transitional stage in the process. The fourth bagatelle, for example, is a folksong transcription which begins by accepting the aeolian character of the melody before setting it in a 'modern' context of parallel dissonant chords.

Stravinsky's discovery of new possibilities inherent in Russian folklore came, like Bartók's, at the very time when he seemed to be drawing close to atonality in *Le Roi des Étoiles* and *The Rite of Spring*. The initial impulse towards folklore was his discovery of the free accentual properties of Russian popular verse when it is sung, a discovery which was perfectly attuned to his growing preoccupation with rhythmic asymmetries. The outcome of this new enthusiasm was a technique of continuously oscillating motivic fragments, folk-inspired and above all *tonally centred*, whose principal means of propulsion is through rhythmically displaced *ostinati* of the kind developed in *The Rite*. After a number of shorter vocal works this technique culminated in the masterpiece of Stravinsky's 'Russian' period, *Les Noces*. Completed in preliminary sketch in 1917, *Les Noces* represents, together with Bartók's Second String Quartet of the same year, a perfect translation of a nationalist aesthetic into a firmly tonal language which combines the 'primitivism' of folkloristic material with an uncompromisingly 'advanced' harmonic idiom.

Stravinsky turned away from an overtly nationalist style shortly after his voluntary exile from Russia following the revolution. Already in *The Soldier's Tale* (1918) there are intimations of the stylistic parody (the word is used in its original, non-pejorative sense) which was to form an essential characteristic of his so-called 'neo-classical' period. But it was the ballet *Pulcinella* (1919–20) which decisively opened this new phase in Stravinsky's development, during which he made use of the external characteristics of established styles to create a new and personal tonal language. His music from this period (1920–50) is characterized by a creative tension between a recognizably traditional tonal-triadic background and his own modification or distortion of that background, often by means of 'tonal interferences' similar to those in *Le Roi des Étoiles*. To a large extent Stravinsky's aesthetic commitment during his neo-classical period reflected a much wider movement in the arts, some of whose most characteristic expressions in music have been noted in the work of Busoni.

Important features of Stravinsky's tonal language in the music from this period may be examined in the opening movement 'Hymne' from one of his earliest neo-classical works, the *Serenade in A* (1923). The melodic contours, phrase structure and textural patterns of the movement are recognizably 'classical' in outlines though they are subject to distortions similar to those found in the work's harmonic language. Typical of the tonal-harmonic tensions which are generated in the music is that between A phrygian and F major in the first nineteen bars of the movement (Ex. 14i). F major is strongly suggested by characteristic melodic formations and by the prominence of its tonic triad, but the spacing and doubled thirds of the F major triads emphasize the pitch A. The tension is heightened at cadence points such as (x) where the leading note in F major, expected to rise to its tonic, behaves instead as the fifth of A minor; the phrase cadences on an A minor triad while an F major triad is outlined melodically in the bass. Apart from some

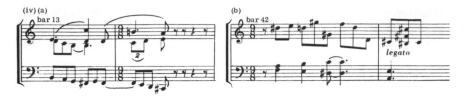

sharpened supertonic and sharpened sub-mediant interferences, these nineteen bars are completely 'diatonic' to A phrygian/F major, paralleling a later extended section (bars 52–62) which is diatonic to E phrygian/C major. Characteristic of these passages is the unrestricted combination of all the diatonic notes of the tonality, a concept which was already present in *Petrouchka* and which is common in the neo-classical works. Such pan-diatonic textures may of course lead to various distortions of traditional tonal functions, in particular the use of simultaneities in which polarized harmonic elements such as tonic and dominant triads are presented together, neutralizing their traditional tonal attractions.

The extended pan-diatonic sections in the 'Hymne' will be heard in relation to the chromatic elements which surround them and are brought into conflict with them (Ex. 14ii). Often these take the form of distortions of triadic harmony through tonal interferences employed consistently within an unchanging harmonic area, as with the A sharps, B sharps and E sharps in the A major context of bars 44–7 (Ex. 14iii). In a movement which depends for its coherence upon an interplay of diatonic and chromatic material the cadence is clearly of paramount importance. Stravinsky's attitude to the cadence, in this as in other middle-period works, underlines the essential nature of his neo-classical tonal language (Ex. 14iv). It is still the chief means of structural articulation and tonal affirmation and it still employs recognizably traditional cadential features but these are almost invariably disguised or distorted by means of unorthodox spacings and doublings, or through tonal interferences.[13]

Unlike Stravinsky, Bartók remained a 'nationalist' throughout his life and his musical language, while developing in the direction of more and more concentration of thought involving a closely organized process of motivic evolution and extensive use of elaborate contrapuntal procedure, remained tonal if not triadic. It has been observed that in the *Fourteen Bagatelles* Bartók was already seriously undermining the importance of the triad and this development continued in the severely linear style of his middle-period music. Here tonal centres are established as pitches rather than triads but, much more than in Busoni's Second Sonatina, the tonal argument is a dramatic and integral aspect of the structure and is closely related to the melodic and harmonic language of the work as a whole. The nature of this rethinking of tonality in a non-triadic context will be examined in some detail through close analysis of one of Bartók's more 'difficult' middle-period works, the Second Violin Sonata, composed in 1922, one year earlier than Stravinsky's *Serenade*.

Like the other chamber works of the 1920s, the Second Violin Sonata consistently avoids the major/minor triad (apart from the final cadence), exploring a range of alternative harmonic types characterized by their emphasis on a particular interval or intervals. Interval identity, expressed through the chord rather than the motive (cf. the third and fourth string quartets) is clearly an important source of integration in the sonata. Bartók's concern for interval identity interacts constantly, however, with his concern for pitch identity, as established by the repetition of, and rhythmic emphasis on, specific pitches and by the recapitulation of material at its original pitch. It is this interaction which defines the role of the pitch centre in relation to its immediate and overall context and which gives rise to the tonality of the work.

A close inspection of the opening pages of the sonata reveals the nature and subtlety of the process. In the first section (bars 1–19) there is a concentrated harmonic emphasis on the perfect and augmented fourth intervals, giving a distinctive and homogeneous harmonic colour to the section itself while presenting at the outset one of the principal elements in the intervallic organization of the work as a whole. Ex. 15i is a 'skeleton' outline of the opening harmonies, indicating how the disposition of these fourths serves to emphasize the pitches F and F sharp, themselves related by a perfect and augmented fourth to the work's tonal destination C. The closing bars neatly summarize the argument—intervallic and tonal—by superimposing perfect and augmented fourths while recalling the opening pitch structure with its alternation of F and F sharp in the bass (Ex. 15i). Throughout this opening section the violin establishes characteristic melodic formations which avoid the fourth interval, the most prominent being the initial thematic idea (x) whose grouping of whole-tone steps and semitone acts as a source for later thematic material. The tension between these melodic formations and their harmonic support is achieved here, and throughout the work, by means of frequent semitonal contradictions. In addition to its thematic functions the violin gives particular prominence to the pitch E; it opens and closes the section and is further emphasized throughout the first movement and at the work's final cadence.

The section immediately following Ex. 15i establishes a second, contrasting harmonic type which superimposes major and minor thirds in groupings which give rise to semitonal tensions. The cadence preceding fig. 7 affirms this harmonic type and marks a significant stage in the evolution of the tonal argument in that its superimposed thirds are built upon the pitches F and F sharp, while the violin returns to its opening pitch E (Ex. 15ii). Here, as elsewhere in the sonata, the cadence —the point of *tonal* clarification—is a natural outcome of the preceding *intervallic* argument.

The overall tonal structure of the work emerges from constant emphasis on these and other harmonic types in relation to specific pitch areas. A third harmonic type is explored in the section beginning at fig. 12 where the parallel major seconds of the violin result in semitonal contradictions with the piano. At fig. 15 the harmony reverts to thirds and the section culminates dramatically in a cadence which draws together several strands in the argument. It is a strongly dissonant harmonic structure in which the crucial importance of the semitone as a harmonic determinant is underlined. Ex. 15iii, a summary of the progression, indicates how the augmented fourths in the piano part have been superimposed on adjacent semitones (emphasizing C and F sharp in the bass), while the violin splits each tritone into minor thirds. The resolution of this dissonance relates closely to the second harmonic type of Ex. 15ii, with minor thirds superimposed at the semitone.[14]

Ex. 15

The final section of the movement represents an important clarification of the overall tonal direction of the music. In the 'dominant' statement of theme (x) which follows Ex. 15iii the perfect fourths of the original accompaniment have been inverted to form stable open fifths built on F sharp and C sharp, though the violin characteristically undermines the tonal stability with increasingly frenzied semitonal contradictions (Ex. 15iv). There is a final reference to (x) at its original pitch in which the perfect and augmented fourths are for the first time diatonic to C major, with semitonal contradictions beginning to suggest a bitonal opposition of C and F sharp (Ex. 15iv).

The second (and final) movement of the sonata is concerned with the transformation of first movement material and with further clarification of the tonal structure in preparation for the concluding C major triad, the only unclouded triad in the work. The recapitulation of theme (x) which dramatically interrupts the argument at fig. 34 and which later forms a coda to the movement is one of several explicit links with the first movement. The extended passage based on parallel major seconds at fig. 29, for example, is a reworking of fig. 12 and related material, while the opening thematic idea of the movement is itself a transformation of (x), significantly alternating F and F sharp.

On a more fundamental level the movement continues to explore the harmonic types established in the first movement. Ex. 15v presents two harmonizations of the 'second subject' which relate respectively to the first and second harmonic types of the first movement. Similarly at fig. 15 an harmonic area based on perfect fourths centred on A is contradicted by a tritonal E flat in the violin part, an opposition clearly deriving from the first harmonic type. Even the semitone clusters which are prominent in the movement are a logical outcome of the progression from fourths, via major and minor thirds to the major second and semitone.

This close integration of harmonic material relates to the tonal structure of the movement in that clearly defined tonal areas are established through *ostinato* patterns which invariably derive from familiar interval groupings (see after figs. 6 and 11). Such tonal areas offset the growing tendency of the music to focus on C as principal tonal centre in preparation for the final cadence. When the 'second subject' returns in a harmonization of fourths at fig. 16, the bass emphasizes and centres on C while the violin persistently stresses F sharp (Ex. 15v). The passage leads directly to a strongly emphasized 'structural downbeat' at fig. 18 on a 'dominant' open fifth, though this is almost immediately absorbed

into an area of perfect fourths. An important tonal and thematic landmark occurs at fig. 34 when (x) returns in its first movement form and is
accompanied by the tritone C/F sharp, a dramatic anticipation of the
coda to the sonata. Much of the ensuing harmony stands in a quasi-
bitonal relationship to these pitches culminating in a climactic cadence
at fig. 43. In the final pages C is firmly established as a tonal centre
within a context of perfect fourths harmony; an important stage in the
process is the traditional V—I progression in the bass at fig. 46. In the
closing bars of the work the accompanying fourths and fifths in the
piano part are directed towards an open fifth on C while the violin E
is approached thematically and recalls the first movement's emphasis on
that pitch (Ex. 15vi). It is a triadic cadence which arises naturally out
of a non-triadic argument.

This analysis has made no attempt to investigate in any detail the
structural role of tonality by relating tonal centres to formal outlines
and thematic process. Its purpose has been to demonstrate that the tonal
scheme not only articulates the work's overall structure but shapes and
co-ordinates its individual events to the extent that the cadence emerges
as their natural outcome. In a context where the harmonic relationships
of the major-minor key system no longer function, this amounts to a
reinterpretation of the tonal principle comparable, though stylistically
very different, to the mature music of Debussy or the neo-classical idiom
of Stravinsky.

Part Two

Paths to Atonality

Part Two

4

'A pull within the art'

During the first two decades of the present century major-minor tonality, already threatened by a chromatic expansion and modification of tonal functions in the nineteenth century, was conclusively undermined. Composers from many different cultural backgrounds were united in their rejection of 'the tyranny of major-minor keys' though divided on the consequences of that rejection. It was, in Stravinsky's phrase, 'a pull within the art' whose far-reaching effects on the language of music few composers felt able to ignore. In tracing several individual 'paths to atonality' we inevitably risk isolating a small number of composers from the broad stream of European music whose many and diverse stylistic currents helped to support and direct them. Some attempt to survey the background to the achievements of these composers will be a necessary corrective, and will serve to emphasize that the decline of traditional tonality was a widespread phenomenon.

THE FIRST DECADE

The artistic and intellectual life of Austro-Germany, unlike that of France, had no single geographical centre during the first decade. The pre-Expressionist ferment in the literary and visual arts was associated as much with Munich as with Berlin, as much with Prague (administratively an Austrian city at that time) as with Dresden. These were the years of Strindberg and Wedekind performances in the German theatre, of the formation of *Die Brücke* in Dresden and, at the end of the decade, of *Der Blaue Reiter* in Munich. They were years, too, in which the life-affirming call of Nietzsche's Dionysus and the exploratory research of Sigmund Freud into the workings of the subconscious mind each had the widest possible repercussions in German art and thought.

Vienna made a significant, though often a reluctant, contribution to the prevailing spirit of change, and not only as the home of Freud. Kokoschka spent his early years in the great capital; Adolf Loos carried

out his architectural experiments there; the works of Schnitzler, Alten-
berg and Kraus were all products of the city. Above all, as the seat of
the great symphonic tradition, Vienna was the undisputed musical
capital of Austro-Germany, and it was here that Schoenberg and his
pupils posed the most direct of several challenges to tonality in the first
decade. Schoenberg was himself closely associated with many of the
leading progressives in the other arts. His ideas on art were influenced
—quite specifically—by the new architecture of Loos, the theories of
language held by Karl Kraus and the views of his close friend Wassily
Kandinsky, whose *On the Spiritual in Art* amounted to a kind of bible of
Expressionism.

Schoenberg was one of the most 'progressive' composers of his
generation, but he was also one of those most acutely aware of his
country's musical tradition and most concerned with its logical continuation. There is no contradiction here. It was indeed his very respect for
tradition which made him all the more sensitive to the need for constant
change and evolution within a tradition if it is to remain alive. Moreover, Schoenberg apparently felt that he was fitted in a rather special
way for the role of legitimate heir to the great Austro-German tradition,
a view which was perhaps reflected in the increasing tendency of his
early compositions to relate a chromatically expanding, Wagnerian
harmonic language to a closely argued thematic process influenced by
Brahms. Yet whatever interpretation Schoenberg may have placed on
the historical significance of his own early music and of his subsequent
break with tonality, a close inspection of the impulses involved in tonal
decline would prompt many of us to question, or at least to qualify, the
notion of any single 'mainstream' development towards atonality.
Even Reger and Mahler, whose contributions were recognized by
Schoenberg, played essentially separate roles in breaking down the firm
lines of tonal harmony. The widening range of chromatic harmony in
Reger and the growing contrapuntal independence of Mahler developed
two tendencies inherent in the language of Austro-German late-
Romantic music. While they both certainly influenced Schoenberg,
they can hardly be regarded as progressive stages in a consistent, evolutionary development from *Tristan* to *Das Buch der hängenden Gärten*.

Other Austro-German composers stressed a further aspect of the
Romantic legacy, exploring the expressive or illustrative qualities of
dissonance, very often unresolving. Occasionally this went beyond the
'emancipation' of higher tertiary dissonances—ninth, eleventh or
thirteenth chords—to include fourths harmonies, added sixth chords

and material based on the whole-tone scale. In some works unresolving, 'expressive' dissonance has been emphasized to the extent that tonality and the triad seem in danger of being submerged without giving way to the alternative unifying procedures which ensure comprehensibility in Schoenberg's transitional works. In such cases coherence would depend to a marked extent on what Schoenberg described as 'a sort of emotional comprehensibility', usually relatable to a supporting text or programme.

The intensely expressive dissonances of 'Die du Gott Gebarst' from Wolf's *Spanisches Liederbuch* or of 'Seufzer' from the *Mörike-Lieder* reflect this development in its early stages. Admittedly the dissonances do not as yet obscure an underlying tonal structure, but their acceptance as self-sufficient harmonies whose justification is their expressive quality contributed to the 'emancipation of the dissonance' and permitted a further chink in a weakening tonal armour. Similarly in the tone poems of Richard Strauss unresolving dissonance was often employed for programmatic purposes, though the overall context is invariably triadic and usually surprisingly diatonic.

In the public estimation and in the view of many contemporary composers Strauss epitomized the *avant-garde* of Europe during the first decade. His commitment to the ideals and the techniques of the 'New German School' was total and that at a time when these were still crudely dubbed 'progressive' at the expense of Brahms and his supporters. If his symphonic poems were widely and accurately considered to surpass previous essays in the *genre*, both in their structural breadth and their illustrative detail, the one-act operas *Salomé* and *Elektra*, completed respectively in 1905 and 1908, seemed at the time to be the ultimate extension of the operatic methods of Wagner. Certainly the conception of the works is Wagnerian. The orchestra (itself an extension of Wagner's) carries the weight of the musical argument by means of an intricate network of *leitmotiven*, while the vocal lines are content with a type of melodic declamation superficially similar to Wagner's though rarely achieving the subtlety of Wagner's intimate correspondence of word and note. But the level of dissonance permitted by Strauss in response to the savage passions unleashed on the stage is far in excess of anything in Wagner and had a marked impact on other young composers at the time. The importance of these works for Schoenberg's 'expressionistic' music of 1908–9 may well have been underestimated.[1]

The sustained dissonance which depicts Elektra's numbed reaction on recognizing her brother Orestes, believed dead, is typical of the complex

61

harmonies, including fourths chords, hints of bitonality and whole-tone material, which occur throughout *Elektra*, many of them scarcely relatable to an underlying tonality. Yet such passages are countered by moments of diatonic simplicity such as the lyrical A flat major section which immediately follows this passàge, or the transparent F major of the serving men's dialogue in the 'Orest ist tot' scene, contrasting sharply with the brutal dissonance of the preceding passage. The more advanced harmonies in *Salomé* and *Elektra* undoubtedly helped to pave the way of atonality, but when they are heard in context they appear as deviations from an accepted norm rather than a destruction of that norm.

The impact of *Salomé* was an important factor in the new harmonic freedom which appeared in the works written by the Austrian composer and teacher Franz Schreker in the final years of the decade. Schreker's early songs are in a traditional Brahmsian mould, though with occasional expressive dissonances reminiscent of Wolf (the pungent diminished octaves in *Wohl fuhl' ich*, Op. 4, No. 3, are characteristic). In his first opera, the one-act *Flammen*, Op. 10 (1902), it is perhaps only the fourth scene which seems to be straining beyond this idiom towards the colouristic dissonance of his best-known work, *Der Ferne Klang*. Here the new harmonic idiom is a response to the type of effete, mystical subject matter which was increasingly to attract Schreker. *Der Ferne Klang* occupied him intermittently from 1903 until 1909 and it is the first work in which we find those unchanging dissonant harmonic areas, at times supported by *ostinato* patterns and embellished with ornamental melodic figurations, which appear in his later music, betraying his sympathies with French Impressionism. The extended passage of whole-tone harmony in Act III, Scene 9, graphically depicting a dawn scene, is a particularly explicit instance of this technique, but it is perhaps less characteristic of Schreker's music as a whole than the harmony of Act I, Scene 1, with its major second pedal point, its parallel chord structures and its discreet hints of bitonality.[2]

During 1911 Alban Berg prepared the vocal score of *Der Ferne Klang*, and its impact on *Wozzeck* has often provoked comment. The most explicit area of influence is the instrumentation of the work, for Schreker evolved a highly personal orchestral style (again owing something to French music) which first manifests itself in his 1908 ballet *Der Geburtstag der Infantin*.[3] A comparison of this score with the earlier *Ekkegard Overture* (1902) indicates clearly how far he has travelled from the efficient but conventional scoring of the earlier work. Egon Wellesz has further pointed out, moreover, that the use of closed forms in *Wozzeck* may have been suggested to Berg by the sonata structure of the second act of *Der Ferne Klang*,[4] and there are additional similarities such as the use in both works of an out-of-tune piano. But Berg's early music demonstrates a further and deeper affinity with Schreker and with the Strauss of *Salomé* and *Elektra*. He shared with these composers a liking for unresolving dissonance employed for its expressive qualities, very often at the expense of traditional tonal functions. Indeed the last of Berg's *Four Songs*, Op. 2 (completed 1909), takes the step which had been threatened but not accomplished in *Salomé* and *Elektra* and in *Der Ferne Klang*. Here a dissonant harmonic language of almost unprecedented expressive intensity has been developed to the point at which the triad has been eclipsed and tonality submerged.

Many of the more radical harmonic developments of the decade took place in France, and specifically in Paris, the unrivalled artistic capital of Europe at the turn of the century. From the 1860s Paris had remained a centre for the most innovatory trends in painting and sculpture. In the mid eighties such trends gathered increasing momentum, with important artistic movements and groupings springing up with bewildering rapidity, many of them held together by no more than an ill-defined anti-establishment sentiment. Less dazzling in its variety, but of equal importance, were the achievements of her poets and musicians. If the symbolist poets helped to free the language of poetry from the shackles of precise meanings, the music of Debussy successfully freed the individual harmonic event from a traditional tonal syntax. He may have been the greatest but he was by no means the only, or even the first, French composer to have moved in this direction. The independence of earlier French music from the most characteristic expressions of classical tonality in Italy and Austro-Germany was re-established in the mature music of Fauré, after a period when French composers seemed unable to loosen the stranglehold of Teutonic influence. The tonic-dominant polarity of classical tonality was undermined in Fauré's music by a revival of modality (attributable in part to his training under Niedermayer) and by imperceptibly changing enharmonic progressions which serve to loosen the syntactical connections between chords. Already in his songs of the eighties and nineties—above all in his settings of Verlaine—Fauré was developing an unobtrusively original harmonic idiom whose unmistakable flavour is at least partly due to a preference for 'false relations', added sixth harmonies and freely interchanging major and minor sevenths and ninths. The boldness of that idiom is subtly concealed by a fluid, non-accentual rhythmic language and an evenly flowing accompaniment configuration.

More radical, and often cited, were the harmonic innovations of Erik Satie's early piano pieces, the *Sarabandes* of 1887 and the *Gnossiennes* and *Gymnopédies* of the early nineties. It seems entirely probable that Satie's removal of the chord from a diatonic context—the unresolving sevenths in the *Sarabandes* have no expressive connotations but function simply as vertical 'colours'—had a liberating effect on Debussy in his works of the early nineties, though Debussy was to draw quite different, and infinitely wider, implications from the procedure. Later in his *Rose Croix* works, Satie formalized some of the harmonic fingerprints of earlier compositions, employing rigid formulae based on parallel triads, 6/3 chords, sevenths and ninths and, occasionally, fourths harmonies (e.g. the opening of his incidental music for *Le Fils des Étoiles*). His harmonic methods in these works—frankly experimental and remote from traditional procedure—have been examined in detail by Satie's most knowledgeable researcher, Patrick Gowers.[5] Throughout his life it was Satie's achievement and his limitation that his innovations were to a remarkable extent unhampered by an allegiance to tradition. Although many higher claims have been made for his music, his modest role in musical history has surely been to point the way, both technical and spiritual, to greater and more successful composers. The extent and nature of his influence on Debussy might certainly be questioned but there can be no doubt of the importance of his later music for a younger generation of French composers working between the wars. The incorporation of music-hall and ragtime idioms into his compositions of the first two decades, culminating in the ballet *Parade* of 1917, reflects a much wider enthusiasm for the popular culture of the café-concert and cabaret in *fin-de-siècle* Paris, an enthusiasm which was also given artistic expression in the drawings of Toulouse Lautrec and the songs of Aristide Bruant. As an antidote to the world of Symbolism and Impressionism, the music of *Parade*, its popular tunes presented in vivid, unmixed orchestral colours, was proclaimed by Jean Cocteau as a new starting point for French music, though the deeper implications of Satie's aesthetic position have only been realized—in music at least—since the Second World War.

Satie's experimentalism was paralleled rather than echoed in the music of Charles Koechlin, though the exploratory harmonies in Koechlin's early music mingle with elements derived from more traditional French styles and, occasionally, from Debussy. His early works, particularly the songs of the nineties, betray clearly enough their debt to his teacher Fauré. The successions of chromatic triad progressions in *Les Clairs de Lune*, Op. 9 (1893), or *La Prière du Mort*, Op. 17, No. 2 (1895–6), are typical, though both songs already employ progressive tonal schemes. In the songs of the first decade more advanced harmonies creep into the texture; the quasi-bitonal harmony of *L'Astre Rouge*, Op. 13, No. 4, for example, or the 'layered' dissonance of 'Hymne à la Nuit' from the *Cinq Chansons de Bilitis*, Op. 39 (1908). The latter feature draws attention to Koechlin's enduring preoccupation in his later, more characteristic, music with harmonic structures built of superimposed fourths and fifths (in some late works all twelve chromatic notes are superimposed in perfect fourths). Such structures, similar at times to procedures in the music of Casella's 'secondo stile', appear frequently in the *Four Songs*, Op. 28, the *Six Songs*, Op. 31, and the *Four Songs*, Op. 35. They are also found occasionally in the short piano pieces, notably the *Esquisses*, Op. 41, which bridge the two decades. Here they take their place beside modal or diatonic material of an almost folk-like simplicity, recalling Satie with its sparse textures and irregular barring.[6] The second piece from the second series of the *Esquisses* is characteristic of this unique blend of layered dissonance and innocent diatonicism.

Other French composers working during the first decade owed much to Debussy's technical achievements, however remote they may have been from his aesthetic or spiritual world. One of those most often and most unjustly accused of Debussyism was his great contemporary Maurice Ravel. Influence there certainly was, but it flowed in both directions and in some matters priority is notoriously difficult to establish. The parallel is perhaps closest in some of Ravel's earlier music, such as *Miroirs* (1905) and the *Introduction and Allegro* (1906) where it is as much a matter of textural sonority as of harmonic procedure. There are of course shared harmonic characteristics, even where the significance of these is different for each composer; a preference for modality, often in an 'exotic' context, for internal pedal points and for parallelism—of bare fifths, triads and higher numbered discords. But as a rule Ravel avoided both the whole-tone harmony and the sustained dominant-quality dissonances favoured by Debussy. He preferred the piquancy of the higher diatonic discords and liked to 'sharpen' his harmonic palate with the seconds and fourths of unresolving appoggiaturas. Ultimately, however, the more astringent harmonies in his music are an extension and enrichment of a traditional type of tonal thinking rather than a re-shaping of tonality along new, radical lines.

With only slightly less inspired results, Debussyan harmonic finger-prints appear in several works composed by Dukas during the first decade, in particular his opera *Arianne et Barbebleu*, heavily indebted to *Pelléas*, and in the early music of Roussel, his *Quatres Poèmes*, Op. 3 (1903), *Poème de la Forêt*)1904–6) and *Évocations* (1909–10) Even composers as diverse in temperament and style as Roger-Ducasse and Florent Schmitt [7] responded in some measure to the challenge of Debussy's harmonic innovations. Admittedly the 'Impressionist' harmonies employed in much of this music serve only to offset rather than to destroy diatonic procedure, but they did at least help composers to free their detailed harmonic working from the 'laws' of a traditional tonal syntax.

At this level the impact of Debussy's harmony extended far beyond France, acting as a liberating influence on composers whose search for a national style turned them away from prevailing German models. It is reflected in the gently dissonant harmonies and parallel chord structures of Kodály's early songs and piano pieces—the eleventh of his Op. 1 songs, for example, or the eighth of his Op. 3 Piano Pieces, both composed in 1907. It was also in 1907 that the young Manuel de Falla met Debussy in Paris and the fruits of that meeting were to be gathered in his *Three Songs* of 1909 and in his *Nights in the Garden of Spain* for piano and orchestra (1909–15).

Much of the ground had already been prepared for Falla in his development of a Spanish style which avoided provincialism. Already in the late nineteenth and early twentieth centuries his teacher Felipe Pedrell had been tentatively developing a harmonic language which could suitably accommodate the modalities of Spanish folksong, formerly forced into a diatonic straitjacket. Pedrell was a direct inspiration to Albeniz and Granados who, again influenced by French composers, took the next step in the progress towards a modern Spanish music, most notably in the twelve pieces comprising Albeniz's *Ibéria* for piano (1906–9).

Like Spain, England saw a revitalization of her music during the first decade. Despite the highly personal character of Elgar's music, its roots were deeply embedded in the soil of German Romanticism. As in Spain it was the dual stimulus of French music and folkloristic materials which proved a liberating influence for English music; the former in the work of Delius and both in that of Holst and Vaughan Williams, whose achievements lie close to the foundation of a modern English style. The rejection of early Wagnerian influences in Holst's music and his development, particularly in the one-act opera *Savitri* (1908), of a characteristic modal chromaticism and a flexible rhythmic procedure welded to the English language, proved of the utmost importance for the future of English music.

The modalities associated with such national styles confirmed the decline of traditional tonality while firmly resisting any inclinations towards atonality. The tonal languages of Kodály, Falla and Holst may fall far short of the fundamental reinterpretation of tonality which we find in Debussy, Bartók and Stravinsky, but they have equally been extended well beyond the confines of classical tonality. Modality is a feature, too, of the music of Leos Janáček, though it hardly accounts for the remarkable originality and power of his *œuvre*. His mature musical language, as established belatedly in *Jenufa* (completed 1904), retains many of the ingredients of classical tonality (above all the triad) but radically changes their relative functions and significance. The 'accompaniment' patterns in Janáček are often familiar from earlier music, for example, but they are given a prominence which totally changes their relationship with melodic line, endowing them at times with something like equal status. The on-going movement of his music is similarly achieved by unorthodox means—often a discourse of short, 'unfinished' phrases comprising constant repetitions of short motives which gather momentum in a cumulative manner. The melos itself has a flexibility of rhythm and contour which derives from Janáček's close study of speech rhythm and inflections (carried much further than Mussorgsky), while the unorthodox spacing of his harmony ensures that it sounds equally fresh and original whether based on thirds and sixths or on seconds and fourths. Like Mussorgsky, Janáček prefers the abrupt juxtaposition of 'unrelated' harmonies and tonal regions to the more organic procedures of conventional part-movement and modulation. Yet however far-reaching his modification of tonal *practice*, Janáček remained faithful to the tonal *principle*. His own comment on the subject could well have been made by other twentieth-century 'nationalists': 'There is no music without key. Atonality abolishes definite key, and thus tonal modulation. . . . Folksong knows of no atonality . . .' [8]

One 'nationalist' school which remained uniquely distanced from the great European traditions was already stirring in the 1890s and was being consolidated during the first decade in the music of Charles Ives. Although the direct influence of Ives was limited during the earlier part of the century, he was the first representative of a 'tradition' of experimentation in America which was to lead to an intensive exploration of technical resources between the wars in the music of Cowell, Ruggles, Varèse, Partch and early Cage. Classical tonality, like other aspects of European achievement, was treated by Ives as one resource among many which could be used or rejected freely in a musical translation of the totality of existence—its order and its chaos; the necessity for integration which characterized European art for four centuries played a subsidiary role throughout his work.[9] Certainly from his earliest music the 'rule' of classical tonality is honoured more in the breach than in the observance. Indeed Ives's early experiments in 'polytonal' and 'atonal' textures preceded similar developments in Europe by several years, although the significance of these experiments was profoundly different from anything in Stravinsky or Schoenberg. He even developed a rudimentary form of serialism in *Tone Roads No. 3* (1915) some ten years before Schoenberg's development of the method. Many of the complexities in Ives's music, including its notorious rhythmic difficulty, are consequences of what Reti has described as a 'polyphony of groups', a technique seen at its crudest in the simultaneous brass bands of *Putnam's Camp*, but in fact a central aspect of his musical language from *The Unanswered Question* to the Fourth Symphony. The horizontal 'splitting' of musical entities which have within them an independent harmonic and contrapuntal life suggests a parallel with Stravinsky's multi-layered textures and relates to later developments in the music of Elliott Carter and Michael Tippett.

THE SECOND DECADE

The second decade absorbed more completely into the mainstream of its musical development many of the compositional techniques which had seemed new and unfamiliar in the first. Undoubtedly many of the more 'difficult' compositions continued to reach only a severely restricted audience, but the performance of contemporary works at concert series in major European capitals and in New York went some way towards preparing a wider musical public for even the most intractable scores. New harmonic procedures were 'in the air' during the second decade. For an older generation of composers such procedures could enrich their musical language while in no way concealing its basically traditional character; it was quite possible for Puccini to borrow freely from Debussy, even from Stravinsky, without changing the fundamentals of his style. For younger composers, on the other hand, the impact of a wide range of new techniques, their significance often imperfectly

68

understood,[10] coincided in many cases with the crucial formative stages in their stylistic development. The dangers are obvious, and for many the seductions of novelty delayed, where they did not actually prevent, the emergence of an individual voice.

The great social and political upheavals of the decade left on its artistic life a mark whose true extent cannot be gauged, such are the intangibles which immediately present themselves when we seek that elusive point of contact between the external and internal impulses informing the creative act. Certainly it would be dangerous to attribute to war and revolution more than a catalytic role in the significant stylistic changes which are apparent in the work of so many composers at the time. But the after-effects of social and political change did have a more tangible influence on the music of those young composers whose early compositions date from the latter part of the decade and whose most characteristic work belongs outside the scope of the present study. With the collapse of the older social order in Europe, fresh attitudes and with them new styles and techniques could disengage themselves more easily from vestigial traces of late Romanticism. Cocteau's *rappel à l'ordre* embodied an anti-Romantic commitment which had widespread influence at the time though it has hardly been sustained as the century has progressed. Its musical expression was very often a dry, mercurial idiom, employing a 'witty' bitonality, a rhythmically vigorous contrapuntal writing, and a harmonic dissonance which has lost all expressive connotations. The style had perhaps most importance in France in the music of certain members of *Les Six*, but it should be remembered that the early music of Hindemith, Křenek and Martinů as well as that of Milhaud and Poulenc appeared within the second decade.

In Austro-Germany, Strauss was still regarded by many as the virtuoso among contemporary composers, though his 'betrayal' of modern music angered many progressive spirits. The tuneful diatonicism and lilting waltz rhythms of *Der Rosenkavalier* signalled a retreat from the extreme position of *Elektra* and led directly to the highly original harmonic language of his later music, a language characterized by a continuous, if discreet, dialogue between chromatic and diatonic styles. By contrast Franz Schreker consolidated the harmonic acquisitions of *Der Ferne Klang* in his second decade music. The experience of that work has been registered fully in the harmonic language of his *Five Songs* of 1909, particularly in the third song 'Die Dunkelheit sinkt schwer wie Blei', with its highly dissonant textures, and it was confirmed in the later operas from *Das Spielwerk und die Prinzessin* (1909–12) to *Die*

Schatzgraber, completed in 1919. It is a telling clue to the impulses underlying Schreker's more complex harmonies that the instrumental
Chamber Symphony of 1917 returns to a relatively more relaxed harmonic idiom.

One composer whose harmonic language changed dramatically
during the decade was Alexander von Zemlinsky, best known today for
his early association with Schoenberg, but a considerable opera composer in his own right. His fourth opera *Ein Florentinische Tragödie*, Op.
16, first performed in 1917, admits a degree of savage, expressionistic
dissonance which was unprecedented in his work and which strongly
recalls *Salomé* and *Elektra*. As in the Strauss operas, however, the more
extreme dissonances are balanced by triadic and diatonic material.
Zemlinsky's early instrumental music owed more to Brahms than
anyone [11] and it culminated in a work of considerable emotional and
intellectual power, his Second String Quartet, Op. 15 (published
1916). The quartet combines a richly chromatic harmonic procedure
with concentrated motivic working clearly indebted to Brahms (almost
all the material in the work can be related to its opening idea) in a
manner strikingly similar to Schoenberg's First String Quartet, Op. 7.
The parallel with Schoenberg is strengthened by the fact that both
quartets are single-movement structures incorporating *scherzo* and
adagio material and by the appearance in Zemlinsky's work of a recurring harmony (a D minor triad with G sharp) which plays an important
part in several of Schoenberg's early tonal compositions. For all its
concentrated chromaticism, however, the second quartet seldom
achieves the freely dissonant harmonic movement of Zemlinsky's later
instrumental compositions such as the Third String Quartet (published
1925), whose slow movement makes effective play with unresolving
major seconds, and the magnificent *Lyric Symphony* (published 1926).

The early music of Egon Wellesz also dates from the second decade
though it was some time before he achieved the stylistically integrated
musical language of his maturity, a language which combines in Bergian fashion the emotional climate of late Mahler with the tightly
organized thematicism of his teacher Schoenberg. Wellesz's early
extended works—the First and Second String Quartets, for example—
are in the expanded tonal idiom of early Schoenberg and Zemlinsky,
but already by the Fourth String Quartet (published 1920) organic
tonal thinking has been replaced by harmonic points of reference which
punctuate non-tonal, but traditionally conceived, textures in the
manner of some of Schoenberg's atonal, pre-serial pieces. The quartet

consolidates some of the harmonic resources which had already been mapped out by Wellesz in shorter piano pieces, ranging from the Debussy-inspired, impressionistic textures of *Der Abend*, Op. 4 (1909–1910), to the pungent, Schoenbergian dissonance of the *Drei Skizzen*, Op. 6 (1911).

Paris in the second decade remained the most thriving cultural centre of Europe though its glory was reflected as much from resident foreign artists as from indigenous talent. It was after all in Paris that the spectacular performances of the Russian Ballet, including *The Rite of Spring*, gained widespread recognition for the most radical developments in music as well as in the visual arts. As the decade progressed notable stylistic changes became apparent in the music of some of the most important French composers. There are indications in Debussy's *Jeux* and in his late *Études* that he did not remain indifferent to his contacts with the early music of Stravinsky, but it is above all in his three late sonatas that his music leans noticeably in the direction that French music was about to take. In these works literary and pictorial considerations have been totally subordinated to an overriding concern with abstract formal and linguistic problems. Their harmonic language has been pruned of the lingering, dominant-quality dissonances of earlier works and the triad (seldom completely suppressed in Debussy's music) assumes a renewed importance as basic harmonic unit.

France was indeed to become a major centre for the dissemination of neo-classicism between the wars, both among her own composers and the many foreign—in particular American and Polish—musicians who studied there. It is certainly no coincidence that the countries which found it easiest to adopt the 'neo-classical' manner were those in which classical tonality had at best shallow roots. The term 'neo-classicism' has been used to describe a wide diversity of styles—within France alone it has been used of the instrumental music of composers as different as Milhaud and Roussel—but they have in common an involvement with the *external features* of classical tonality, a separation of outward form and inward principle which would have been more difficult for the Central European. If Debussy's late sonatas seem prophetic of neo-classical developments, the second decade music of Ravel strongly confirms this tendency. Ravel's innate classicism, expressed in a clarity of line and a simplicity of formal outlines, is given full rein in the *Trois Poèmes de Mallarmé* (1913), the Piano Trio (1914) and the *Tombeau de Couperin* (1914–17). Later works were to find, and to some extent helped to create, a sympathetic context in the aesthetic climate of inter-war Europe. In the broadest possible sense, neo-classical tendencies are also discernible in the music composed by Roussel towards the end of the decade, particularly his Second Symphony of 1920, though his full-scale adoption of classical forms, albeit used in a personal way, came only in the 1920s.

The later music of Koechlin characteristically refused to conform to the general trends in French music at the time. His main output until 1909 had been songs, but in the second decade he turned to chamber music. Works such as the Flute Sonata, Op. 52, the Violin Sonata, Op. 64, and the Viola Sonata, Op. 53, are couched in a more uncompromisingly dissonant harmonic idiom than the early songs. The Viola Sonata in particular is characterized throughout by bitonal writing and pungent dissonance, its third movement typical of Koechlin's layered, Casella-like sonorities. Although the work was composed between 1912 and 1915, sketches, including bitonal passages, date from as early as 1905, three years before the first of Bartók's *Bagatelles*.

French influences were an important element in the impressive achievements of English composers during the second decade. Holst himself responded to the music of Debussy in parts of his orchestral suite *The Planets* (1916), notably in the 'Saturn' and 'Neptune' movements with their quasi-bitonal harmonies and impressionistic sonorities. So, too, did Vaughan Williams whose early mature compositions, with their highly characteristic blend of impressionism and pastoral modality, date from the end of the first decade and the beginning of the second. His was an idiom which could leave traces on distinguished composers such as Ireland, Bax and early Bridge (later to explore more radical territory, influenced by Bergian expressionism), but which could, and often did, descend to the most trivial and enfeebled provincialism in the hands of minor imitators.

Exploratory harmonic techniques were common among minor English composers of the period. The songs and piano pieces of Cyril Scott betray an obvious indebtedness to Debussyan harmony, though few of them show the refinement and technical 'finish' of the impressionistic piano miniatures of William Baines, owing more, it would seem, to Skryabin than to Debussy. More eccentric are a number of works by John Foulds and some of the piano pieces of Lord Berners, notably the wittily dissonant *Trois Petites Marches Funèbres*. Of particular interest is the early music of Bernard Van Dieren, a Dutch composer who made his home in England. In his early songs and piano miniatures, Van Dieren developed a highly original harmonic language in which dissonant combinations result from contrapuntal writing of extreme complexity.[12] This is already a feature of songs such as 'Come, I will sing you some low sleepy Tune' (1909), but it is carried much further in the second decade songs; in his *Chanson* of 1919 the polyphony is so complex that small and large print has been used as an aid to the performer. In the opening movement of his Second String Quartet (1917), the rhythmic independence of the parts is of an almost unbelievable complexity (like much of his early music it does not use bar lines) and the level of dissonance is consistently high, despite the final D major cadence. In later works, including subsequent quartets, Van Dieren's style relaxed considerably, both rhythmically and harmonically.

During the second decade the achievements of Bartók and Stravinsky were becoming sufficiently familiar to serve alongside those of Debussy and Ravel as an inspiration to nationalist composers in Eastern Europe. It seems likely that Janáček assimilated elements from these composers in the music he wrote towards the end of the decade and subsequently, though there is clearly no question of his personal idiom being in any way sacrificed. His younger compatriot Boleslaw Vomáčka similarly responded to new techniques in his early, exploratory works, the Violin Sonata, Op. 3 (1912), *Hledeni*, Op. 4 (1913), and the Piano Sonata, Op. 7 (1917), though his later music was markedly to dilute the dissonant harmonic language of these works.

The importance of Russia as a centre for progressive thinking in the arts at the turn of the century has only recently been fully appreciated. In music the radical harmonic achievements of Skryabin had a widespread influence on younger and lesser-known Russian composers. This was in some ways comparable to Debussy's influence on French composers in that it often amounted to no more than an external colouring of basically traditional styles; his influence on Myaskovsky and even Steinberg was of this nature. But some three decades before *Prometheus* the Russian composer Rebikov had already been composing pre-Impressionist miniatures whose parallel seventh and ninth chords often suggest intriguing pre-echoes of Debussy.[13] The true extent of progressive activity in early twentieth-century Russian music is not known, even today, but there can be no doubt that it was a time of intensive experimentation for many composers (both before and after the Revolution), from the microtonal experiments of Georg Rimsky Korsakov to the exploration of electronic sound sources by Theremin. The atonal Violin Sonata and proto-serial *Three Piano Pieces* of Rosslavetz,[14] both dating from 1913–14, and the mechanistic compositions of Mossolov

73

and Deshevov in the early twenties help to place in some sort of perspective the second decade achievements of Stravinsky and Prokofiev.

Many of Prokofiev's characteristic stylistic fingerprints are already present in the work with which he first gained acclaim and notoriety, the First Piano Concerto of 1911, whose cleanly articulated piano writing seems determined to destroy any prevailing sympathies with impressionism and is certainly in sharp contrast to the piano style of Skryabin. Yet before the concerto Prokofiev had already composed shorter piano works of more radical cast, including the *Four Studies*, Op. 2 (1909) and, above all, the *Four Pieces*, Op. 4 (1908–10). The last of the Op. 4 pieces 'Suggestions Diaboliques' foreshadows Bartók's *Allegro Barbaro* in its tough, percussive dissonance and its *ostinato* patterns of strong rhythmic profile. The piano works of the second decade extend this harmonically pungent, rhythmically vigorous idiom, from the Second Piano Sonata of 1912 to *Sarcasms* of the same year (its third piece an early study in bitonality) and the Second Piano Concerto of 1914. Other exploratory works of the period include the ballets *Ala and Lolly* (1914) and *Chout* (1915–20), both composed under the influence of the Stravinsky of *The Rite of Spring*. But like the early music of Bartók, Prokofiev's second decade music cannot realistically be classified within a single stylistic category, however broadly conceived. The percussive dissonance of the piano works expressed one aspect only of his musical personality during these years, years which also produced compositions of such exquisite and gentle lyricism as the First Violin Concerto. It was an aspect which would be given a new lease of life in the works composed in Paris during the twenties before becoming absorbed into the more successfully integrated language of Prokofiev's later music.

In deriving its inspiration from the modern city, from the machine and the factory, Prokofiev's ballet *Le Pas d'Acier*, together with other Parisian works of the twenties, established a point of contact with the 'urbanism' of Mossolov and Deshevov and of many other European and American composers working between the wars. The origin of the preoccupation was the Futurist movement which emerged in Italy in the early years of the century under the aegis of the poet Marinetti. It was Italy's most important contribution to the modern movement in the arts. Although the greatest influence of Futurism was exerted in the visual arts, the experiments of Luigi Russolo in the *Arte dei Rumori* were influential at the time and stand in an important antici-patory relationship to the later development of *Musique concrète*. But there were Italian composers of progressive sympathies who felt unable to identify with the Futurists on the one hand or with Puccini and the *verismo* composers on the other. For these Busoni offered a more congenial source of inspiration, though it was more of an ideological than a purely musical nature. He gave the greatest encouragement to the *generazione dell' ottanta*, of whom the two most important composers were undoubtedly G. F. Malipiero and Casella.

During the second decade both composers rejected the conventionally diatonic idiom of their earlier music, a rejection which resulted in Malipiero's two dramatic works of 1919, the one-act stage works *Pantea* and *Setti Canzoni* and in the music of Casella's|so-called '*secondo stile*'.[15] It is worth examining the Casella works in some detail as they illustrate particularly clearly the difficulties facing young composers in the light of a wide diversity of new styles and techniques.

The first work in which such techniques are fully explored by Casella is the set of *Nine Piano Pieces*, Op. 24 (1914), though the earlier *Notte di Maggio*, with its creeping chromatic scales, its bare fifths, its superimposed fourths harmonies and its passages verging on polytonality, had already suggested new paths. The first of the Op. 24 pieces is a compendium of many of the techniques which have been examined in the music of Debussy, Bartók and Stravinsky—parallelism, whole-tone and other symmetrical structures, 'polychords' and multi-layered textures (Ex. 16). Although most of these techniques have the effect of temporarily suspending tonality, a centre of B flat, as a pitch rather than a triad, is discernible though of subsidiary importance. The most distinguishing characteristic of the piece, and of much of Casella's music from this period, is its extreme vertical density, with parallel eight-note chords and a counterpoint of chordal blocks moving on different planes. Casella himself remarked that 'Our music has sprung from the patient, incessant and progressive penetration of the laws of resonance. . . . Harmonic consciousness is incontestably the vital centre of modern musical sensibility.'[16] The first of these piano pieces is minutely sectional in construction, each section distinguished by a particular harmonic colour, ranging from simple triads or bare fourths and fifths to the most complex dissonances. Harmonically it owes something to Debussy, but it is more directly indebted to developments in Stravinksy's music, and in particular *The Rite of Spring*.

Stravinsky's influence is even more apparent in two works composed during 1915, *Pupazzetti* and *Pagine di Guerra*. The use of a dissonant chord as a non-developmental harmonic area, an *objet sonore* providing the raw material for rhythmic patterning, is found in the fifth piece from

Ex. 16

Pupazzetti, where the reiterated chord bears a striking resemblance to that used in the 'Danses des Adolescentes' from *The Rite of Spring*. Similarly the first of the *Pagine di Guerra* frequently telescopes major and minor triads in the manner of Stravinsky (Ex. 17). Both pieces also use *ostinato* accompaniment patterns as a means of asserting tonal centres, recalling both Bartók and Stravinsky. The first piece from *Pupazzetti*, again using an *ostinato* accompaniment, is an experiment in bitonality similar to that in the second of the Op. 24 pieces, 'In Modo Barbaro', whose sharp dissonance and rhythmic drive recall Bartók's *Allegro Barbaro*. One technique commonly found in Casella's 'second manner' is the distortion of familiar dance patterns, akin to procedures in Busoni and Stravinsky, but possibly also influenced by Satie, whose music

Ex. 17

Casella heard while studying in Paris. The fourth piece from the *Pagine di Guerra*, the 'Serenata' from *Pupazzetti* and the sixth and eighth pieces from Op. 24 are all examples of this style.

These short pieces by Casella, like some of the Bartók *Bagatelles*, were as close as their composer ever came to atonality. His own comments could perhaps apply, with appropriate modifications, to early Bartók and Stravinsky and even to Busoni: 'I have never written a truly atonal piece. I could have done so but my nature prevented it. But if my old and firm Latin instincts preserved me from the extremes of the Viennese composers, I can still frankly admit that for several years I regarded atonality as a natural and inevitable outcome of the whole evolution of music.'[17] The remark is particularly interesting in the light of works such as the Piano Sonatina (1916) and *Elegia eroica* for orchestra (1916) whose concentration of the total chromatic hints occasionally at twelve-note structures.

Casella was rather less successful when he tackled an extended work making use of the harmonic acquisitions of the short, exploratory pieces of the 'second manner'. The harmonic structures of his programmatic work for piano *A Notte Alta* (1917)[18] are similar to those of Op. 24, No. 1, but the sectional construction here results in a serious lack of continuity, despite a skeletal tonal scheme outlined by pedal points. Casella, standing on the brink of atonality, may well have learnt from *A Notte Alta* the necessity of finding methods of organization which would be sufficiently broadly based to give unity and cohesion to an extended work containing a resourceful and varied harmonic vocabulary. Bartók and Stravinsky had succeeded in finding such methods in their development of new tonal languages. Their aesthetic commitments suggested two possible solutions to the problem of a unified musical language which followed the decline of traditional tonality; both 'nationalism' and 'neo-classicism' supplied the raw material for a musical language while allowing scope for a composer to develop along individual lines. If an overtly 'nationalist' aesthetic contains within itself the seeds of its own exhaustion, 'neo-classicism' was a specific manifestation of a more enduring preoccupation of the twentieth-century composer, his attempt to define a creative attitude to the past. For many composers working between the wars who rejected the path of serialism, the *rappel à l'ordre* took the form of an alignment to a neo-classical style. Casella was one of these. After *A Notte Alta* there were several years of relative creative silence during which his radical style was evidently on the way out. The *Concerto for String*

Quartet (1923–4) marks the beginning of a new 'neo-classical' orientation in his music which was to be confirmed by the *Partita* of 1925 and the *Concerto Romano* of 1926.

5

Skryabin

The achievements of the nineteenth-century Russian nationalists proved of immense significance as an incubator for many of the new techniques developed by twentieth-century composers working outside the Austro-German tradition, composers such as Debussy, Bartók and Stravinsky. At the same time a more 'cosmopolitan' tradition centred on the Moscow conservatoire rejected the inward-looking attitudes of 'the mighty handful', though the divergence in aims and styles grew less marked towards the end of the nineteenth century. Skryabin's early training was in the 'cosmopolitan' tradition and the stylistic sympathies of his early works clearly reflect his orientation towards Western Europe. Formative influences on his musical language ranged from Chopin and Liszt to Wagner and César Franck, but as his music matured such influences gradually gave way before a remarkably individual harmonic language which is notable for its comparative isolation from contemporary trends elsewhere in Europe.

The aesthetic convictions which informed Skryabin's later music were moulded much more by his contacts with the Russian Symbolist poetry of Balmont and Blok and with the mystical philosophy of Solovyov in Russia and Madame Blavatsky in Western Europe than by any developments within music.[1] Skryabin's mystical beliefs, undoubtedly the most serious obstacle to a reasoned assessment of his music in the past, should be viewed in the context of a much wider preoccupation with mysticism among artists and intellectuals at the time, though the influence of this on music remained largely peripheral. It found artistic expression not only in the work of the Russian Symbolists, but in the paintings of Watts, Moreau and Mellery and in the poetry of George Russell and Yeats. The important series of *Salons de la Rose Croix* held in Paris between 1892 and 1897 were an artistic counterpart to Madame Blavatsky's Theosophical circle with which Skryabin maintained close connections.

The profound association of Skryabin's musical and spiritual develop-

79

ments is indicated by the correspondence of major turning-points in both—in 1903 and 1909–10—and by specific technical fingerprints whose programmatic significance is revealed through directions in the scores, explanatory notes and the poems composed in association with major works.[2] But it is all too easy to over-simplify the nature of this association. Stylistic change in Skryabin's music was the result of a complex interaction of 'extra-musical' impulses acting upon the musical language and an evolutionary momentum generated from within the language. It is with the latter that we shall be primarily concerned.

THE EARLY MUSIC

Skryabin's earliest compositions are piano miniatures in which chromatic elements usually function as decorative or expressive enrichments of fundamentally diatonic progressions. Very often the more chromatically saturated the texture in these early pieces, the simpler their harmonic foundation and the slower the harmonic rhythm. This feature, together with Skryabin's marked tendency to postpone any orthodox cadential resolution to the tonic until the final bars of a piece, was of course common to much late-Romantic harmony. But there are harmonic characteristics in the early preludes and studies which help to distinguish them not only from contemporary influences but from the music of Chopin which was their major source of inspiration. Above all there is a preference for harmonies based on the intervals of a fourth and seventh which, although they are treated as dissonances, give the music a distinctive and prophetic harmonic colouring. Skryabin tended, moreover, to give such harmonies particular prominence by stating them at the outset of the piece and permitting them to function referentially, very often as a 'resolution' to cadential preparations.

The opening minor seventh of the second, A minor, prelude from the Op. 11 set (1893–6), for example, acts as a 'resolution' to the two cadential preparations of A minor which precede the only explicit reference to the tonic triad at the final cadence (note that at bar 21 the minor seventh is 'filled in' to create a fourths chord). In the first of the *Two Preludes*, Op. 27, the opening harmony, like the later so-called 'mystic chord' from *Prometheus*, is constructed from various types of fourth—augmented, diminished and perfect—and, although treated as a dissonance, it appears in different transpositions eleven times during the short piece and is used as a 'resolution' to the two cadential preparations of the G minor tonic.

But there are more specific harmonic fingerprints in these early pieces which look ahead to the mature Skryabin. In Op. 11, No. 2, for example, a momentary transposition of the 7/3 unit at the tritone interval is suggested by the harmony of the second bar, anticipating a progression—we shall call it (a)—which was to play a prominent part in the evolution of Skryabin's later harmonic method (Ex. 18i). Similarly in the opening of the second Op. 27 prelude the use of diatonic sevenths on the tonic and subdominant degrees of B major foreshadows an important aspect of the harmonic language of the fourth and fifth piano sonatas (Ex. 18ii).

Ex. 18
(i) Op. 11 no. 2
(ii) Op. 27 no. 2
(iii) Op. 32 no. 2

Apart from such harmonic fingerprints, and from a tendency to emphasize specific dissonant sonorities by allowing them to function referentially, the early piano miniatures give little hint of the harmonic methods of Skryabin's maturity. In the works composed in 1903, however, there are indications of significant stylistic change, partly resulting from the impact of Liszt and Wagner on Skryabin's harmony at that time, but discernible in his melodic language too. The fragmentation and characteristic shaping of melodic material in a piece such as the second of the *Two Poems*, Op. 32 already foreshadows the *Poem of Ecstasy* and *Prometheus*. The piece also represents a step forward in Skryabin's progress towards an individual harmonic language. The 7/3 unit, here accepted as a consonance, has become the foundation of the harmony, often with the fifth of the chord flattened or sharpened to create strong whole-tone implications; indeed whole-tone harmony is given particular prominence in this piece. Ex. 18iii indicates, moreover, that in addition to progression (a), Skryabin employs a related, and equally prophetic, progression—(b)—in which the evasion of cadential resolution to the tonic is achieved by the retention of dominant harmony over a traditional V—I movement in the bass. Like the other harmonic fingerprints which have been examined, the importance of this progression lies less in its contextual role in Op. 32, No. 2 than in the extent to which it anticipates later developments.

Of the works written in 1903 it is the Fourth Piano Sonata which offers us the clearest glimpse of future harmonic worlds. Skryabin had already composed several extended works before 1903, among them three piano sonatas, a piano concerto and two symphonies, but they are less adventurous harmonically than the shorter pieces, articulating traditional sonata or ternary structures by means of clearly defined tonal regions, whereas the preludes and studies often arrive at a clear statement of their central tonality only at the final cadence. The Third Piano Sonata (1897) is an impressive synthesis of the formal and thematic processes of the early extended works and (in the second subject of the first movement and the slow movement) the harmonic acquisitions of the shorter pieces. The formal outlines are traditional; a sonata-form first movement with second subject in the relative major and mono-tonal recapitulation, an Intermezzo and trio (revealing an indebtedness to Schumann and Brahms rather than Chopin), ternary slow movement and Sonata-Rondo *finale*. At the same time Skryabin does show concern to interrelate the basic themes of the work by means of motivic derivations and transformations, establishing close thematic links between the movements.

The new directions suggested by the Fourth Sonata and other works of 1903–4 were doubtless in part a response to changes in Skryabin's personal and intellectual life. It was in 1903 that he abandoned his teaching post at the conservatory and devoted himself entirely to composition. In the same year he began the liaison with Tatyana Schloezer which was to lead to the breakdown of his marriage two years later. It was also in 1903 that he intensified his readings in philosophy and began to evolve a 'mystical' view of art, though this was only fully developed when he became involved with Theosophy some years later. Already, however, he was beginning to share the apocalyptic consciousness and 'magical' philosophy of art which we find in Solovyov and the Symbolist poets and which was common enough in Russian intellectual circles at the time. Extra-musical connotations are apparent in the titles of works such as *The Divine Poem* (its individual movements given the somewhat Nietzschean titles 'Struggles', 'Delights' and 'The Divine Game') and of the *Poème Satanique*, the first of several compositions to betray the influence of Liszt's Mephisto Waltzes. Similarly Skryabin described to Eugen Gunst the metaphysical 'meaning' of the opening melody of the Fourth Sonata as 'the striving upwards towards the Ideal Creative Power and the motive of resultant Languor or Exhaustion after effort'.[3]

This opening melody foreshadows closely important themes in both the Fifth Sonata and the *Poem of Ecstasy*, while the fragmented melodic lines of the second movement, their sudden ascending flights and longer, drooping descents, look ahead to general characteristics of his mature melodic style. Thematically the work reveals a more concentrated inter-relationship of material than the Third Sonata; the principal thematic ideas of the second (and final) movement have been derived from the work's opening lyrical melody. But it is above all in its tonal-harmonic aspects that the sonata is prophetic of later developments. Tonally it may be regarded as a long preparation for the point at which the F sharp tonic, present as a 'background' throughout, emerges into the foreground of the musical argument with the recapitulation of the second theme of the second movement. It is the first extended work by Skryabin which consistently postpones any explicit reference to the tonic triad until the later stages of the composition in the manner of earlier preludes and studies. In the short first movement alone there are three strong cadential preparations for F sharp which fail to resolve. Although the continuity of the music still depends upon a directional harmonic movement towards such cadence points, whether or not there is an orthodox resolution, the rate of fundamental harmonic change has become extremely slow, with the 'pull' towards the cadence weakened by unresolving dominant-quality harmony.

Close analysis reveals that the sonata has gathered together within a single work several of the harmonic fingerprints which have been noted

83

in earlier miniatures. The work opens with a diatonic seventh on the subdominant of F sharp major which is later stated over a tonic pedal when the opening theme is recapitulated. The link with Op. 27, No. 2 (Ex. 18ii), is strengthened at the opening of the second movement where the same harmonic area is presented first in its original form and then transposed to the fourth degree (the tonic pedal remains unchanged) (Ex. 19i). A characteristic feature of this opening passage is the basically

Ex. 19

(i) **Prestissimo volando**

(ii) **Andante**

slow harmonic rhythm underlying the rapid chord changes, for the triads are heard as belonging to a single harmonic 'area' in which the higher tertiary dissonances have been given harmonic status. In the Fourth Sonata such harmonic areas have not yet been emancipated from a traditional tonal setting, but by blurring the consonance/dissonance distinction and retarding the harmonic rhythm they serve to push the tonality further into the background.

The Fourth Sonata, and in particular its first movement, takes further than Op. 32, No. 2 the tendency to treat the 7/3 unit, with its strong dominant quality, as the foundation of the harmony, often with whole-tone implications. Progressions (a) and (b), both making use of the 7/3, occur in clear form in the passage immediately preceding the recapitulation of the opening theme (Ex. 19ii). The sonata therefore brings together two contrasting harmonic types—Ex. 19i and ii—which had been crystallizing in earlier compositions; they are distinguished from each other above all by the contrast of major and minor sevenths. These harmonic types still operate within a tonal context and by no means account for the entire harmonic language of the work, but the increasing prominence given to them in this and other works written in 1903–4 suggests that Skryabin was already turning towards a new concept of harmonic unity which might replace the weakening influence of traditional tonality.

THE EVOLUTION OF A METHOD

The short pieces written between 1904 and 1908 are of crucial importance for an understanding of Skryabin's later harmonic method. They continue and increase the tendency of the Fourth Sonata to emphasize the unresolving 7/3 chord as harmonic foundation and, at a time when tonal functions were being undermined, they give more and more prominence to progressions (a) and (b) at the expense of other harmonic possibilities. In the *Poème Fantasque*, Op. 45, No. 2 (1904), for example, the harmony is consistently dominant-quality, but Skryabin refuses to allow an orthodox resolution to the tonic until the final cadence. A closer examination reveals that progressions (a) and (b) account for the entire harmonic language of the outer sections apart from a recurring whole-tone chord which acts as a point of punctuation; statistics underline the point, with (a) occurring four times and (b) three times. Similarly in the outer sections of the *Scherzo*, Op. 46 (1905), the unresolving dominant-quality harmony incorporates both progressions. Examples can be multiplied. The progressions are prominent in the *Poème Ailé*, Op. 51, No. 3 (1906), in *Ironies*, Op. 56, No. 2 (1908), and in *Désir*, Op. 57, No. 1 (1908).

It is instructive to compare the final bars of *Désir* with those of the *Poème Fantasque* (Ex. 20). Both pieces have a tonal centre of C, and in the earlier piece the final progression (b) resolves, by way of the recurring whole-tone chord, onto a C major triad. In *Désir*, on the other hand, Skryabin leaves the progression unresolved so that it acts as a final cadence progression—a substitute for the traditional perfect cadence. The same procedure is adopted at the final cadence of the last of the

Ex. 20
(i) Op. 45, no. 2

Four Pieces, Op. 56, again composed in 1908. In this short piece the tendency to emphasize increasingly progressions (a) and (b) reached a culminating point, with the progressions constituting almost the entire harmonic language—(a) occurs fifteen times and (b) three times. Here the unity and coherence of the music derive as much from the consistency of its use of a single harmonic type as from its relationship to a tonal centre.

The last of the Op. 56 pieces is an extreme expression of the general tendency of these short works to replace *tonal* unity with *harmonic* unity. It would be misleading to represent this as a totally consistent, step-by-step development and one which affected all the music Skryabin was composing during these years. But it is a clear indication of the direction of his thought that where a second, contrasting harmonic type is introduced, as in the *Quasi Valse*, Op. 47 (1906), and the second of the *Four Pieces*, Op. 56, this tends to be employed with equal consistency. The harmonic language of the latter piece is strikingly reminiscent of the *Poème Fantasque*. Like that work the outer sections consist entirely of progressions (a) and (b), occurring in the same C major context and punctuated by the same whole-tone chord. But the middle section of the Op. 56 piece introduces a second harmonic type, characterized by its emphasis on the major rather than the minor seventh; the piece as a whole is experienced against a background of these contrasting harmonic types.

In the *Poem of Ecstasy* and Fifth Piano Sonata, both completed in

1908, Skryabin incorporated the harmonic techniques of these short pieces within extended structures. The visionary programme of both works is expressed in Skryabin's prose poem *Poem of Ecstasy* [4] and by the inscription at the head of the sonata; 'I call you forth to life, hidden influences, sunk in the obscure depths of the Creative Spirit, timid germs of life, I bring you boldness.' The programme, reflecting his growing interest in Theosophy, already looks ahead to *Prometheus*, the later sonatas and the projected *Mysterium*.

Technically, the sonata in particular stands in a fascinating pivotal relationship to the earlier extended works, in which tonality is still the chief means of articulating a structure, and the later works, whose constructive basis lies above all in their derivation from a single chord or set. Although formally it more closely resembles the later sonatas, the Fifth Sonata has much in common with its immediate predecessor. Like the Fourth Sonata, there is a closely argued thematic integration in which important motives may be derived from the 'first subject' (Ex. 21i). There is, too, a dramatic recapitulation of the introductory themes at the end of the work which is reminiscent of the coda to the Fourth Sonata (there are in any case specific thematic links between the two

Ex.21

87

(iv)

Harmonic Type 1

(v)

Harmonic Type 2

works). Again like the Fourth Sonata the key signature is F sharp, though the work begins and ends with a tonal centre of A.

But the most striking parallel is undoubtedly that between the opening harmonies of the 'first subject' of the Fifth Sonata (Ex. 21ii) and the beginning of the second movement of the earlier work (Ex. 19i). Again the juxtaposed triads of B major, D sharp minor and G sharp minor have been built over an F sharp pedal,[5] while the composite 'area' has been transposed to the fourth degree. The whole is diatonic to B major and the aural impression (despite the key signature) is of tonic and subdominant 'areas' of that key in which the sixth and seventh have been given harmonic status. This impression is strengthened by the emphasis in the preceding prologue on the 7/3 chord on F sharp, though this is characteristically clouded by whole-tone added notes.

The 'second subject' of the Fifth Sonata, with a key signature of B flat major, moves to a contrasting tonal area, but again avoids any explicit affirmation of key through traditional harmonic progressions. The B flat tonality is suggested rather by unresolving dominant harmony in which the fundamental harmonic rhythm is very slow indeed. In a context where tonal regions tend to remain in the background in this manner, the two 'illuminations' of E flat, immediately preceding and immediately following the second subject, have a heightened structural significance, the more so as they correspond to important stages in the thematic argument of the work (bars 114 and 140). As the recapitulation is transposed down a fifth, there is a corresponding tonal progression from E major to illuminations of A flat, while the sonata ends as it began with a tonal centre of A. An interesting, if perhaps unplanned, feature of this tonal scheme is its close relationship to the short 'motto' motif which opens and closes the work and which makes two dramatic appearances in the middle section (Ex. 21iii).

Although tonality still has a structural role in the Fifth Sonata, it is no longer supported by traditional diatonic harmonic progressions which would direct the course of the music in a dynamic way. It is expressed rather through long—at times almost motionless—harmonic 'areas' in which the higher diatonic and dominant discords have achieved harmonic status, requiring no orthodox resolution even at the final cadence. As in the shorter piano pieces, the underlying unity of the work depends as much on the consistency of these harmonic areas as on a tonal structure. The close affinities between the harmonic language of the sonata and that of the shorter pieces can be illustrated by an harmonic analysis of the second subject. Ex. 21iv outlines the basic harmonies, indicating that progressions (a) and (b) account for the entire harmonic language in the familiar context of whole-tone/dominant-quality harmony (I shall refer to this as Harmonic Type 1). This harmonic unity is equally apparent, moreover, in the first subject. It has been noted that this begins (Ex. 21ii) with an identical harmonic area to the opening of the second movement of the Fourth Sonata. An analysis of the continuation of the first subject reveals that this harmonic area (Harmonic Type 2) is used almost exclusively throughout, giving a homogeneous harmonic colouring to the section as a whole (Ex. 21v). The transitional material between the first and second subjects (bars 96–119) begins with Type 1 harmony (progression (a) is prominent), but shifts abruptly to Type 2 for the first appearance, *quasi tromba*, of an important new motive, reverting again to Type 1 and progression (b) as the second subject approaches. There are even more dramatic alternations of both harmonic types in the middle section, notably at bars 280–8.

It is perhaps ironic that the finest of Skryabin's extended works, the Fifth Piano Sonata, should have been composed before the evolution of his later harmonic method had been completed. It is a measure of the quality of the work that its unity and coherence can be demonstrated in terms of several independent dimensions of the musical argument—tonal, harmonic and thematic—which are in no way mutually contradictory. We may, for example, experience the first subject as a succession of Type 1 harmonies and at the same time remain aware of its relationship to a background tonality of B major. The sonata is arguably the last of Skryabin's extended works in which the sonata-form outlines still have an integral connection with the content of the music. The need for a complete and almost unvaried recapitulation may certainly be questioned, but the tonal structure of the exposition makes some sort of transposed recapitulation appropriate and justifies a middle section which avoids any clear tonal commitment. This middle section provides, moreover, a necessary reworking, with its rapid juxtaposition of thematic fragments and harmonic types, of material which was stated in bare outline in the exposition. More important, however, is the introduction of a second harmonic type which emphasizes the major rather than the minor seventh and which enables the Fifth Sonata to make dramatic and structural use of harmonic contrast. The absence of such contrast had already weakened the impact of the *Poem of Ecstasy* and it was to prove a serious defect in *Prometheus* and the later sonatas.

The *Poem of Ecstasy* occupied Skryabin intermittently between 1905 and 1908 and was completed just before he began work on the Fifth Sonata. Formally it is an expanded sonata-form movement with a second 'development section' and coda following the recapitulation— like the Fifth Sonata there is a prologue whose two ·themes recur throughout the work. But the shaping of the work is dictated much more by the approach to, and relaxation from, its three main climaxes, each more 'ecstatic' than its predecessor and culminating in the final C major apotheosis (the first two climaxes occur respectively in the first and second development sections). Skryabin's fidelity to a sonata-form background is matched here and in the sonata by his retention of the four-bar phrase as the chief architectonic unit, though there are some indications in these works of an increasing rhythmic flexibility within the phrase. The implications of his allegiance to a traditional formal and thematic process and to a traditional phrase structure in his later music will be considered in a later chapter.

Tonally the *Poem of Ecstasy* is an expression on the largest scale of that process of postponing all reference to the tonic triad until the final bars, which has been examined in the early piano miniatures. The entire work is a long and continuous preparation for the final C major triad, the only one in the work apart from a brief hint in the prologue. Despite the surface activity of much of the music, its basic harmonic rhythm is extremely slow, with progression (a) employed over a long time-span (usually with flattened or sharpened fifth and other whole-tone added notes) to give the harmony its curiously suspended character. The consistent use of progression (a) creates long tritone oscillations in the bass, giving stability to the music as a sort of twin pedal point but delaying further its commitment to a single tonality. Other tonal 'areas' in the work are articulated at the cadence by progression (b) and established by long pedal points. Ex. 22i outlines the basic tonal framework of the composition.

The close affinity between the *Poem of Ecstasy* and the Fifth Piano Sonata lies above all in their emphasis on Type 1 harmony, whose importance in the shorter piano pieces of 1908 has already been established. The extent to which this dominates the harmony of the *Poem of Ecstasy* can be illustrated by an harmonic 'skeleton' of bars 16–70 (Ex. 22ii), where the entire harmonic language is made up of progressions (a) and (b). This emphasis on Type 1 harmony has already taken

Ex. 22
(i)

(ii)

the *Poem of Ecstasy* very far in the direction of a new constructive method which might replace traditional tonality. There is a narrowing of the range of harmonic possibilities—a harmonic selectivity—which results in an ever slower rate of change from one harmonic 'area' to the next. As the traditional tonal expectations aroused by dominant-quality harmony are consistently frustrated, the weakening influence of tonality is gradually replaced by a strengthening harmonic unity, though this has not yet crystallized into an empirical system.

To anticipate somewhat, it will be demonstrated that the evolutionary nature of the changes in Skryabin's harmonic language is due above all to the continuing importance of Harmonic Type 1 and in particular progression (a) in his later works. The in-built ambivalence of progression (a), in which a tonally evocative harmonic unit is used actually to weaken or suspend tonality, is central to the character of Skryabin's music, both before and after *Prometheus*. It weakens the tonal direction of a work such as the *Poem of Ecstasy* which is still composed against a tonal background and, conversely, provides telling reminders of traditional tonal procedures in the later music.

6

Schoenberg

Unlike Skryabin, Schoenberg sustained neither the benefits nor the drawbacks of a rigorous conservatory training. He turned to composition as a natural extension of his early experience of performing chamber music and, apart from some lessons in counterpoint from Alexander von Zemlinsky, he was entirely self-taught as a composer. The musical language of his earliest surviving works—a movement from a String Quartet in C major (1894) and a four-movement quartet in D major (1897)—demonstrates an obvious stylistic sympathy with earlier German composers, though there are occasional (and perhaps surprising) Slavonic inflections. The later work is immeasurably the more successful. If the influences are at times obtrusive (the *finale* in particular is uncomfortably close to Dvořák), there is none the less a secure grasp of form and an ambitious yet clearly focused tonal organization.

The stylistic gap which separates the D major quartet from the string sextet *Verklaerte Nacht*, composed only two years later in 1899, is immense. Admittedly the intervening songs—Opp. 1 and 2—had already moved far beyond the conservative idiom of the quartet. They permit a much higher concentration of chromatic harmony and adopt an attitude to word-setting which is closer to the 'New German School' than to Brahms. As in Wolf, the poetic idea is usually translated into motives which unfold independently in the piano part while the voice's dialogue with this 'accompaniment' is free and widely ranging. But it is in *Verklaerte Nacht* that Schoenberg's identification with the music of Wagner, and with *Tristan* in particular, is first made explicit. His consummate mastery of the whole range of Wagnerian harmony at this early stage in his creative life is indeed remarkable and it was to be consolidated in two ensuing works, the cantata *Gurrelieder*, most of which was composed in 1900–1, and the symphonic poem *Pelleas und Melisande*, completed in 1903. In these later works influences from other late-Romantic composers, notably Mahler and Richard Strauss, blend with that of Wagner.

93

In 'My Evolution', Schoenberg referred to the dual importance of Wagner and Brahms for the music of *Verklaerte Nacht* and Willi Reich has gone so far as to claim that in the internal structure of the work the influence of Brahms is stronger than any other.[1] Yet the predominant influence here, as in *Gurrelieder* and *Pelleas*, is surely that of Wagner, both in the general sonority of the music and in its detailed melodic-harmonic construction—in particular its 'model and sequence' technique and its deceptive cadences.

It is only in the ensuing First String Quartet, Op. 7 (1904–5) that the importance of Brahms for Schoenberg's stylistic evolution becomes clear. Indeed this work marked a decisive stage in his development. From 1899 to 1903 Schoenberg, like many other young composers at the time, was under the spell of Wagner, and his music from this period belongs to the twilight of German Romanticism. While he never fully exhausted the potentialities of a Romantic aesthetic, Schoenberg did seek increasingly to harness those potentialities to a growing preoccupation with problems of form and unity and their changing solutions from one period to the next, a preoccupation with the meaning of an evolving German tradition in its profoundest and most universal aspects. In this Brahms proved a major source of inspiration and, from the Op. 7 quartet onwards, as the influence of Wagner declined in Schoenberg's music, it made room for the more enduring influences of Brahms and the earlier German masters. It is ironical, though perhaps predictable, that a self-taught composer should have acquired a more highly developed and more creative sense of history than any of his conservatory-trained compatriots. His rejection of tonality was in no sense a reaction against his nineteenth-century predecessors but was rather a result of his desire to build upon and extend their achievements without falling into facile imitation of them. Much of Schoenberg's later development may be understood in terms of his enduring search for a means of restating the fundamental tenets of the German Classical tradition in the absence of tonality, his attempt to forge a twentieth-century link in an evolutionary chain stretching back to the early German masters.

THE FIRST STRING QUARTET, OP. 7, AND FIRST CHAMBER SYMPHONY, OP. 9

In Schoenberg, as in Skryabin, the progressive weakening of tonality cannot easily be separated from the progressive strengthening of those compensatory disciplines which replaced it. Unlike Skryabin, however, Schoenberg only succeeded in formalizing those disciplines into an all-embracing 'system' of composition several years after the break with tonality. The constructive methods which gradually ousted tonality from his music were by no means new. They had been developed within the tonal era but were permitted to assume more and more importance as tonality declined. Chief among them were a closely integrated thematic process achieved through elaborate techniques of motivic variation and transformation and the renewal of a contrapuntal independence which had been largely eclipsed by the harmonic developments of the nineteenth century. Subsidiary to these thematic procedures, but also important, were structures based on symmetry or 'notes equally related among themselves' and the use of characteristic sonorities as non-diatonic referential features.

The increasing concentration of thought which characterizes the thematic organization of Schoenberg's early extended works is no less apparent in their formal planning. Apart from the prentice pieces and *Gurrelieder* the general tendency is towards ever greater compression of material within single-movement structures. *Verklaerte Nacht*, Op. 4, and *Pelleas und Melisande*, Op. 5, are both symphonic poems in which formal considerations have been closely linked to programmatic requirements, though Schoenberg was less concerned with a Straussian literalism than with the attempt to 'express the idea behind the poem'.[2] The overall impression of the earlier work is of a freely evolving movement in which the development, transformation and combination of *leitmotiven* have been dictated by the poetic programme, but closer inspection reveals that the framed dialogues of Dehmel's poem have suggested the more specific formal scheme of two interlocking sonata movements. *Pelleas und Melisande*, despite several literal transcriptions of programmatic details, manipulates its programme sufficiently to permit a four-in-one structure comprising a 'first movement', *scherzo*, *adagio* and *finale-cum*-recapitulation. As in *Verklaerte Nacht* the *leitmotiven* are developed and transformed as suggested by the programme so that the thematic argument of the work cuts across its formal divisions.

The change of emphasis in Schoenberg's next major compositions, the First String Quartet, Op. 7 and First Chamber Symphony, Op. 9 (1906–8), proved decisive for his future development. Here he abandoned the programme prop and applied himself rigorously to the problems of formal organization which accompany declining tonality. Both works are single-movement structures with continuously developing groups of themes, but the formal divisions have now been related to an overall sonata-form design with development sections woven into the structure. Formally the quartet is the richer of the two works and it remains susceptible to various interpretations. Indeed one of its fascinations is the manner in which it partakes of characteristics of different formal types, the four movement structure, the sonata-form movement and the rondo, a feature which Hans Keller has described as a 'splitting of formal functions'. Perhaps the most obvious structural difference between both works is the changing proportion of the whole which has been allocated to 'development sections'; the quartet finds room for two (Keller regards them as a single, interrupted, section) while the later work is content with a single, relatively short section. This greater formal compression is a direct outcome of changes in the formal functions of nineteenth-century sonata-symphonic works. The blurring of traditional distinctions between exposition, development and recapitulation procedures was partly a matter of thematic treatment— the tendency, particularly strong in Brahms, towards an organic process of continuous development—but it was also one of tonality. While a contrast between tonally stable and tonally unstable passages remained essential to the sonata dialectic in the nineteenth century, there was a much more flexible attitude towards the 'placing' of such passages, further obviating the need for a traditionally conceived working-out section. In these early works of Schoenberg the term 'development section' is hardly appropriate as a description of passages which comprise little more than a heightened expression of those techniques of elaborate motive working and contrapuntal interplay in a harmonically unstable context which are to be found throughout a composition.

In his analysis of the opening ten-bar phrase of the quartet,[3] Alban Berg has demonstrated that from the outset of the composition the listener is confronted with a remarkable concentration of thematic working. An examination of the complete first subject group demonstrates even more conclusively that the traditional separation of exposition and development procedures has here become unreal. This first group could almost be regarded as a small-scale sonata-form movement in itself. The opening thirteen bars would form a 'first subject' in which themes A1 and B1 (Ex. 23i) are stated in combination, giving way at bar 14 to a second pair of themes A2 and A3 in a B flat minor region. The middle section would begin at bar 30 in an E flat minor region, with the opening ideas presented in invertible counterpoint, leading to an intensified working-out section at bar 54 in which A1 and A2 are combined. This moves from a C sharp minor to a tonic region for a varied recapitulation of the opening material at bar 65. In the 'exposi-

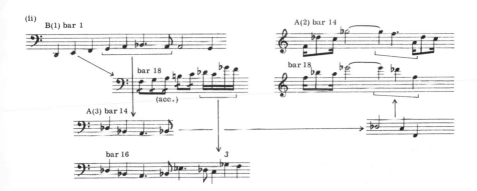

'tion' of this first subject group alone we find the tonal contrast and contrapuntal interest associated with a traditional 'development section'.

A closer inspection of this first subject group reveals, moreover, that a continuous process of motivic evolution underlies these formal divisions —further evidence of Schoenberg's growing preoccupation with thematic integration of material in a context of declining tonality. Schoenberg employed here in concentrated form variation procedures which are all to be found in Brahms, including rhythmic expansion and contraction of the phrase, expansion and contraction of interval patterns and inversion and retrogression of basic motives. The derivation of A3

97

is characteristic. At first hearing it might appear to be an entirely new idea, but it may be derived from B1 (an inversion with interval expansion of the cello motive in bar 2) and it is further related to its companion theme, A2 (Ex. 23ii). The continuation of A3 in bar 17 is an augmentation of the viola accompaniment figure at the end of the preceding bar which is itself a melodic extension of B1 in diminution. This interrelationship of thematic material can be demonstrated, moreover, on the broader canvas of the work as a whole in that many of the principal themes have been linked by a *Grundgestalt* with a prominent interval formation of perfect fourth or fifth and tritone presented in several permutations. This provides much of the inner cohesion underlying external contrasts (Ex. 23i). In the D minor quartet a remarkable degree of thematic integration has been achieved, but other analyses by Alban Berg are sufficient to indicate that such preoccupations had been central to Schoenberg's music since the *Gurrelieder*.

The search for unity in these early works of Schoenberg reveals itself further in his tendency to bring the basic themes of a work into every conceivable contrapuntal relationship with each other. This increasing emphasis on counterpoint is at once an extension of procedures in Mahler and a backward glance at late Beethoven and Bach. In the early songs, Schoenberg's melodies have not yet freed themselves from their dependence upon an underlying harmonic support whose semitonal part-movement obscures but does not conceal a triadic background. It is in parts of *Verklaerte Nacht* that the widely leaping, highly expressive themes begin to cut through the harmonic texture, asserting their independence in combination with other themes. This tendency is carried much further in *Pelleas und Melisande* and the D minor quartet, where the contrapuntal impulse at times seems to dictate and 'explain' the harmony. In the second subject group of the quartet (Fig. A) themes C1 and C2 are developed canonically and combined in augmentation and diminution, giving coherence to the music in the absence of a clearly defined tonality; the lack of tonal definition is underlined incidentally by the symmetrical placing of the entries—at the minor third interval.

The renewal of counterpoint acquires even greater constructive significance in the chamber symphony. Two short examples from the 'development section' will suffice to indicate how important themes have been combined to create complex contrapuntal textures, at times involving canonic procedure (Ex. 24). The uneasy relationship in Ex. 24ii between vertical and horizontal dimensions—between the residue of a traditional tonal-harmonic foundation and the assertion of

Ex.24
(i)

(ii)

thematic identity through contrapuntal combination—is typical of
much of the work. Certainly traditional concepts of consonance and
dissonance are still operative—in determining the pitch at which themes
are stated and the vertical 'placing' of canonic entries. Changes are
often made in the melodic line, moreover, in the interests of harmonic
coherence, as when the minor ninth of the Scherzo theme is modified to a
minor seventh under the influence of prevailing whole-tone harmony, or
when the whole-tone theme is altered to create an F minor triad at the
beginning of bar three (Ex. 14ii). Yet despite such evidence of traditional harmonic thought, Schoenberg's growing preoccupation with the
linear dimension has already begun to overrule vertical considerations
in many parts of the chamber symphony, destroying the harmonic flow
which had formerly generated contrapuntal interplay and replacing it
with an independent 'contrapuntal logic'.

These two aspects of the thematic process of his early music—the
interrelationship of thematic material through concentrated motive

99

working and the combination of thematic ideas into contrapuntal complexes—are complementary dimensions of a single underlying preoccupation. Their common denominator lies in the approach to a 'total
thematicism', in which every thread of the music's texture, including
accompanimental details, has a thematic basis. In the opening bars of
the quartet, for example, the accompaniment to A1, far from simply
providing a harmonic support, is itself thematic and is developed independently later in the work. Webern has described such 'total thematicism' in his essay *Schoenberg's Music*: 'It is marvellous to observe how
Schoenberg creates an accompaniment figure from a motivic particle,
how he introduces themes, how he brings about interconnections
between the principal sections. And everything is thematic!' [4] In his
lecture series *The Path to the New Music*, he compares the concept to
Goethe's primordial plant (*Urpflanze*): 'The root is actually nothing
other than the stem, the stem is nothing other than the leaf, the leaf in
turn is nothing other than the blossom; all variations of the same idea.' [5]
The relevance of the concept to later serial practice will be apparent.

'Total thematicism' was both a cause and a result of the decline of
tonality in Schoenberg's early music, destroying and at the same time
replacing traditional harmonic relationships. The inevitable tension
between tonal-harmonic unifying methods and the thematic-contrapuntal methods which replaced them was expressed in particularly
acute form in the chamber symphony where the tonal direction of the
music is often far from clear. Some effects of this tension have been noted
(Ex. 24), but a fuller understanding of its significance and of the
importance of the work in Schoenberg's evolution will require an
examination of the progressive undermining of tonal harmony in his
earlier music.

In his early songs, Schoenberg, like Wagner and other late-Romantic
composers, employed increasingly complex harmonic phenomena as a
means of enriching the harmony within a single tonal region. In
Harmonielehre and *Structural Functions of Harmony*, he classified many of
these phenomena as chromatic substitutes for, or transformations of,
diatonic harmonies, though he also acknowledged the multiple functions of symmetrical harmonies such as the augmented triad and
diminished seventh, describing them as 'vagrant' or 'roving' harmonies. With the increasing prominence of such 'vagrant' harmonies
and of complex dissonances capable of multiple resolutions, Schoenberg's methods of harmonic classification, derived from a Rameau-
Riemann line of harmonic theory, seem to relate less and less closely to

our aural experience of the music itself. It would be possible to classify the opening harmonies of *Schenk mir deinen goldenen Kamm*, Op. 2, No. 2, within an F sharp region using the methods employed in *Structural Functions of Harmony*, but the ambiguities which would inevitably arise in such an exercise emphasize that the harmonies are more likely to be heard in terms of consistent semitonal part-movement against a triadic background, with a clearly defined 'structural motion' in the outer parts (Ex. 25).

In the interpretation of 'extended' tonal relationships the classification of complex harmonies and the isolation of tonally unstable harmony from its overall context are likely to be of limited usefulness. The harmonies of Op. 2, No. 2 will, after all, be heard in relation to a tonal-cadential framework whose clear tonic cadences leave us in no doubt as to the underlying tonality, though these cadences are obliged to support

Ex.25

harmony in which simple diatonic elements are minimized and the level of dissonance is high.

It is not surprising that in Schoenberg's early extended works the balance between diatonic and chromatic, consonant and dissonant, elements should pose even less of a threat to tonality, for the establishment of clearly defined tonal regions was still the chief means of articulating an extended structure. A very crude summary of the tonal-harmonic language of *Verklaerte Nacht* will indicate the equilibrium of tonal stability and tonal instability which is an essential feature of the structure and which obtains again in the *Gurrelieder* and in *Pelleas und Melisande*. Page numbers refer to the U.E. miniature score.

1–7	7–13	13–14	14–21	21–2	22–5	26–51
D minor		E major		C minor		D[F♯/E♭]D
Stable	Unstable	Stable	Unstable	Stable	Unstable	Stable

The D minor quartet is altogether more complex harmonically, though simple triadic elements still play an important role in affording relief from the complexities, both harmonic and textural, of much of the

Ex. 26

(i)

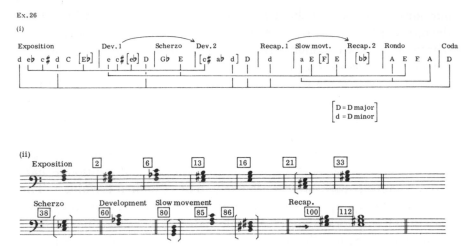

(ii)

music. The first working-out section, for example, opens with a lyrical statement of theme D, accompanied by throbbing E minor chords, which stands in a complementary relationship to the dense thematic saturation of much of the exposition. Similarly the tonally unstable development which follows gives way to a triadic affirmation, however brief, of D major, signalling the return of B2 (cf. page 26 of *Verklaerte Nacht*). The ensuing Scherzo opens, appropriately enough, with a full-blooded triadic version of C2, now diatonic to G flat major (Fig. E).

Such tonal-triadic elements must, however, be viewed in relation to passages, much more prominent than in earlier works, where the tonality is obscure and where the triad has been eclipsed by complex contrapuntal textures. As Hans Keller has indicated, there are moments in the D minor quartet which, if removed from their context, would sound no less 'atonal' than the *finale* of the Second String Quartet (e.g. Fig. C 20–30). Such passages, although they occur within an overall tonal context, emphasize the evolutionary nature of Schoenberg's journey into 'atonality'.

If the equilibrium between tonal stability and tonal instability which was present in earlier works has been disturbed in the D minor quartet by the increasing weight of chromatic and dissonant elements, there is none the less a clearly defined cadential framework by means of which contrasting tonal regions have been established as alternatives to the central tonality (Ex. 26i). In the chamber symphony, on the other hand, the chief alternatives to the central tonality are not contrasting tonal regions (though these exist) but 'non-tonal' passages which are organized contrapuntally or in symmetrical harmonic structures. Both contrapuntal and symmetrical structures embody form-giving principles which are no longer dependent upon tonality and which actually serve to weaken it. It is in fact possible to distinguish in this work between those tonal regions which are established with varying degrees of clarity through a background of diatonic harmony (much of the Mahlerian Scherzo is composed against a C minor background; the 'adagio' shifts from a highly chromatic G to a less distant B major; the third theme of the 'first movement' is in a chromatic A major) and the cadential points of tonal clarification—the 'structural downbeats'—which consistently affirm the E major tonic or its Neapolitan relative F (Ex. 26ii). Often these points of tonal clarification, which articulate the major structural features of the work, no longer emerge as a natural outcome of the preceding harmonic material, for the most part highly chromatic and dissonant. Furthermore the use of a 'non-tonal' theme in fourths, recurring at important junctures of the work and influencing much of its harmony, suggests that referential features could replace tonal cadences now that traditionally functioning harmonic construction has been abandoned for large stretches of the music.

The emphasis on contrapuntal procedure in the chamber symphony and its corrosive influence on tonal harmony has been examined, but the prominence of symmetrical structures, based on 'notes equally related among themselves', as a means of offsetting tonal hierarchies deserves some consideration at this point. Comparable structures have already been observed in the later music of Liszt and in some works by Busoni and Debussy. In Schoenberg's chamber symphony they are of two types, based on the perfect fourth interval and the whole-tone scale (Ex. 27).

This example indicates how, as with the contrapuntally organized textures, there is often an uneasy relationship between these tonally

Ex. 27
(i)

fourths and mirrored augmented triads

fourths

symmetry diatonic

fourths and whole-tone scale

symmetry diatonic symmetry diatonic

whole-tone scale

evasive symmetries and diatonic elements. If this ambivalence is a source of fascination in the chamber symphony, it none the less prevents the work from achieving the quality of the D minor quartet. Too often it seems to waver unhappily between its memories of a tonal past and its prophetic glimpses of an atonal future, retaining the tonal cadence but rejecting for long stretches the harmonic progressions which would have established the cadence as a natural outcome of the work's harmonic language.

THE SECOND STRING QUARTET, OP. 10

It would have been difficult for Schoenberg to have followed the chamber symphony with another *tonal* composition retaining the four-in-one single movement structure, for in that work the tonal cadence often retains only a slender relationship to the surrounding harmonic material. In the Second String Quartet, composed in 1907–8, he returned instead to the four movement form which he had not used since the early D major quartet. The scheme not only gave him a smaller framework which was conducive to harmonic exploration but also allowed a progression within a single work from the clearly affirmed tonality of the first movement to the tonal evasion of the *finale*, a consciously transitional journey towards 'new worlds of sound'. Even in the *finale*, however, Schoenberg did not completely abandon tonality, though it clearly could not have been expanded further without collapse. He himself made this clear in a note on the work: 'The decisive progress towards so-called atonality was not yet carried out. Every one of the four movements ends with a tonic, representing the tonality.' [6]

After the formidable complexities of the D minor quartet, the first movement of this work appears much more readily assimilable, both in its harmonic and its thematic organization. The thematic groups of its exposition section are short and self-contained, and Schoenberg makes little attempt to develop them extensively in the early stages of the work as he had done in the earlier quartet and in the chamber symphony. For this reason, and also because the exposition moves through clearly defined tonal regions (foreshadowing, incidentally, the tonalities of the second and third movements), a working-out section is more essential and makes for a more effective contrast with the outer sections in this work than in either Op. 7 or Op. 9. The section (bars 90–159) begins with a 'false repeat', after the manner of the first movement of Beethoven Op. 59, No. 1 and other nineteenth-century sonata-form movements, before turning to an exhaustive contrapuntal exploitation of the principal thematic material, in particular that of the second subject group. At bar 160 the central F sharp tonality returns and there is a condensed recapitulation in which the order of thematic presentation differs from that in the exposition.

Harmonically the first movement has been composed more consistently against a triadic background than either the first quartet or the chamber symphony. An harmonic summary of the opening bars (Ex. 28i) reveals an underlying chromatic triad progression with 'pivot note' connections which is typical of much of the harmony in the first movement and which is in sharp contrast to the dense motive working of Op. 7. A glance at the opening textures of both works underlines this contrast. Whereas in Op. 7 the subsidiary voices had fulfilled both a harmonic and a thematic role, their function in Op. 10 is almost exclusively harmonic (Ex. 28ii). Even the contrapuntal complexes which play an important part in the working-out section, where there are canons by inversion and augmentation, seldom obscure the triad

105

Ex. 28

(i)

(ii) Op.7

Op.10

(iii) bar 51

quaver groupings

as they had done in the earlier work. The predominantly triadic textures are to some extent offset, however, by harmonic constructions
based on the whole-tone scale and the perfect fourth interval. The
second theme of the second subject group (bar 58) carries a strong
whole-tone harmonic implication (all but one of its notes belong to the
whole-tone scale) which is fully exploited by Schoenberg on the theme's
first appearance. This passage interrupts the overall progression of the
exposition section from an emphasis on the third interval, both melodically, harmonically and tonally, towards an emphasis on the perfect
fourth at bars 66–70.

Within its sonata-form outlines the movement is particularly subtle
in its phrase structure and rhythmic language, extending Brahms's

preoccupation with rhythmic asymmetries. Ex. 28iii indicates the characteristic counterpoint of irregular phrase groupings both in the larger thematic statements and the internal quaver groups. A similar flexibility informs the broader phrase structure of the exposition as a whole, with four-bar symmetries replaced by juxtapositions and over-lappings of three-, four- and five-unit groupings. Such flexibility is entirely characteristic of a movement whose primary concern is the refinement of traditional procedures rather than an attempt to move significantly beyond them.

At first hearing the Scherzo might seem to have a similarly retro-spective quality, for its striking harmonic originality is partly concealed by a traditional rhythmic surface. The main Scherzo section is made up of a succession of short structures which usually take D minor as their tonal starting point but quickly move into complex harmonic areas. Although these harmonies are governed partly by linear thinking, they do suggest at the same time some alternative types of organization in the form of whole-tone and fourth constructions, familiar from the first movement and from the chamber symphony (Ex. 29), and there are at times prophetic indications of a concern to integrate melodic and harmonic material through intervallic invariance.

Ex. 29

perfect fourths

major thirds and perfect fourths

whole-tone scale 1   whole-tone scale 2

But by couching such unorthodox harmonies in a traditional rhythmic language of Beethovenian energy and drive,[7] Schoenberg created in this movement a sound world which presents close analogies with some of his later serial music. If we compare the movement to passages from the Fourth String Quartet, composed some twenty years later and itself often suggesting D minor, we find that in both instances the on-going energy is generated as much by rhythmic as by harmonic means.[8] The use of 'classical' rhythmic patterns in a context of tonal instability or atonality is an important link with tradition, as the driving dotted rhythms of the D minor quartet and chamber symphony had already revealed. Yet the first movement of the second quartet indicates that Schoenberg was no less preoccupied in these transitional works with asymmetrical phrases and irregular groupings within the phrase which extends Brahms's flexible phrase and rhythmic structure. These opposing directions, towards and away from traditional phrase and rhythmic patterns, continued to gain momentum as tonality was submerged in succeeding works, moving further apart in the process.

It is significant that in working out material no longer governed by traditional tonal functions, Schoenberg should have composed in short bursts of concentrated development such as the short structures of the Scherzo represent. The difficulty of sustaining a musical argument without the support of tonality naturally increased in later works, but Schoenberg was clearly aware of it in the Second String Quartet, and the use of a text in the last two movements is closely related to it. The introduction of a soprano soloist in these movements strengthens our impression of the work's consciously transitional character, for the text may act as a formal 'prop' as tonality becomes progressively more obscure (it is of course much more than this). The third movement is a setting of Stefan George's poem *Litanei*, a moving and clearly symbolic prayer for strength in a time of weakness, and it has an overall Theme and Variations form. Its 'psychological shape', dictated by the text, strains against the Classical Variations form, however, suggesting rather a progression towards and away from the two major climactic points. Schoenberg provides a key to this formal tension in his analysis of the work: 'I must confess it was another reason which suggested this form. I was afraid that the great dramatic emotionality of the poem might cause me to surpass the borderline of what should be admitted in chamber music. I expected the serious elaboration required by variation would keep me from becoming too dramatic.'[9]

The movement represents a culminating point in a technique of exhaustive motive working through variation and contrapuntal procedure which Schoenberg inherited from Brahms and it is the most uncompromising expression of 'total thematicism' which he had achieved up to that time. (As the motives making up the 'theme' are taken from the first two movements, the third movement as a whole might be regarded as a 'development section' for the quartet and has been called so by Webern.) [10] Indeed the affinity with Brahms is often of a detailed phraseological kind, as indicated by Ex. 30i, a comparison of melodic elaboration in the fourth variation with part of the earlier composer's Third Symphony. The complexity of the contrapuntal

Ex. 30
(i) Brahms Third Symphony (2nd. movement)

Schoenberg Op. 10

(ii) Principal Motives
(a) (b) (c)
(d) (e) derived motif
(a) (b) (c)

Contrapuntal Combination
bar 22 (e) varied
(c) with inversion
bar 29 (d)
(a)
(c)
(e)

bar 36 (b) (e)
3 3
(c) (d)
(a)

organization, involving elaborate canonic procedure, has been illustrated in Example 30ii. It is undoubtedly this thematic saturation of the texture which acts as the most important unifying feature in the music, as traditional harmonic relationships are given little opportunity to establish themselves and, apart from the final cadence, the E flat minor tonality is restricted largely to an implication which arises out of the opening fragment of the Theme. Schoenberg was here exploring the motivic methods of earlier works in an almost atonal context, giving them increased constructive status and anticipating an important aspect of early atonality.

In the final movement of the quartet, Schoenberg explored further the implications of those 'non-tonal' passages, contrapuntally and symmetrically organized, which had played an important part in the First Chamber Symphony, building them into greatly extended musical paragraphs and reducing to a minimum the complementary references to an F sharp tonic. Ex. 31 summarizes the tonal-harmonic structure of the movement, showing the interplay of tonally affirmative and tonally evasive material. The introduction carefully avoids any tonal implications though it does at times employ pedal points as non-diatonic points of reference. The first preparation of the F sharp tonic is the open fifth on C sharp at the end of the introduction which leads to the first F sharp major triad in bar 25. The transitional passage between this 'dominant' and 'tonic' consists of a linear statement of chord (x) (Example 31), reminiscent of the horizontalization of the 'Tristan chord' at the end of Wagner's Prelude and the beginning of the love duet. The parallel extends further in that chord (x) itself functions as a non-tonal referential sonority, similar to both the 'fate' chord from *Pelleas und Melisande* (whose construction is almost identical) and the 'Tristan chord'. The succeeding phrase with the first entry of the voice is typical of much highly chromatic and atonal harmony in its tendency to 'strengthen' the harmony by employing progressions where successive chords have no or few notes in common. The importance of this concept in twelve-note harmony has been pointed out by Theodor Adorno who refers to the 'law of complementary harmony'.[11]

With its interaction of tonal elements—assertions and preparations of the F sharp tonic—and non-tonal elements, this movement continues the methods employed in the chamber symphony, differing from that work solely, but crucially, in the balance between both types of material. To recall Schoenberg's own comment: 'The overwhelming multitude of dissonances cannot be counterbalanced any longer by occasional returns

Ex.31

III

to such tonic triads as represent a key.' By giving tonality little chance to establish itself, Schoenberg had to consider the problem of organizing and shaping the long paragraphs of tonally evasive material, a problem which clearly became more acute in later compositions. The text is of the greatest importance in this respect, shaping both details of texture and large-scale structure; so too is the use of contrapuntally derived textures, the independent part-movement which could no longer be forced into the 'Procrustean bed of tonality'. But it is the greatly increased prominence of symmetrical structures, already important in the chamber symphony, which forms the most striking response to the problem. Long paragraphs whose symmetrical construction ascribes equal importance to each of the chromatic notes helped to free Schoenberg from the pitch hierarchies which are a condition of tonality. It is worth noting that when they had achieved this purpose they declined in importance in his work.

The introduction is such a paragraph and it is the more suitable for examination in that there is as yet no vocal line to give the music dramatic shape. Schoenberg's own description of the introduction vividly conveys the notion of freedom from the 'pull' of tonality by referring to the text of George's poem: 'Becoming released from gravitation—passing through the clouds into thinner and thinner air, forgetting all the troubles of life on earth—that is attempted to be illustrated in this introduction.' [12] Ex. 31 indicates that motive (a), comprising incidentally eight notes of the total chromatic, is repeated in a pattern of ascending fifths which gives way to a sequence of descending, interlocking fifths. This symmetry, from which the music derives its order and coherence, ends with motive (b) which acquires a cadential function and is repeated at the end of the second symmetrical structure. This time it leads, after an increase in rhythmic and dynamic tension, to a chord of D minor with major seventh which relieves the tension and whose cadential function is emphasized by a quasi-tonal V—I progression in the bass. This cadence illustrates not only the replacement of tonal cadences by other forms of punctuation, be they distinctive motivic shapes or strongly characterized sonorities, but also the added importance in a non-tonal context of rhythm and texture as a means of creating the tension and relaxation formerly attributable to harmonic procedure. The third structure is a necessary contrast to the first two symmetrical constructions, employing a twin pedal point as the foundation for a chromatically ascending figure which soon begins to hint at D minor and which gives way to a chord similar in construction to (x).

This leads to a further symmetrical structure using open fifths at the major third interval in a pattern which culminates in a chord built on C and comprising two superimposed fifths—on C and E flat. Both fifths close inwards onto a chord built on C sharp which opens the next paragraph and which functions as a dominant preparation for the first reference to the central tonality of the movement.

The final three movements of the Second String Quartet were each of the greatest importance for Schoenberg's development as a composer. The Scherzo revealed the extent to which harmonic dissonance could be 'explained' by traditional phrase and rhythmic patterns, foreshadowing the almost 'neo-classical' characteristics of some of his serial music. The Variations represented a landmark in his development of a totally integrated thematic and harmonic process, an important link between the concentrated thematicism of the D minor quartet and the total thematicism of 'Nacht' from *Pierrot Lunaire*. The *finale* tackled the problem of shaping extended paragraphs of music in the absence of tonality and, in doing so, foreshadowed several of the preoccupations of the early atonal music—the constructive significance of counterpoint, the use of rhythm and texture as a means of shaping and directing the phrase, the replacement of the tonal cadence by other referential features and the subtle integration of tonal reminiscences into a predominantly non-tonal musical language.

7

Berg and Webern

Predictably there are close affinities between the early music of Berg and Webern and that of their teacher Schoenberg. Especially close to Schoenberg are the early instrumental compositions of Berg where there is a marked tendency for 'total thematicism' to replace tonality as the most important form-giving principle in the music. The convenient grouping of all three composers into a so-called 'Second Viennese School' was inevitably encouraged by their later adoption of the serial method, but the very real affinities between them should not be allowed to obscure fundamental differences of musical instinct and idiom which separate their individual achievements.

If the decisive influences on Schoenberg's development were those of Brahms and the early Classical masters, Berg's music is closer in spirit to the world of the later German Romantics, to Mahler's impassioned lyricism and to the exploration by Strauss and Schreker of a richly dissonant harmonic language for its emotive and colouristic qualities. Even in his early Piano Sonata, where much of the texture has been thematically derived, Berg employs harmonic phenomena which cannot be explained in terms of a tonal background or of thematic derivations, having their *raison d'être* in a search for heightened expressiveness. The predilection for expressively dissonant harmonies and emotionally charged melodies persisted throughout his creative life, forging strong links between the tonal compositions, the atonal music and the later serial works. But there was a further dimension to his musical sensibility —an intellectual concern for a closely argued thematic process and strict, at times rigid, structural control (often this has a cryptological basis). Already in the early works there are intimations of a tension between both dimensions of his work, a tension which was to be given creative expression in the serial music.

Webern, too, was inspired by the late-Romantic world of Mahler, though his relationship to that world was quite different from Berg's. Schoenberg perfectly expressed the nature of the relationship when he wrote in a foreword to Webern's *Bagatelles*, Op. 9: 'To express a novel in a single gesture, a joy in a breath—such concentration can only be present in proportion to the absence of self-pity.' [1] The expressivity of Webern's melodic writing may indeed be regarded as an ultimate distillation of the widely spanning, emotion-laden lines of Mahler's symphonies which he learned to love during his formative years in Vienna. At the same time his musicological research into the work of Heinrich Isaac was ultimately to play an equally important part in helping to mould his unique artistic sensibility. In the serial works that sensibility was given its clearest expression; an 'expressive' late-Romantic melos, almost, in Joyce's phrase, 'refined out of existence', is fertilized by, and in a sense objectified by, a contrapuntal process inspired by the techniques of Renaissance polyphony.

BERG'S EARLY SONGS AND PIANO SONATA, OP. I

The collection of *Seven Early Songs* was grouped together from songs which had been composed separately by Berg over a period of three years from 1905 to 1908 (a larger collection of unpublished songs dating from these years exists in the *Österreichische Bibliothek* and betrays for the most part mid- to late-nineteenth-century German Romantic influences, notably that of Brahms [2]) and a development of style may be traced from the traditional, if very beautiful, early songs such as 'Die Nachtigall' (1905–6) to the more forward-looking 'Nacht' (1908) which opens the cycle. 'Die Nachtigall' belongs squarely within the German *lied* tradition of Brahms and Schumann, though there are echoes of Mahler in the character of its principal motive, developed sequentially in the outer sections of a simple ternary structure, and in the cumulative overlapping of its entries at climactic points such as bar 12. At no point do the richly expressive harmonies disturb a clearly defined tonal structure with a characteristically 'Romantic' move to a mediant region for the middle section. The second song 'Schilflied' is more elaborate chromatically, perhaps reflecting Schoenberg's influence, though there is again a clear tonal structure stressing the mediant relationship F-A flat-C.

It is in the opening song 'Nacht' that Berg begins to move decisively away from the traditional harmonic language of earlier songs. His natural leaning towards expressively dissonant harmonies undoubtedly made him more susceptible than Schoenberg to the harmonic developments of Debussy, and 'Nacht' reflects his new awareness of the French composer in its use of the whole-tone scale and allied harmonic com-

ponents—alternating augmented triads and parallel major thirds—
as the principal harmonic resource of the song. Unlike Schoenberg
in his First Chamber Symphony and Second String Quartet, Berg
dwells upon the whole-tone scale and savours it as a harmonic colour,
giving it added prominence by systematically alternating both transpositions (Ex. 32). In addition to its whole-tone colouring the song

Ex.32

A = whole-tone scale I   B = whole-tone scale II

emphasizes the unresolving 7/3 unit and enjoys the sensuous qualities
of passages in major thirds, a Straussian feature of Berg's music which
persists into his later harmonic idiom and one whose frank Romanticism again points the contrast with Schoenberg (excepting the deliberately nostalgic thirds of the last movement of *Pierrot Lunaire*). Ex. 32
also illustrates the tonal scheme of the song, with the augmented triad
on E forming an important hinge in the argument in that it belongs to
the first whole-tone scale and may at the same time be directed towards
the central tonality of A major. There is a careful balance throughout
the song between the tonal evasion of whole-tone harmony and the
tonal attraction of orthodox cadential preparations, while the latter
are often enriched by a resolution to an added sixth chord on the tonic.

Although 'Nacht' avoids any explicit reference to its tonic triad, a
tonal scheme is outlined by cadence, and the triad is still the basic
harmonic unit, however chromatically embellished. The Piano Sonata,

117

Op. 1, composed during the same period (1907–8), begins and ends with a statement of its B minor tonic, but the stability of the triad is constantly undermined here by unresolving dissonance and by a tendency for thematic considerations to dictate much of the harmony. The sonata was Berg's first mature extended work and it is in a single sonata-form movement of traditional outlines (not a four-in-one expanded sonata-form movement such as Schoenberg's Op. 7 and Op. 9) with a repeated exposition, development section, varied recapitulation and coda.

An analysis of the first eleven bars (Ex. 33i) will establish the stylistic premises for the work as a whole. Bars 1–3 serve to set out the three most important motivic cells while at the same time establishing the B minor tonality. Motive (b) recalls the first of the *Seven Early Songs*, but motive (a), combining the intervals of a perfect fourth and tritone, is a new fingerprint in Berg's music and its use, both melodically and harmonically, was to be of some importance as he moved into atonality, outlining as it does such 'non-tonal' intervals as the tritone and major seventh. The opening three bars are followed by an immediate development of these motives (Ex. 33i) which demonstrates the extent to which thematic saturation of the texture provides much of the coherence of this music. Yet even in a context of almost total thematicism, the harmony is 'filled in' with characteristic passages in major thirds moving chromatically or by whole-tone steps to create whole-tone harmonic areas. Example 33i also demonstrates the prominence of the augmented triad not only as a melodic shape but as a recurring harmonic feature. There is a strong bass preparation (bars 9–12) for the seventh chord on D which, in a chromatic and dissonant context, acts as a cadential point of relative stability and signals the beginning of a new theme. The blend of thematic, harmonic and tonal elements which characterizes this passage continues throughout the work; it is by no means always successful.

The concentration of motive working in Berg's sonata is by far its most important unifying feature and it dictates the vertical dimension to a considerable extent. Much of the texture of the work cannot be explained thematically, however, and one of the most interesting aspects of its harmonic language is the frequent replacement of the triad by more complex dissonant harmonies which none the less behave in a manner analogous to traditional tonal progressions; they 'resolve' onto other dissonant chords by means of stepwise, predominantly semitonal, part-movement (Ex. 33ii). Here a traditional phrase and rhyth-

Ex. 33

(i)

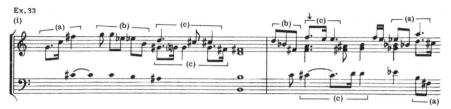

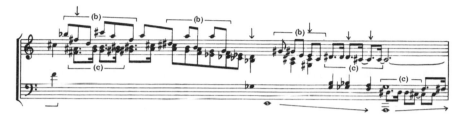

D7

(ii) bar 66

(iii) Exposition

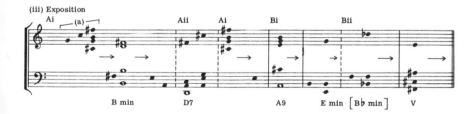

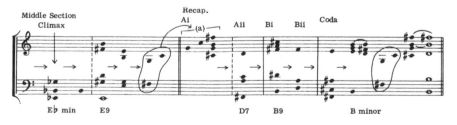

mic structure and strongly directional melodic and bass motions reinforce the quasi-tonal nature of the chord progression. Often in such
progressions Adorno's 'law of complementary harmony' appears to be
functioning. In addition Berg makes use of fourths harmonies (bar 27)
and parallel chord progressions, another Debussyan procedure which is
rare in Schoenberg, while a pervading and to some extent unifying
harmonic colour is created by the prominence of the augmented triad
and whole-tone scale.

   The uneasy relationship which exists in much of the sonata between
thematically derived textures and independent harmonic elements is
further complicated by the attempt to accommodate both to a freely
tonal framework centred on B minor. The development towards 'total
thematicism' tends to be tonally disruptive, as are several of the independent harmonic procedures which have been observed; in particular
dissonant chord progressions and harmonic constructions based on the
whole-tone scale. Yet despite disruptive elements, the significant structural features of the sonata are articulated by tonal cadences (Ex. 33iii).
The clearest tonal progression is from a tonic to a subdominant region,
though the mediant region is stressed at the main climax of the development section. These tonal regions are confirmed by triadic harmony, but
it is significant that at other points Berg employs seventh and ninth
harmonies as cadential points of relative consonance, falling as they do
on 'structural downbeats' (i.e. approached by traditional cadential
phrase and rhythmic patterns) and acting as the starting point for new
material. In Ex. 33i, where there is a strong cadential preparation for
the second theme, the tonal 'pull' of the seventh chord on D is immediately cancelled by the whole-tone character of the theme. Such ambivalence is highly characteristic of this sonata. It is one of the fascinations
of the music that the very moments which appear to be the most directional tonally tend to dissolve into unstable whole-tone harmonic areas
(e.g. bars 68–70).

   Both Schoenberg's First Chamber Symphony and Berg's Piano
Sonata are sonata-form works in which the unifying influence of tonality
has weakened considerably. Stylistic comparison of two such transitional
works can usefully illuminate the important differences in their musical
languages at a similar stage of their evolution. In the Schoenberg, the
coherence depends to a large extent on an interplay of tonally stable and
tonally evasive material, the latter in the form of contrapuntally dictated
or symmetrically organized textures. In the Berg the premises are less
clear. To the extent that the work approaches total thematicism as a

unifying method which might replace tonality, it reflects the influence of Schoenberg and anticipates the thematic concentration of the first movement of the String Quartet, Op. 3. Thematic procedures cannot easily be separated, however, from a harmonic background of expressively dissonant chord progressions which respect traditional part-movement and traditional patterns of harmonic tension and relaxation, and therefore tend to suggest a distant tonal background. Rather than an interplay of 'tonal' and 'non-tonal' material the work presents a harmonic flux in which points of tonal clarification occur and alternative types of non-tonal organization are suggested, but where the most characteristic material hovers precariously between both worlds. Perhaps the most serious weakness is the resulting lack of harmonic differentiation; the development section, for example, differs in no essential respects in its tonal-harmonic language from the outer sections.

BERG'S FOUR SONGS, OP. 2

Berg's next composition was the set of *Four Songs*, Op. 2, composed in 1909. The last three songs are settings of poetry by Mombert, their blend of the mystical and the sensuous reflecting Berg's sympathies with a particular aspect of German pre-Expressionist verse. Indeed the Op. 2 songs are close to the heart of Expressionism. In its desire to search out the 'inner spirit', Expressionist poetry heightened the emotional content of late-Romantic verse to the point at which conventional formal constraints were sacrificed, just as the intensity of some of Van Gogh's later canvases strained to the limits traditional notions of formal balance in painting and suggested new directions to younger painters such as Kandinsky. There is a tempting parallel between such developments in the other arts and Berg's rejection of tonality in the last of the Op. 2 songs.

Like the four movements of Schoenberg's Second String Quartet, the tonal foundations of Berg's songs become progressively less secure, from the relatively stable D minor of the first song, a setting of Hebbel, to the tonal evasion of the last. Even the first song, however, quickly moves outside the D minor sphere of influence. Like the other three songs it makes use of those quasi-tonal dissonant chord progressions which have been examined in the Piano Sonata, where traditional part-movement is supported by an equally traditional rhythmic structure (Ex. 34i). The familiar fourth and whole-tone constructions also play a part in the song's harmonic language as does a characteristic sonority—chord (x)—which first appears in the fifth bar and which functions as a referential feature. Chord (x), comprising the 7/3 unit and a verticalization of motive (a) from the Piano Sonata, is resolved in quasi-tonal manner by an 'appoggiatura' onto a major ninth chord on D. The use of the chord as an unchanging point of reference in a harmonically complex context relates it to those referential harmonies which have been noted in Schoenberg's early music. A further detail which foreshadows later procedures in Berg's music is the use of the pitches C sharp and E flat (bar 11) to imply the unstated tonal centre D (the vocal line supports this with a dominant-quality appoggiatura B flat—A). In later atonal works, Berg frequently 'closed in' on a pitch centre through its semitonal neighbour notes in this way.

Ex. 34

Although the first song begins and ends with a tonic triad, the intervening harmonies cannot be related easily to the underlying tonality. In the other three songs the triad, already obscured by the unresolving dissonances of the first song, is further undermined. The outer sections of the second song provide an early example of Berg's fascination with rigorous constructive patterns. A harmonic structure of which the 'French sixth' [3] is the fundamental unit is transposed at the perfect fourth interval throughout the total chromatic, an essay in non-tonal harmonic symmetry which Berg may well have modelled on parts of Schoenberg's First Chamber Symphony. The systematic nature of the construction (Ex. 34ii shows how the grouping of seven ascending and five descending fourths serves to outline the tritone B flat–E) is disguised by the distribution of parts and by the introduction of passing-notes and some added notes. The middle section, like parts of 'Nacht' and the Piano Sonata, explores the whole-tone characteristics of consecutive major thirds. The final 'French sixth', built on E flat, becomes a dominant seventh when the A natural is released and resolves onto the A flat minor melody which opens the third song.

In some respects the third song recalls the first, not least in its reiteration of the descending fifth A-D and in its reference to a D minor tonality (Ex. 34iii). Despite the complex harmonies of the song there is a strongly marked II—V—I bass progression which strengthens the central cadence into a D minor region. Admittedly this cadence is clouded to some extent by the vocal line's added sixth but the region is none the less established clearly enough and it acts as a link in the overall tonal progression from A flat to E flat. This tonal scheme is therefore closely related to motive (a) from the sonata and the motive itself forms part of the thematic material of the song (Ex. 34iii), furnishing yet another link with the first song.

In the final song Berg abandoned a key signature and with it tonality. The overall progression from the harmonic area (y), firmly established at the opening by repetition (Ex. 34 iv), to the final chord (x), again reiterated and already familiar from the first song, has something of the character of a remote Neapolitan relationship. But despite its character as a triadic combination and its emphasis as a harmonic point of reference, the final chord is here without tonal function. Moreover the continuation of the opening harmony with parallel major sevenths suggests that it is best understood as a harmonic area independent of tonality. When a modified version of chord (y) returns in bar 5, after a series of parallel minor sevenths which effectively destroy any tonal feeling which may have been established in the opening bars, its spacing emphasizes its relationship to chord (x) with the notes C, F and F sharp grouped together in the upper register. The additional sevenths result in a severely dissonant harmonic area which dissolves in a descending cascade (with obvious pictorial significance) onto a bare tritone E flat-A (Ex. 34 iv). The tritone figure is developed in bar 11, now thickened into open fifths, while a passage in thirds gives way to the semitonal part-movement which leads to the main climax of the song. Motive (a) is presented harmonically, shared between voice and piano, and at the climactic point the pitches B flat and A are emphasized, emerging exposed after the climax has dissolved in a whole-tone passage again using major thirds. A series of chords follows in which the bass rises in perfect fourths—an obvious reminiscence of the second song—while motive (a) is verticalized and descends in semitones until it reaches chord (x) (Ex. 34 iv).

This description—it is not an analysis—has isolated those harmonic features which, in the absence of a more thorough-going unifying principle such as tonality or total thematicism, act as landmarks in an unfamiliar terrain. Chordal progression by semitonal part-movement (bars 12–13) and harmonies based on thirds (bars 9–12 and 17) give coherence to the music because they relate to traditional tonal procedure; parallelism and whole-tone harmony because they are based on the principle of symmetry; the recurrence of a particular motive or harmonic area precisely because they recur. The fact that such harmonic procedures do not account for the musical language of the entire song—that there is no underlying linguistic principle to which they can all be related—localizes and weakens their unifying influence. Accordingly the Form of the music—its tensions and relaxations, its contrasts, its sequence of events—depends to an unprecedented degree on the composer's intuitive grasp of formal balance, which in tonal music had been allied to a set of universally accepted conventions. The free association of ideas on an intuitive level which we find in Berg's song is 'expressionistic' in the sense that its concern is the concentrated expression of the individual moment of intense emotion. The music is an extension of the spirit and language of late-Romanticism; it employs the phraseology of the late-Romantics—their expressively dissonant harmonies and widely leaping melodies—but without their underlying constructive foundation, tonality. In such a context a pre-existing dramatic shape is all-important as a structural 'prop', and it is Berg's response to the text of Mombert's poem which dictates not only details of texture but the overall shape of the song.

Where the Piano Sonata was already exploring new ways of organizing material which could replace tonality—its approach to a totally integrated thematic and harmonic language represented one direction among several which culminated in serialism—the final song of Op. 2 revealed a different aspect of declining tonality. Here tonality has been submerged by the weight of 'expressive' dissonance, without giving way to the alternative thematic disciplines found in the sonata. The composer was therefore obliged to rely to an unprecedented extent on his subconsciously functioning sense of form to achieve the *Zusammenhang*—the unity or cohesion—which in tonal music was at least partly ensured by definable tonal-harmonic relationships. More than ever 'he must be convinced of the infallibility of his own fantasy and he must believe in his own inspiration'.[4]

A NOTE ON WEBERN'S TONAL MUSIC

Without forcing the point unnaturally, it is difficult to detect many intimations of Webern's future stylistic direction from a study of the works composed before his *Passacaglia*, Op. 1.[5] These consist for the most part of songs written between 1899 and 1908 and it is tempting to compare them with the songs composed by Berg during the same years. Like Berg's, Webern's early songs are heavily indebted in their general conception to German Romantic *lieder*, and in particular to the songs of Brahms, but the lyrical expansiveness of Berg's settings contrasts with Webern's greater concentration of expression giving rise at times to highly unorthodox harmonic procedures, particularly in the frequent appearance of 'semitonal contradictions'. The earliest surviving songs range from a conventional setting of Avenarius's *Vorfrühling* (1899) to the strikingly adventurous *Heimgang in der Frühe* (1901). Here an overall tonal progression from a D major region (after a tonally ambiguous opening) to a D flat region incorporates chains of parallel augmented triads, while orthodox cadential resolutions are avoided until the final cadence. Parallel augmented triads are indeed a recurring feature of the early songs, notably *Nachtgebet der Braut* (1903) and *Helle Nacht* (1908), a setting of Dehmel which comes to rest on an unresolved augmented triad.

Although the predominant stylistic influence in the early songs is that of Brahms, several of them, including *Gefunden* (1904), demonstrate an awareness of Wagner and Richard Strauss in their use of extended chromatic sequences. These influences are much more explicit, however, in the instrumental works of the formative years, especially in the tone-poem *Im Sommerwind* and the Wagnerian 'Slow Movement' for String Quartet (1905). Stylistically the relationship between this quartet movement and the single-movement String Quartet composed later in the same year is not dissimilar to that between Schoenberg's *Verklaerte Nacht* and his D minor string quartet. There are indeed several indications in the music of the later quartet that Webern may have modelled the work on Schoenberg's quartet, completed in the same year. Apart from a marked similarity in thematic material, the motivic working and contrapuntal density of Webern's work is comparable to that in the Schoenberg. It is perhaps worth noting that the principal motive of the work is the three-note cell which was to assume special prominence in Webern's serial music.

The same motive appears again as a second idea in the Piano Quintet which Webern composed two years after the quartet in 1907. In this work, too, there are close thematic resemblances to Schoenberg's Op. 7 quartet, notably between the impressive, widely spanning opening melody and the beautiful viola melody from the 'slow movement' of Schoenberg's work (Fig. K bar 53). It is perhaps a tentative indication of Webern's emerging musical personality that although the piano accompaniment textures are Brahmsian in conception, they are often organized into tightly knit contrapuntal configurations such as the canonic interplay with inversion at bar 31.

The concentration of thought which marks the Quartet (1905) and the Piano Quintet derives essentially from Brahms, both directly and through Schoenberg, and a similar concentration is apparent again in the last two of his compositions to retain a key signature and the first two to bear an Opus number. Indeed the *Passacaglia*, Op. 1 (1908), may well have used Brahms's Fourth Symphony *finale* as a starting point, though it goes even further than that movement in the compression of its structure and the concentration of its motive working. Like Schoenberg's later Op. 31 Variations, the 'theme' of the *Passacaglia* remains in the foreground of the argument just long enough to be clearly assimilated, before giving way to derived melodic material. Tonally the work remains stable, despite chromatic elaborations, forming a tripartite tonal structure centred on D minor—D major—D minor.

The chorus *Entflieht auf leichten Kahnen*, Op. 2 (1908), on the other hand, pays only token respect to its G major key signature. It is intriguing that the work which should have preceded Webern's first venture into atonality should have been canonic, just as his last composition before adopting the serial method should have been 'the *Five Canons*, Op. 16, composed some sixteen years later. But canonic procedure only assumed real importance for Webern with his adoption of serialism and it would be easy to attach too much significance to its appearance in such an early, and not entirely characteristic, essay. Certainly contrapuntal integrity is maintained throughout the work at the expense of orthodox harmonic progression, but at the same time the harmonies may still be understood in terms of the more remote transformations of diatonic functions. Even more than Schoenberg's chorus *Friede auf Erde*, Op. 13, of the previous year, a work with which it has affinities, *Entflieht auf leichten Kahnen* occupies a fascinating borderland between tonal and atonal harmony. Indeed the concentration of chromaticism is such that Walter Kolneder has suggested that Adorno's 'law of complementary harmony' is almost the only independent harmonic constraint.[6]

Unlike the early music of Schoenberg and Berg, that of Webern does not lend itself readily to a study of stylistic evolution towards atonality. The stylistic gap between Op. 1 and Op. 2 is wide, as is that between Op. 2 and his first atonal work, the *Five Songs*, Op. 3. Indeed it is perhaps this very feature of the early music which most clearly foreshadows his maturity. Throughout his creative life Webern's stylistic evolution, far from being translated into finished works which would be to some extent 'pivotal', was achieved silently—in the mind, as it were (hence the importance of his sketches for a thorough understanding of the nature of his achievement). Only when the stylistic advance had been consolidated in the mind, was it given creative expression, resulting in compositions whose conception and realization are uniquely attuned.

8

Szymanowski

The earliest surviving compositions by Szymanowski, the seventh and eighth of his *Nine Preludes*, Op. 1, date from the final years of the nineteenth century. It is the remarkable technical assurance of these and other early works which makes it all the more surprising that his achievement of a fully mature and stylistically integrated musical language should have been delayed until the works of 1915. The reasons for this long period of stylistic uncertainty can be grasped only when we have appreciated the enfeebled state of Polish music after the death of Chopin. There is a paradox but no contradiction in the fact that Szymanowski was acutely conscious of his obligations towards Polish culture and yet remained an eclectic, drawing freely upon contemporary European styles and techniques. He made the vital distinction between nationalism and the provincialism which had accounted partly for the low vitality of much Polish music in the later nineteenth century. Composers such as Noskowski and Zelenski had spared no effort to make their music sound 'Polish'—Szymanowski referred to '*oberek*-mazurka paper-cuts'—while steadily losing touch with the deeper spirit of the nation.

Admittedly socio-political difficulties in late nineteenth-century Poland affected music much more than the other arts. Szymanowski's article *Thoughts on Polish Criticism in Music Today* [1] indicates clearly the stifling effects of partition on the musical life of the three provinces, with the conservatism of teaching institutions, critics and concert managers effectively moulding the conservatism of public taste. Such factors add up to the external trappings of a musical tradition, and on this level at least we may justifiably claim that the ground was not fertile enough for a composer of Szymanowski's calibre. He realized that to be a significant *Polish* composer he must first become a significant *composer*; that he could only rebuild Polish music from the highest vantage point, an understanding of the great achievements of Western music. Hence the long period during which he composed his way through European styles, assimilating those features of established traditions which might help him renovate a Polish tradition. Nor did he ever isolate himself from new developments in Western Europe, though his view of what was relevant to his needs changed radically.

Szymanowski was one of several young Polish composers who, in 1901, formed a group known as 'Young Poland in Music', inspired perhaps by the 'Young Poland' movement in literature, with whose aesthetic views he identified to a limited extent. The literary movement was both a conscious reaction against the 'Positivism' of an earlier generation of Polish novelists and a response to Poland's renewed contact with the mainstream of European artistic and intellectual life in the nineties, following a period of relative isolation. As with an emerging group of Russian poets, the impact of the French 'Symbolists' proved to be a particularly crucial determinant in the direction Polish poets were to take at the turn of the century. The most extreme expression of the underlying philosophy of 'Young Poland' was the *Confiteor* of Przybyszewski, author of the notorious *Homo Sapiens* and the central figure of the movement: 'Art has no aim, it is aim in itself . . . it cannot serve any idea, it is dominant, it is a source from which all life comes. . . . Art stands above life; penetrates the essence of the universe. . . . Art so conceived becomes the highest religion, and the artist becomes its priest. . . .' [2] While it would be quite wrong to confine Szymanowski's aesthetic sympathies within the limited sphere of the 'Young Poland' circle, there can be no doubt that the aims and philosophy of 'Young Poland' did have considerable bearing on the underlying impulses which shaped his musical language, particularly in the works composed before 1920. One senses that as his music increased in refinement and sophistication, he grew less concerned with the communication of new musical resources than with their exploration. This 'withdrawal from the world', very much in the spirit of 'Young Poland', was to lead to a serious spiritual and creative crisis in later life.

The musical expression of that crisis centred around the role of tonality in his work. Despite obvious points of contact with many contemporary styles, Szymanowski developed a highly individual musical language as his creative personality matured, a language notable for its flexible melodic lines, elaborately shaped chromatically, its refined harmonic palette exploring a wealth of nuance within a predominantly dissonant context, and its avoidance of regular phrase structure and strong rhythmic accent. Tonality, the unchallenged unifying principle in his early works, was gradually undermined in several of the middle-period works by a growing preoccupation with an exotic, 'Impressionistic' dissonance and a highly chromatic melisma. But unlike Skryabin and Schoenberg, Szymanowski felt no need to replace tonality by an alternative self-consistent method of organization. The decline of tonality in his music is perhaps closest to one aspect of the early music of Berg and to the work of Franz Schreker—their exploration of the colouristic qualities of dissonance at the expense of tonal functions. It is indeed precisely because Szymanowski adopted no thorough-going alternatives to tonal organization that his music is of particular interest to the present study. It highlights in especially clear form the difficulties of concept and terminology which arise in music where the harmonic tensions and relaxations and the melodic phraseology have clear origins in tonal procedure, but where an underpinning tonal framework has been almost or completely dissolved away.

THE EARLY MUSIC

'Szymanowski composed at the piano . . . Above all he loved and worshipped Chopin and, after Chopin's music, the piano works of Scriabin. When he was working on his First Piano Sonata, Op. 8, I found him frequently at the instrument studying in minute detail the structure of passages in Chopin and Scriabin.' [3] Rozycki's comments on Szymanowski's working methods in the early years are borne out by the stylistic atmosphere of his early piano preludes and studies, many of which are similar in form and conception to the early piano miniatures of Skryabin. They give little indication of the composer's later harmonic development, but exhibit none the less a skilful workmanship, a command of *métier*, which belies the simplicity of their forms and which reveals itself in a careful balancing of materials, an economy of thematic elements and in unexpected harmonic twists and rhythmic subtleties. The flexibility of the phrase rhythm and the subtle balance between the exposition of motives and their varied restatement in the second prelude from the Op. 1 set (1897–1900) are characteristic of that avoidance of the obvious gesture which is a hallmark of Szymanowski's finest music, from whatever period. The prelude is a short rondo structure and, like most of the early pieces, is tonally unambiguous, moving from a D minor region through regions of F major, D flat major and G minor to a coda in the tonic.

The third prelude, again in D minor, illustrates how an expressive interweaving of parts in fluid rhythms can be governed by the chromatic scale while still remaining within the orbit of its unchanging tonal region. Like many of Skryabin's early preludes, it is a simple ternary structure in which the middle section is an extension, using sequential patterns, of the opening material. The sixth prelude is more adventurous tonally, its recurring augmented sixth chord finding a tonic resolution only in the final bar. It also demonstrates the sort of harmonic inconsistency which occasionally mars these early works, as Szymanowski explored more 'advanced' harmonic idioms. The stark octaves and pungent dissonances of the opening section seem curiously out of place beside the 'Wagnerian' sequences,[4] centred on the diminished triad, of the middle section.

In acquiring a basic fluency during these early years, Szymanowski looked beyond Chopin and early Skryabin to the German Classical and Romantic masters. The influence of Brahms's piano style is particularly apparent in the more extended works of the early period, the Piano Sonata, Op. 8 (1904) and the two sets of variations—Op. 3 (1901–3) and the impressive *Variations on a Polish Theme*, Op. 10 (1900–4). The sonata in particular, for all its formal imperfections, represents a remarkable achievement on the part of a young composer, its preoccupation with motivic unity and cyclical structure clearly based on the more recent German achievements; the final fugue suggests an influence from Reger even at this early stage in Szymanowski's development.

One of the intriguing features of the early works is the stylistic discrepancy which exists between instrumental and vocal compositions, and it tells us much about Szymanowski's creative personality. Although they are no more 'finished' technically, the early songs have infinitely greater character than the fastidiously chiselled, intricately textured piano miniatures. Throughout his life, Szymanowski wrote much of his best music in response to extra-musical stimuli, and the song-cycles remain one of the clearest guides to his evolving creative personality. The early songs draw upon the poetry of 'Young Poland'; Tetmajer in the *Six Songs*, Op. 2, Kasprowicz in the *Three Fragments*, Op. 5 and *Salomé*, Op. 6, Berent in *Labedz*, Op. 7 and Micinski in the *Four Songs*, Op. 11 and the *Six Songs*, Op. 20. The Op. 5 songs, composed in 1903, are settings of extracts from Kasprowicz's free-verse hymns which appeared in 1902 in two volumes—*To the Perishing World* and *Salve Regina*. The blend of mystical fervour and violent imagery in these poems is 'earthed' by a preoccupation with the tragic existence and unique sensibility of the Polish peasant, his revolt against, and at the same time his stoic acceptance of, a cruel fate. Szymanowski's response was a setting of remarkable dramatic power and lyricism, catching the overtones of a Russian rather than a German vocal idiom.[5]

At the opening of the first song the stepwise melodic movement, simple homophonic textures, exploring the most sonorous register of the piano, and regular, treading rhythms immediately establish some of the most characteristic features of the cycle as a whole, expressing perfectly the profound pessimism of a peasant lament during a time of plague ('O Lord, King of Kings, Immortal One, have pity on us'). When the opening 'motto' theme returns at bar 17, creeping chromatic scales in the bass hint at the smouldering bitterness which underlies this lament, a bitterness which explodes violently in the third stanza's cry of accusation against God—'Why do my lips speak to you only of sorrow? Why must my path always lie under the cruel, burning sun? And why must I drag myself without happiness or repose always towards your awful cross?' Despite such chromaticisms and some pungent dissonance (bars 31–40), the tonal direction of the song is seldom obscured; it tends indeed to remain almost obsessively within the orbit of a B minor tonal region, although a V—I affirmation of the central tonality is consistently avoided. In the second and third songs we encounter the element of fantasy which was to become an essential aspect of Szymanowski's artistic sensibility, though here it is firmly rooted in Polish folklore. The poems conjure up a vision of dreaming spirits 'searching for their tombs in the misty autumn', shortly to be joined by a procession of all nature, the fields, trees and flowers marching forward in the mysterious shadows. The music is much more diatonically founded than in the first song, achieving some of its more telling effects through a combination of modal melodic patterns and simple root position triadic successions.

During the years following his father's death in 1906, Szymanowski travelled extensively in Europe, spending much of his time in Berlin and Vienna. His artistic development reflects these travels in that he came more and more under the spell of German Romantic culture, steeping himself in the works of the German poets and in the music of Strauss and Reger. The influence of German composers is perhaps most apparent in the instrumental works of these years, from the *Concert Overture*, Op. 12 (1905) to the Second Symphony (1909–10) and Second Piano Sonata (1910–11). The contrapuntal density of the overture is relieved only intermittently by passages such as the 'dolce amoroso' of Fig. 10, with its delicate accompaniment patterns on violins and harp. Such contrapuntal density was taken even further in the symphony and sonata which, together with the one-act opera *Hagith* (1911–14), closely modelled on Strauss's *Salomé*, mark a culminating stage in Szymanowski's so-called 'Viennese Period'. Although the overall structures of both instrumental works pay homage to the German symphonic tradition in that their three movements are respectively a sonata-form allegro, a set of slow variations incorporating some scherzo-like material, and a final fugal movement, their use of cyclic devices reflects more recent influences. Moreover the conception of 'variations' and 'fugue' in a highly chromatic context immediately invites a comparison with Reger which is justified by other aspects of the sonata's construction and indeed by its detailed phraseology (Straussian phraseology is no less explicit in parts of the symphony, e.g. bars 46–52). Like the earlier *Concert Overture*, the textures in these works are closely knit contrapuntally in the manner of Reger but they have a tendency to build into complex webs of sound which are almost impressionistic in effect, anticipating the harmonic language of the middle-period music.

The symphony is much more tonally wayward than the earlier overture and its chromatically shifting textures and contrapuntally dictated harmonies often obscure the underlying tonal-cadential structure. For all the breadth of its formal lay-out and the ingenuity of its thematic working, the conception of the work seems to run counter to Szymanowski's deepest instincts as a composer, instincts which were later to be channelled into more suitable forms. His genius lay in the creation of subtly drawn, flexible and intensely expressive melodic lines and in devising appropriately sensitive and refined harmonic accompaniments, and it was not best served during these years by his preoccupation with intricate part-movement and complex contrapuntal combinations on the German model.

The continuity of Szymanowski's development towards more and more chromatic elaboration in these early works is at least as significant as the impact on his music of new styles and techniques and makes the extent of such an impact often difficult to determine. This continuity can best be demonstrated in the song-cycles of the 'Viennese period'. The semitonal part-movement and motivic integration of the first song from his *Four Songs*, Op. 11 (1906) (Ex. 35) already foreshadows the later *Twelve German Songs*, Op. 17 (1907), where the influence of Strauss is particularly strong, while the Op. 17 songs themselves seem to be straining towards the harmonic language of the middle-period works. Already in the fourth song 'Zuleikha' from the Op. 13 cycle (1905–6), there are hints of the composer's later fascination with oriental subjects and quasi-oriental musical techniques. It is a portrait of the familiar Zuleikha, with whom nothing can be compared, not the angels in

Op.11 no.1

Heaven's blue tent, not the roses in perfumed flower beds, not even the eternal sunshine. The augmented seconds and short melismatic 'tails' in the vocal line, together with a highly coloured harmonic palette giving prominence to the augmented triad and to whole-tone harmonies, contribute to the 'exotic' atmosphere of one of Szymanowski's most delightful songs. It is a perfectly shaped miniature, with the opening section built over a tonic pedal D flat and the middle section and recapitulation over a chromatically descending bass line which 'fills in' an octave over an extended time span. Such strongly directional bass lines were to become an important feature of his later style.

The first eight of the Op. 17 songs are settings of Dehmel and the last four of Mombert, Falke and Greif. Several of the poems are conventional love lyrics, light in tone, while others are imbued with a sense of the mystery of nature and of the solitariness of the poet which brings them close to recurring preoccupations of the 'Young Poland' group. The harmonic language of these songs has moved far beyond the diatonic idiom of the Op. 5 songs and the early piano pieces, with the marked influence of German composers leading the musicologist Jachimecki to refer to 'Straussian tricks'. Ex. 36i presents a harmonic

Ex.36
(i) Op.17 no.1

(ii) Op.17 no.5

'skeleton' of part of the opening song, illustrating the semitonal part-movement which, together with unresolving appoggiaturas, doubtless prompted Jachimecki's remark, and indicating further the presence of harmonic structures conceived empirically in a manner which suggests the direction Szymanowski's music would take in the future. The use of symmetrical harmonic structures based on the augmented triad is of particular importance in this respect, providing a link with later procedures, though in Op. 17, No. 1 such structures merely act as a temporary suspension of a tonal argument centred on B flat. They are an appropriate musical expression of the feeling of release from gravitation conveyed by Dehmel's description of a visionary moment on the mountain-side in early morning—'Look how we climb towards the stars, Our eyes dazzled by the gleaming snow on the mountain-side reflecting the burning sun . . .' [6]

The emotive, expressive dissonance of this song is taken even further in parts of the fifth song 'A Glance', a poem about disillusioned lovers, where unresolving appoggiaturas and semitonal contradictions in the harmony (Ex. 36ii) are characteristic of the musical language, reaching a shattering climax at the phrase 'Is everything dead now, and dismal?' The second song 'Secret' is even less securely rooted to its A flat tonic than either of these, however. Its most important unifying features are the prominence given to the tritone interval both melodically and harmonically, the firm bass foundation and the consistency of its traditionally conceived accompaniment configuration. The A flat cadence emerges only inconclusively at the final bars. The consistent evasion of this A flat tonic is matched, moreover, by an irregular metrical scheme which creates an unending textural flow without strongly marked cadences to give tonal and rhythmic punctuation.

The chromatic density of the Op. 17 songs, although it is tonally accommodated and retains the triad as fundamental tonal-harmonic unit, undoubtedly suggested to Szymanowski the expressive potential of a richly chromatic harmonic language remote from a restrictive diatonic background and no longer necessarily the outcome of traditional part-movement. Already in several of the Op. 17 songs, a fascination with expressive or colouristic dissonance was weakening the attraction of traditional tonal relationships to the extent that the cadence—the point of tonal clarification—did not always function as a natural outcome of the work's most typical harmonic language (e.g. the second song). This development persisted in ensuing works, but it was by no means a consistent, evolutionary process, being determined in large measure by the expressive demands of the text or programme. Each of the *Bunte Lieder*, Op. 22, for example, is more firmly tonal than Op. 17, No. 2, although they were composed some three years after that song in 1910. But the *Bunte Lieder* represent an important step forward in other respects. The title is significant for, although the cycle retains for the most part traditional accompaniment patterns, it rejects the intricate part-movement of the Op. 17 songs in favour of a more colourful, transparent keyboard style. The first song 'The Hermit', depicting the gay dance of a hermit who has cast off his religious habit, is particularly prophetic, with its picturesque 'guitar' accompaniment and sharp points of dissonant colour (Ex. 37) anticipating similar 'dance' movements from the later cycles.

Ex.37
Op.22 no.1

The *Love songs of Hafiz*, Op. 24, composed in 1911, is the most distinguished and mature of the early cycles. The choice of fourteenth-century Persian poetry is symptomatic of the composer's new enthusiasm for the culture and mythology of the East, stimulated by travels to Sicily and North Africa. Szymanowski chose his colourful love lyrics in a German translation by Hans Bethge, whose translations from the Chinese are well known to musicians through settings by Mahler and Webern. The occasional crudities of the Op. 17 songs—extravagant chromatic effects and textural congestion—have been dissolved away in the Hafiz cycle, but in other respects the idiom has not changed significantly. The use of parallel 7/3 chords in the final section of the last song and of augmented triads and whole-tone harmony in the second foreshadows later developments while at the same time recalling Op. 17, No. 1. Throughout the second song, 'The Only Cure', cadential resolution is avoided, tonal regions of E, B, F sharp and E being suggested through dominant harmony and the final dominant seventh in E minor failing to resolve. At the opening of the third song 'The Flaming Tulips' an unorthodox attitude to dissonance is concealed by a traditional rhythmic surface and a conventional accompaniment con-

137

figuration. The song has a firm underlying tonal structure articulated by cadences in E flat and B flat and a carefully shaped melodic structure, generating a single extended curve which reaches a peak note A at the main climax. At this climax the dominant-quality harmony dissolves into a whole-tone area which remains static because of an exact sequence at the tritone, a feature which strikingly anticipates Szymanowski's 'Impressionist' harmonic style, and which recurs in identical form in the first of the *Songs of a Fairy-tale Princess*, Op. 31. But for the most part the Hafiz songs represent a refinement of the musical language of the Op. 17 and Op. 20 cycles rather than a new stylistic departure.

'IMPRESSIONIST' WORKS

A more decisive stylistic break is apparent in several of the works composed in 1915, in particular the *Métopes*, Op. 29 for piano, the *Mythes*, Op. 30 for violin and piano and the *Songs of a Fairy-tale Princess*, Op. 31. These works ushered in the most fertile period of Szymanowski's creative life, a period characterized by the influence of oriental culture on his choice of subject matter and by the impact of the 'impressionistic' textures of Debussy, Ravel and late Skryabin on his musical language. It has already been suggested that in earlier compositions such as Op. 17, No. 1 and Op. 24, No. 2 there were prophetic hints of the harmonic structures of the middle-period works, while the colourful textures of the *Bunte Lieder* foreshadow to an extent the piano style of Szymanowski's maturity. The period of stylistic transition was by no means chronologically consistent, but the works which most obviously bridge the gap between the 'Viennese' and 'Impressionist' periods are the second (orchestral) set of *Hafiz Love-songs*, Op. 26 (1914), the *Nocturne and Tarantella*, Op. 28 for violin and piano (1915) and the *Three Davydov Songs*, Op. 32 (1915). In the new settings of Hafiz [7] accompaniment configuration tends to hover between the traditionally conceived textures of Op. 24 and the vivid, pictorial accompaniments of the later song-cycles. The *Nocturne and Tarantella* and Op. 32 songs are similarly transitional in character, retaining an underlying tonal framework (Op. 28 still has a key signature), but with a sharp, quasi-bitonal dissonance (Ex. 38) which indicates that Szymanowski was freeing himself from the constraints of traditional harmonic relationships.

The *Songs of a Fairy-tale Princess* are representative of Szymanowski's attitude to tonality in the more progressive works of 1915. Through the exotic love poetry of these songs, written by the composer's sister Zofia,

Ex. 38

Szymanowski retreated still further into a private world of fantasy than in the Hafiz cycles. The coloratura soprano line, with its agile melisma and quasi-oriental chromatic flexibility, is a fully formed example of his mature melodic style, to be found in its clearest form in the violin pieces and songs of the period. The opening 'vocalise' and first stanza of the second song illustrate this type of melodic writing, while the piano introduction is typical of the colourful, impressionistic accompaniments devised by Szymanowski to match the fantastic imagery of the poetry (Ex. 39i). This crystallized into a pianistic style of remarkable originality which was to be more fully explored in later piano compositions such as the *Masques*, Op. 34 and the Third Piano Sonata, Op. 36.

Ex. 39

The short transitional passage preceding the first stanza of this song demonstrates the importance which the unresolving 7/3 unit has attained in Szymanowski's music at this time (Ex. 39ii), a development which may be traced back to the Hafiz songs and to some of the Op. 17 songs. He was concerned in particular to explore the ambivalence which can exist between the strong dominant quality of the 7/3 and its whole-tone characteristics. In Ex. 39ii the bass line, each note with a 7/3 built upon it, has itself a whole-tone character, while tonal feeling is further undermined by whole-tone added notes, creating a single whole-tone harmonic area which is broken only by the final two chords. When the fifth of the final chord is added we feel unmistakably the 'pull' of B minor. Such harmonic procedures suggest close parallels with developments in the music Skryabin was composing around 1908 (see chapter 5), works in which the 7/3 was similarly established as a harmonic foundation, very often in a whole-tone context. It is entirely characteristic that the highly dissonant harmonies of the first stanza of Szymanowski's song should be underpinned by open fifths in the bass. As his harmony grew increasingly complex in the middle-period music and was less easily relatable to an underlying tonality, it tended to be underpinned and stabilized by strong bass lines, descending chromatically or in the form of long pedal points, often thickened into open fifths. Such is the harmonic sophistication of this and other middle-period works that the second song consistently avoids the simple triad, outlining its 'suppressed' tonal scheme by means of dominant preparations and ending with the pitch and not the triad of F sharp. This sophistication is paralleled in the phrasing of the song, with frequent changes of metre and tempo effectively concealing any underlying regularity.

The first song demonstrates particularly clearly how tonal centres, although they may still exert an influence on the harmonic material, have been pushed far into the background of the musical argument in much of the music from this period. The song unfolds against a tonal background with alternating centres of E and E flat, although no triads of either tonality appear. It opens in an undefined tonal area using a harmonic structure which again emphasizes the 7/3 unit and its whole-tone associations. The symmetrical descent of this structure at the minor third interval (Ex. 39iii) comes to rest on a 'French sixth' chord on F which is transposed at the tritone, creating a harmonic stasis until the fifth of the chord is sharpened to produce a dominant seventh in E minor. This ends the symmetrical, 'non-tonal' pattern and for the first time relates the music to a tonal centre, though the E minor is implied rather than explicitly stated. After the second stanza, in a highly chromatic E flat minor, there is an extended middle section built on an F sharp pedal, its dissonant harmonies centred around an alternation of the augmented triad and the 7/3 unit. At the climax of the song, the soprano's peak note A sharp signals the dissolution of the harmony into a whole-tone area, recalling the climax of Op. 24, No. 3. A highly dissonant ensuing section leads to a final reference to the opening material and the song ends on a dominant minor ninth chord in E minor.

Tonally, the most adventurous of the Op. 31 songs is the last. Despite its final affirmation of D flat, the harmonies, making frequent use of fourths chords and parallel dissonances, can seldom be related to an underlying tonality, however remotely, and are held together by extended bass pedals in open fifths and by the energy generated by the rhythmic structure. Ex. 39iv illustrates in summary form some of the harmonic procedures of the song, indicating the prominence of chords built of superimposed fourths and fifths, whole-tone constructions and parallelism of complex dissonances and bare fourths. In this song Szymanowski has allowed his intoxication with the colouristic qualities of dense, layered dissonance to have its full expression, to the extent that the tonal assertions of the final pages do not emerge as a natural out-come of the harmonic language of the piece as a whole.

In both the *Métopes* and the *Songs of a Fairy-tale Princess* tonal ele-ments are present with varying degrees of emphasis. In the first of the songs and the last of the piano pieces, the harmonies may still be related, albeit tenuously, to an underlying tonal structure. In the last of the songs and in 'Sirènes' from the *Métopes*, on the other hand, tonal ele-ments play only a subsidiary role in the musical argument. Even in these pieces, however, the *vocabulary* of traditional tonality has by no means completely disappeared; dominant-quality formations and even plain triads are prominent in their harmonic language, while dissonance/consonance relations are still an important means of creating tensions and relaxations. It will be observed that even in those later works where all traces of an underlying tonal structure have been eliminated, Szy-manowski continued to employ harmonic structures whose origins in tonal thinking are unmistakable.

9

Cross-currents

An examination of the impulses involved in the decline of traditional tonality reveals many technical points of contact between composers whose stylistic paths were in other respects very different. Procedural parallels inevitably resulted from approaches to common difficulties and from mutual influences. Nor were such parallels confined to composers who went on to develop atonal musical languages. The rejection of traditional tonal functions did not necessarily entail a rejection of tonality as an underlying principle and there was much in common between the tonal expansion which led to *a*-tonality and the tonal modification which led to *neo*-tonality. Such an examination will draw together several themes which have been developed independently in the earlier stages of this study.

The gradually increasing infusion of chromatic elements into a diatonic framework was common to a great deal of music composed around the turn of the century. In this respect Wagner and Brahms were each important forerunners. In *Tristan* semitonal part-movement against the triad is emphasized to the extent that extended passages have no clear tonal direction, though temporary tonics are implied, if not always stated, at cadence points. But the increasing concentration of chromaticism *within a single tonal region*, an important feature of Brahms's harmony in some works, was ultimately an even more serious threat to tonality than Wagner's 'enharmonic continuum'. In later works such as Reger's *Fantasy and Fugue on the Name BACH* and Schoenberg's *Schenk mir deinem goldenem Kamm*, Op. 2, No. 2, the emphasis given to chromatic elements within unchanging tonal regions was beginning to weaken tonality-defining diatonic hierarchies. Certainly Reger and Schoenberg explored more fully than any of their immediate predecessors in Austro-Germany the implications of increasing chromaticism as related to the overall tonal structure of a work, and both felt the need to discipline an all-pervading chromaticism by thematic-contrapuntal means.

The development towards a totally integrated thematic and harmonic process, itself traceable to Brahms's obvious concern in some works to bring 'melody' and 'accompaniment' into a more integral relationship with each other, played an important part in the music not only of Reger and Schoenberg but of other young composers working in Austro-Germany in the early twentieth century. The second string quartets of Zemlinsky and Wellesz, the Piano Sonata, Op. 1 by Berg and the 1905 quartet of Webern are only four of many compositions which demonstrate this preoccupation with thematically derived textures. So, too, do the instrumental compositions written by Szymanowski between 1906 and 1909, in particular his Second Symphony and Second Piano Sonata.

This concern to relate closely vertical and horizontal dimensions—to achieve a 'unity of musical space'—has an obvious anticipatory connection with serialism. But it is interesting to observe a similar preoccupation among composers working outside Austro-Germany as traditional tonality declined. Many of the works of Stravinsky's 'Russian' period, culminating in *Les Noces*, employ folk-inspired motives as a means of creating the harmonic as well as the melodic material of extended passages. Similar techniques in some of the shorter Debussy pieces (*Voiles* is the most obvious example) may have been an inspiration here, but so too may have been Mussorgsky. In Bartók's *Bagatelles* and in several of Casella's *Nine Piano Pieces* (e.g. No. 4 'In Modo Burlesco') harmonic dissonance is often justified by means of a close intervallic relationship between chord and motive. Particularly intriguing is the way in which Skryabin arrived at a 'unity of musical space' by an almost diametrically opposed route to that of Schoenberg. Where Schoenberg's 'total thematicism' led eventually to the serial method in which the note-row generates harmonic as well as melodic material, Skryabin's development of consistent dominant-quality harmonic 'areas' culminated in a harmonic system in which the basic 'chord' is also the source of thematic material.

The reassertion of a contrapuntal impulse was an important and widespread factor in the weakening of harmonically directed, melodically focused tonality. The inclinations of an 'absolute' polyphonic style are towards an elimination of tonality as expressed through rhythmically propelled chord progression and melodic priority. One of the fascinating aspects of sixteenth- and seventeenth-century music is the interplay between a declining polyphonic idiom and an emerging tonal concept. In the late nineteenth century the roles were reversed as the approach of an undifferentiated counterpoint threatened the gravitational urge of tonality. In this respect Mahler's 'dissonant counterpoint' led directly to the linear independence of Schoenberg's First Chamber Symphony and Busoni's Second Sonatina, both works in which 'contrapuntal logic' tends to undermine and indeed to replace harmonic tonality. For a younger generation of composers a rhythmically vigorous contrapuntal independence was an essential characteristic of an anti-Romantic commitment which directed them beyond the nineteenth century to the contrapuntal style of Bach as a primary source of inspiration. Much of the music composed by Hindemith, Prokofiev and Milhaud during the twenties relates to some extent to this development, and their use of bitonal textures is often no more than an extension of the contrapuntal impulse. Undoubtedly Busoni was of the utmost importance for many such composers, both as an ideological and a purely musical inspiration.

Passages based on the principle of symmetry—on 'notes equally related among themselves'—were employed by several composers at the turn of the century as a means of offsetting tonal hierarchies and offering an alternative method of structuring extended paragraphs. Very often such passages are based on uni-intervallic harmonic formations such as the augmented triad, the diminished seventh chord or the whole-tone scale. Such symmetrical formations may perhaps be traced to decorative passage-work in the piano music of Chopin, Liszt and other pianist-composers in the early and mid-nineteenth century, but in the later works of Liszt and in some of the music of Rimsky-Korsakov they have become a much more integral part of the musical structure. In the early twentieth century formations based on 'notes equally related among themselves' took many different forms—the mirror patterns in Busoni's sixth elegy and Bartók's second bagatelle, the fourths constructions in Schoenberg's First Chamber Symphony, Berg's Op. 2 No. 2 and Busoni's Second Sonatina, or the whole-tone constructions particularly common in Debussy, Szymanowski and Skryabin, but also found in Schoenberg's chamber symphony and Busoni's sonatina.

Parallelism is a specific form of 'equal relations' which was frequently used as a principle of progression capable of replacing diatonic relationships. It forms an integral aspect of Debussy's harmonic language, but it is also prominent in the 'advanced' works of Busoni, in early Berg and Szymanowski, in the music of Casella's 'secondo stile' and in the Bartók *Bagatelles*. It was indeed one of the so-called 'Impressionist' fingerprints which were worked to near-exhaustion at the beginning of the present century by composers from widely different backgrounds, many of them unable to perceive the full implications of the device and its potential weakness when incorporated within an otherwise orthodox diatonic context.

In respect of 'contrapuntal logic' and symmetrical organization, a comparison between Schoenberg's First Chamber Symphony and Busoni's Second Sonatina reveals some interesting parallels and some important differences. Much of the texture of both works derives its coherence from these two 'non-tonal' principles, and the symmetrical constructions tend in both cases to be based on the intervals of the perfect fourth and the major second. Such technical parallels may well reflect the interest shown by Busoni in Schoenberg's music, including several of the atonal compositions such as the *Three Piano Pieces*, Op. 11 and *Pierrot Lunaire*.[1] But there are fundamental differences of style and attitude underlying the parallel. The Second Sonatina is the closest that Busoni ever came to atonality and it is significant that it should be one of his few compositions to consolidate and extend a late nineteenth-century idiom, as distinct from reinterpreting earlier traditions in the spirit of 'Young Classicism'. Busoni's sonatina does not represent an important stage in the evolution of an atonal musical language, but rather the most extreme expression of a single direction in his music, a direction, moreover, too limited in its expressive range to form the basis for a broadly based language. For Schoenberg, on the other hand, the chamber symphony was a logical outcome of his development and extension of the techniques of the German Classical and Romantic masters; with its roots firmly embedded in such a tradition, his evolving musical language had the widest possible range of expression. Having composed the chamber symphony and second quartet, Schoenberg could not have returned to a tonal-triadic idiom as Busoni frequently did after the sonatina.[2] Indeed his own words with reference to the chamber symphony betray his preoccupation with a gradual evolution of style; he believed that he had achieved a '*major step* towards the emancipation of the dissonance' [3] (my italics).

The 'emancipation of the dissonance' was itself an important aspect of declining tonality and one which is in no sense synonymous with, or even a direct result of, the increasing prominence of chromatic elements. As the ear becomes acclimatized to a sonority within a particular context, the sonority will gradually become 'emancipated' from that context and will seek a new one. The emancipation of the dominant-quality dissonances has followed this pattern, with the dominant seventh developing in status from a contrapuntal note in the sixteenth century to a quasi-consonant harmonic note in the early nineteenth. By the later nineteenth century the higher numbered dominant-quality dissonances had also achieved harmonic status, with resolution delayed or omitted completely. The greater autonomy of dominant-quality dissonance contributed significantly to the weakening of traditional tonal functions within a purely diatonic context.

There are striking parallels between the music of Debussy, Skryabin and Szymanowski which result from their preference for unresolving dominant-quality dissonance, in a context which very often stresses the whole-tone associations of the 7/3 unit. The parallel 7/3 chords in the second song from Szymanowski's *Songs of a Fairy-tale Princess* (Ex. 39ii) recall similar procedures in Debussy, while the tritonal transposition of the 7/3 in the first song is reminiscent of procedures in Skryabin's 1908 works.[4] Yet these points of contact have a quite different significance in the work of each composer. Where Szymanowski was moving in the Op. 31 cycle towards a freer, more 'instinctive' harmonic language, no longer confined by major-minor keys, Skryabin was developing in the *Poem of Ecstasy* a stricter, more disciplined harmonic process which would eventually crystallize into a constructive method capable of replacing tonality. Where both Skryabin and Szymanowski were exploring worlds of sound no longer governed by the tonal principle, Debussy was evolving a musical language involving a creative re-interpretation of that principle.

Other dissonant formations beside those of dominant quality assumed harmonic status in the late nineteenth and early twentieth centuries. The changing status of the 'added sixth' chord, from Chopin's F major prelude, where it behaves diatonically, to Mahler's *Das Lied von der Erde*, Schoenberg's *Gurrelieder* and Debussy's *Pagodes*, where it forms an independent harmonic resource of pentatonic character, is a further instance of the law of harmonic evolution. Similarly the 'expressive' dissonance of unresolved appoggiaturas, suspensions and anticipations led to an emancipation in Strauss and Schreker of highly unorthodox combinations, including fourths chords and unresolving seconds. The harmonic language of Berg's Op. 2, No. 4 can best be understood as a natural development of this aspect of declining tonality, its expressive dissonance developed to the point at which the triad has been eclipsed by more dissonant harmonies and tonality submerged.

Szymanowski, too, was preoccupied with the expressive and colouristic qualities of dissonant harmonies other than those of dominant quality. The similarity between some of his middle-period music and the work of Franz Schreker is partly a result of such 'expressive' dissonance, but it does in fact extend beyond this to include a common interest in quasi-oriental melodic writing and a preference for delicate, arabesque-like ornamentation. Although in several of the middle-period works, Szymanowski's dissonant harmonies have been emphasized, like Berg's, to the extent that tonality has been submerged, he never rejected traditional thematic working and phraseology in the manner of Schoenberg, Berg and Webern in their 'athematic' compositions. More than any other composer considered in this study, he slipped into atonality without regarding it as a major creative step, much less a problematical one. In the face of an ever increasing melodic and harmonic refinement, an underpinning tonal structure can be detected in some works, but has been dissolved away in others. His middle-period compositions embody one of the most important characteristics of early atonality, its frequent retention of the forms and phraseology of its tonal ancestry.

The revival of modality in the nineteenth century contributed significantly to the decline of classical tonality, whose essential relationships could only find complete expression when major-minor scales had finally shed vestigial modal traces. Clearly any comparison of medieval and modern modality would recognize that the latter takes place against a background of some three centuries of harmonic tonality, permitting, and in the nineteenth century requiring, a dialogue between modal and diatonic procedure. Just as in the sixteenth century the emergence of harmonic tonality necessitated modifications in modal procedure, so in the nineteenth modal elements resulted in a modification of diatonic relationships. Apart from often-cited modal inflections in several works by Beethoven, some of the earliest extensive use of modes is to be found in Chopin, Berlioz and Liszt. All three composers exerted an important influence on the modal pratice of nineteenth-century Russian music, where modality became a much more integral aspect of musical thought than in Western Europe. A direct line of descent can be traced in his respect from the modality of Mussorgsky and Borodin to that of Debussy, Janáček and early twentieth-century 'nationalists'. In the work of Kodály, Holst and Falla, modal elements still tend to act as a 'modification' of a diatonic procedure whose background presence is still clearly felt. In Debussy and Bartók that background has been completely eliminated and modality—medieval and 'exotic'—is given renewed status as an ingredient in a new tonal synthesis.

Part Three

Early Atonality

Concept and terminology

The year 1908 marked an important turning point in the development of Western music. Underlying the many and rapid changes in the language of music since that date, there has been a fundamental dichotomy between those composers who retained, and those who abandoned, tonality as a major constructive principle. It is with the latter that the final part of this study will be concerned. Before embarking upon an examination of early atonality, however, I shall attempt to clarify some of the difficulties of terminology which arise in a study of tonal expansion and atonality.

It will already be clear that the term 'tonality' is commonly used in two senses, referring on the one hand to the specific language of 'classical tonality'—the major-minor key system of the Classical and Romantic periods—and on the other to the underlying principle of tonality, a principle which has been broadly defined (see p. 2) as 'the requirement that all the events in a musical group should be co-ordinated by, and experienced in relation to, a central point of reference'. In a useful historical survey of theoretical views of the meaning of 'tonality', M. D. Beswick has drawn attention to the subtle nuances of meaning which have separated the explanations of Fétis,[1] Helmholz, Riemann, D'Indy, Adler, Yasser and others.[2] Further clarification of the emergence of theoretical concepts of tonality will be found in Matthew Shirlaw's history of harmonic theory,[3] though Shirlaw himself is heavily biased towards a Rameau-Riemann, rather than a Fétis, view of harmonic functions.

The term 'extended tonality' has been used to describe the incorporation of complex harmonic phenomena within a single tonal region, as in much of the music of the late nineteenth and early twentieth centuries. In a great deal of this music the defining characteristics of classical tonality have already all but disappeared, as increasing chromaticism tended to challenge the integrity of the major and minor modes and undermined the strength of the dominant-tonic relationship. Already, then, in the music of the later nineteenth century we are often close to the second and broader meaning of tonality. The clearest expression of this is to be found in the new tonal languages—'neo-tonality'—of the twentieth century, in which the tonal principle has been reinterpreted in a way which excludes, or greatly minimizes the importance of, diatonic relationships.[4]

For some theorists 'tonality' has been understood in such broad terms that the concept of 'atonality' becomes entirely meaningless. Hindemith, for example, viewed tonality as a sort of competition for dominance of the individual tones in a melodic line or a harmonic succession. The conditions of competition in the harmonic sphere would be determined by the vertical distance between notes, by the number of notes superimposed and by the perceptibility of the 'root'. He concluded that 'what is held to be "atonality" necessarily turns out to be another aspect of tonality—the only difference being that the "atonal" work fixes the sequences in another of the various corners of the full tonal area'.[5] Yet, however unsatisfactory the term, 'atonal' has now been widely accepted as a description of music which rejects the *principle* of tonality as defined above.[6] As such it does not imply any specific method of organizing or unifying musical material, but rather the absence of negation of such methods as are rooted in the idea of centricity.

While our definition of the principle underlying tonality forms a useful point of reference in an analysis of twentieth-century styles, it should be recognized that difficulties will often arise in the interpretation of pitch centricity in a context which excludes diatonic functions. Often in such music we can make a clear distinction between *pitch centres*, functioning referentially in an atonal context, and *tonal centres*, pertaining to a more fundamental interrelationship of pitches from which the basic melodic/harmonic material of a work may be derived, directly or indirectly. There are works, however, in which the role of recurring pitch areas is less easily defined; which resist rigid classification as 'tonal' or 'atonal'. Several of Schoenberg's early 'atonal' compositions—the second of his *Five Orchestral Pieces*, Op. 16, for example—grow out of, and are moulded around, stable harmonic centres whose function is not exclusively referential. Conversely a number of 'tonal' works from Bartók's middle period are organized according to unifying methods whose relation to tonality may not be immediately apparent. In the analysis of such works the interpretation of pitch centricity would be a primary aim. It has already been established that the 'tonality' of Bartók's Second Violin Sonata not only articulates its overall structure but shapes and co-ordinates its individual events so that points of tonal clarification emerge as a natural outcome of the preceding musical argument. Using such criteria we would regard the recurring harmonic centre of Schoenberg's Op. 16, No. 2 as a tonal centre or simply as a harmonic point of reference depending upon how strongly we feel that the melodic-harmonic material of the piece as a whole is influenced by it and derives from it.

Further problems of terminology arise with the extensive musical literature which, although it avoids any underlying tonal structure, retains none the less many of the pitch hierarchies of tonal music. The persistence of dissonance/consonance relations as a means of creating the tensions and relaxations which shape a work emotionally and structurally is a characteristic of many twentieth-century works which in other respects reject the principle of tonality. (This in marked contrast to the early twelve-note compositions of Schoenberg which appear to assume the interchangeability of 'consonance' and 'dissonance' in that there is no apparent *harmonic* meaning governing the degree of dissonance.) In the melodic sphere it is common to find phrases which have a clear 'pull' towards emphasized pitches, very often in a manner which establishes close links with traditional modality. The degree of correspondence between any suggested 'tonic' in such melodic lines and the harmonic support will vary greatly from work to work. An attempt to clarify this largely uncharted region in the theoretical literature has been made by Rudolph Reti who has made use of the term 'pantonality'. It is Reti's view that a wide range of twentieth-century music makes use of a new concept of harmony in which 'the ear instinctively singles out the tonics and connects each of them to any successive phrase with which they can enter into a tonically meaningful relationship'.[7] Reti's contribution has been to distinguish between music conceived in a spirit of 'unconditional tonical non-relationship' and music conceived in a spirit of 'indirect tonality—that is, tonality which does not appear on the surface but is created by the ear singling out hidden relationships between various points of a melodic or contrapuntal web'.[8] Reti's belief in 'pantonality' as an emerging general synthesis seems unlikely to carry much conviction in the light of recent developments in the language of music. Yet his distinction is a real one and it offers further grounds for approaching 'atonality' not as a rigid category but as one whose applicability may in certain instances remain a matter of interpretation.

Atonality and tradition

> We haven't advanced beyond the classical composers' forms. What happened after them was only alteration, extension, abbreviation; but the forms remained, even in Schoenberg.[1]

It is often more profitable to examine those features which an atonal work shares with its tonal ancestry than to emphasize the differences. The study which follows begins by exploring that common ground before investigating the changing patterns and relationships and the alternative constructive methods which resulted from the loss of tonal harmony. While it has been considered necessary to examine these aspects of early atonality in three separate chapters, it will be seen that in most atonal compositions they are constantly interacting. The interweaving of traditional and innovatory features which attends any process of rapid change will already have been sensed in the preceding study of declining tonality and it remains a central theme of the chapters which follow.

The rejection of tonality by no means occasioned a rejection of all the concepts and procedures associated with tonal music, and early atonality often relies heavily upon the retention of such traditional features to give it form and coherence. It will be essential in examining these to distinguish between *residual* features, in which coherence depends upon analogy with the tonal past, and *recreative* features, in which traditional procedures have been invested with a new form-giving significance. In the present chapter we shall be concerned with the former—with those aspects of composition which were salvaged from the tonal past, continuing to play an important form-giving role when tonality had been submerged. Few of the composers considered in this study attempted, at least initially, to eradicate all traces of tonal implications from their atonal works, and these frequently play a major part in our aural experience of the music. No less important was the stubborn persistence in many atonal compositions of formal procedures and constructive methods which were developed within the tonal era. There are, too, close analogies between the melodic and harmonic phraseology, the textural disposition and the phrase and rhythmic patterns of tonal and atonal music. Berg was stressing such links when he wrote: 'Even if, with the loss of major and minor, a few harmonic possibilities have been lost, all the other requirements for real and genuine music have remained.' [2]

RESIDUAL TONAL ELEMENTS

If for no other reason than our familiarity with the tonal literature, we frequently impose a tonal interpretation on the local events of even the most severely atonal compositions, often by relating repeated or rhythmically emphasized pitches to their immediate surroundings. The piano coda to Stockhausen's *Kontrapunkte* (1952) might well suggest to some listeners a quasi-Neapolitan relationship between the repeated B natural of bars 515–20 and the B flat of the final bar. Such an interpretation would be strengthened by the fact that the repeated notes fall on rhythmically accented downbeats and by the formation of a 7/3 harmony in bar 520. Although the interpretation of residual tonal phenomena of this sort will be a subjective matter and ambiguities will inevitably arise, there can be little justification for ignoring such phenomena in an analysis which purports to bear a close relationship to our aural experience of the music. Certainly tonal reminiscences are present in many of the early atonal compositions of the 'Second Viennese School', of Skryabin, Szymanowski and other composers without providing a justification for regarding the works as tonal when viewed as a whole.

The later music of Skryabin is particularly consistent in its integration of tonal reminiscences into a language whose real constructive basis lies in its quasi-serial derivation of melodic and harmonic material from a given 'set' of usually six notes, a method which will be examined in detail in a later chapter. The 'sets' of the later music vary in detail from work to work, but Skryabin's normal practice was to dispose them in dominant-quality harmonic areas, with the 7/3 as fundamental harmonic unit. The so-called 'mystic chord' from *Prometheus* (1911) may be

Ex.40

taken as representative, and Ex. 40 illustrates that it can assume a dominant quality on C or F sharp, the all-important tritone link which, as progression (a), had played a major role in his earlier music. The omission of component notes and a distribution which emphasizes the 7/3 unit will serve to reinforce such tonal associations. The evolutionary links between his earlier and later styles will be clarified if we compare the harmonic language of the second subject of the Fifth Piano Sonata (Ex. 21v) with parts of the sixth and seventh sonatas and with the openings of two short pieces from the later years, Op. 65, No. 3 and Op. 71, No. 2 (Ex. 41). It is apparent from Ex. 41 that progression (a) continued to influence the harmonic language of the works composed

after *Prometheus*, forming the strongest connecting link between the early and late music. For this reason the fifth and sixth sonatas are often similar in sound though importantly different in their implications. The former is a tonal work which is stretching beyond traditional tonality towards a new concept of harmonic unity, while the latter derives its coherence from a closed harmonic system, but one which comprises strong reminders of tonal procedure.

Tonal associations are an important aspect of our experience of the individual events of Skryabin's later music, but it is important to recognize that the dominant-quality harmonic areas are usually of long duration and are consistently unresolved so that they cannot be mistaken for functional dominants. By making use of elements of the vocabulary of traditional tonality in order to forge a quite new harmonic syntax, Skryabin formalized those procedures which were crystallizing in the transitional works of 1908 where the principal unit of construction was a tonally evocative, dominant-quality harmony whose tonal attraction was cancelled by tritone transpositions and whole-tone added notes. A similar ambivalence is characteristic of the later harmonic system and is responsible for the suspended, seemingly motionless character of much of the later music, however rapid the rate of surface activity.

More problematical than the momentary tonal implications of Skryabin's later music are the indications in several works of an overall tonal structure, albeit not of a traditional kind, which has been determined by selective transpositions of the basic set. It has been noted that in the *Poem of Ecstasy* extended sections based on progression (a) create tritonal bass movements which function as twin pedal points. In his later music, with the exception of *Prometheus* which ends on an F sharp major triad, such tritone pedal points are no longer heard in relation to a diatonic outcome but begin to assume the stability of independent, quasi-tonal platforms. The transpositions of the basic set in the 'exposition' of the seventh sonata have been outlined in Ex. 42, indicating a hierarchical organization in which an emphasis on C/F sharp progresses to an emphasis on D/G sharp. When the recapitulation is transposed a tone lower so that it arrives at the tonal starting point, we may assume

Ex. 42

1st Subject Group	C	ab	d	bb	C	F♯	D
2nd Subject Group	G♯	D	G♯		F	B	F
Codetta	G♯	e	c		G♯	D	G♯

an overall planning in which transpositions have primary and secondary functions analogous to modulatory procedures in traditional tonality. The 'tonal' structure of the sixth sonata follows a similar pattern, though the clarity of the initial transpositions on G and D flat is blurred by the use of an inversion built on D (this, however, creates a dominant pedal in respect of traditional tonal procedure). Important as such 'tonal' structures are, they fulfil a subsidiary role in Skryabin's late sonatas, subsidiary to the 'unity of melody and harmony' ensured by his system. An analogy with the dramatic and clearly articulated tonal arguments of Bartók and Stravinsky would be misleading; but it would be equally misleading to equate Skryabin's practice with Schoenberg's serial method, where a hierarchical selection of set transpositions may act as a compositional determinant without audible tonal implications.

Tonal associations form a less integral aspect of the atonal music of the 'Second Viennese School', but in the early 'atonal' works of Schoenberg and Berg in particular traces of an underlying tonal structure can often be detected. Berg made it clear that 'the impossibility of harmonically relating this so-called "atonal" music to a major or minor key does not necessarily mean that the "atonal" works of the last twenty-five years are without some harmonic centre'. [3] His own String Quartet, Op. 3 (1910), the work which immediately followed his *Four Songs*, Op. 2, is perhaps slightly anomalous in this respect, its first movement thoroughly atonal,[4] while its second (and final) movement, centred on D throughout, reveals an increasing orientation towards the D minor of its final bar. The tonal structure of this second movement has been outlined in Ex. 43, demonstrating how the centre is constantly

Ex. 43

implied by its semitonal neighbour-notes C sharp and E flat, a device which was anticipated in Op. 2, No. 4 and which was to recur in the first two of the *Five Pieces for Clarinet and Piano*, Op. 5, and in parts of *Wozzeck*; in each case the pitch centre is D. There can be no question in the *finale* of Op. 3 of tonal modulation being employed as a structural device. Much more than in Schoenberg's First Chamber Symphony a single tonal assertion is required to hold its own in a predominantly non-tonal argument. D minor barely survives the experience and even the final D minor triad is rudely, and no doubt symbolically, brushed aside by a succeeding cluster chord. The virtual obsession of the 'Second Viennese School' with D minor (significant in view of the associations of the key in the Classical and Romantic literature) reached a culminating point in the D minor interlude from *Wozzeck*, where again the bass V—I progressions follow pedal points of C sharp and E flat.

Residual traces of tonal structures are particularly apparent in the music composed by Schoenberg in the years immediately following his Second String Quartet, above all in the song-cycle *Das Buch der hängenden Gärten*, Op. 15. An examination of the larger paragraphing of the third song suggests that tonal procedure has rather more than simply a local significance in the construction of the piece. The opening phrase (Ex. 44i) has been shaped tonally through a correspondence of harmonic change and measured rhythmic stress, resulting in a 'classical' har-

Ex. 44

(iii)

monic rhythm which strengthens the tonal pull of the bass progression and encourages us to interpret the part-movement tonally. This interaction of harmonic and rhythmic structures has moreover been projected onto a larger scale to create an interaction of tonal and phrase structures, as expressed through the cadence. When the opening material is restated in a new tonal area, for example, the tonality is defined by means of a cadence or 'structural downbeat' in which the articulation of the phrase structure is achieved through a coincidence of tonal clarification and rhythmic emphasis (Ex. 44ii). The overall tonal framework might be summarized as in Ex. 44iii, an interpretation supported by the directional bass movement in the latter part of the song, culminating in an extended emphasis on the three pitches of the opening progression.

Suppressed tonal structures of this kind can be discerned in other 'atonal' works by Schoenberg.[5] The second of his *Three Piano Pieces*, Op. 11 (1909), is an extended structure in which a recurring bass *ostinato* figure is one of a number of unchanging elements. It establishes three distinct tonal areas before returning to its original pitch for a final statement, an unmistakable residue of tonal thinking. The formal outlines of the piece are to some extent demarcated by this skeletal tonal framework, and Reinhold Brinkmann has shown in some detail how further tonal relationships arise from the juxtaposition of the *ostinato* with other recurring formations.[6] Yet a tonal structure which results from a collision of invariant pitch formations has little in common with the generative processes of traditional tonality. The *ostinato* in Op. 11, No. 2, like other *ostinati* in atonal Schoenberg, offers little opportunity for tonal progression in the traditional sense. It is rather an epitome of the piece's central dialectical relationship between the static and the dynamic, the constant and the variable.

The second of the Op. 11 pieces invites comparison with the second of Schoenberg's later *Six Little Piano Pieces*, Op. 19 (1911) and the second of Berg's Clarinet Pieces, Op. 5 (1913). Both later works are much slighter in conception, belonging as they do to a group of aphoristic

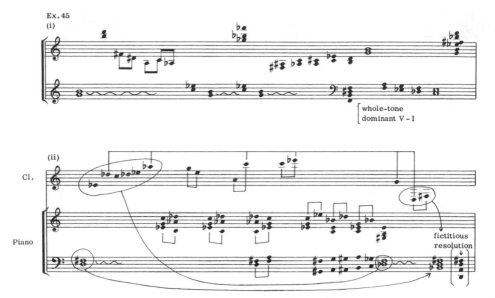

Ex. 45

miniatures composed by Schoenberg, Berg and Webern under the influence of Schoenberg's *Three Orchestral Pieces* (unfinished) of 1910. They present brief melodic and harmonic statements in relation to a fixed point of reference—again the interval of the third. Ex. 45 indicates the similarity in the construction of both works, strongly suggesting that Berg may have used Schoenberg's piece as a starting-point for his own inspiration. Tonally, there is a suggestion in the Schoenberg of the recurring major third functioning as a dominant in C minor with a change to the major occurring in the final bar by way of a whole-tone dominant (Ex. 45i).[7] Berg's piece is much more expansive in concept, however curtailed in realization. The melodic growth of the clarinet line and the developing harmonic ideas in the piano are much more akin to traditional variation procedure than Schoenberg's essay. Tonally there are indications here of a small-scale conflict between D major and D flat major, an echo of a more traditionally conceived tonal argument (Ex. 45ii).

In several of the movements from *Pierrot Lunaire*, the work which summarizes so many technical features of early atonality, there are similar indications of suppressed tonal structures. The final movement, for example, cadences alternately in D and E, with the entire cycle ending on an implied E major cadence. There are, moreover, some indications of large-scale tonal planning throughout the cycle which

162

highlights these tonalities. The fourth and seventh movements, for example, strongly suggest D minor, while the first and fifth hint at a background E major.

Even in those works of the 'Second Viennese School' where there appears to be no underlying tonal framework, the local harmonic working often suggests a background of diatonic procedure, with reference to the vocabulary (though not the grammar) of traditional tonality reinforced by a supporting rhythmic structure. In his reply to the question 'What is "atonal"?', Berg drew attention to the distinction between 'triadic' and 'tonal'.

> 'I think the origin of all this clamour for tonality is not so much the need to sense a relationship to the tonic, as a need for familiar chords: let us be frank and say "for the triad"; and I believe I have good reason to say that just so long as a certain kind of music contains enough such triads, it causes no offence, even if in other ways it most violently clashes with the sacred laws of tonality.' [8]

The coda to the first movement of his own String Quartet, Op. 3, demonstrates the importance of such allusions to tonal vocabulary in a context which suggests none of the broader relationships of tonality. While far from suggesting an approach to F major, as has been suggested by Hans Redlich,[9] the final pages can be reduced to a harmonic background in which the 7/3 unit plays a major role (Ex. 46). This harmonic background is effectively concealed by the dense motive working and contrapuntal complexity of the music but it indicates none the less that a *harmonic* quality, dictated by the persistence of traditional notions of consonance and dissonance, is still discernible in much early atonal music.

Ex. 46

Such allusions to tonal vocabulary are equally prominent in Schoenberg's early atonal compositions. The fourth song from *Das Buch der hängenden Gärten* is characteristic with its triads of C major and D major, its augmented and diminished triads and its opening 'diatonic' seventh on A. No less potent are the tonal allusions in the second of Webern's *Five Movements for String Quartet*, Op. 5 (1909), and particularly the A major-minor of its final bars. Such reminiscences of tonal practice in an atonal context are problematical in that their interpretation, and indeed their importance, remains to a large extent subjective, varying in the aural experience of each listener. (Needless to add that they may be present without the composer himself having intended them or even been aware of them.) Reinhold Brinkmann, for example, regards the first phrase of Schoenberg's Op. 11, No. 1 as suggesting a continuation into D minor, while G. W. Hopkins, hearing the second chord as an unstable A major harmony, suggests a dominant direction.[10] The first eleven bars could equally plausibly be interpreted against a C major background, reading the bass G sharps as A flats. Despite such ambiguities, the analyst is correct to present his experience of a work (which will have much in common with that of other listeners) as fully as possible, in the present instance including residual tonal phenomena.

Szymanowski's development in his middle-period music towards an increasingly sophisticated and elaborate harmonic language and an increasingly flexible and ornate melodic line was often contained by an underlying tonal structure, sometimes traditional in mould but more often remote from traditional prototypes. Equally it often stretched his music beyond such tonal foundations without offering any alternative unifying disciplines. The co-existence of tonally affirmative and tonally evasive works in the middle-period music suggests that Szymanowski did not regard tonal dissolution as a major problem demanding a 'final' solution, but was prepared to allow the harmonic language of each work to be determined by particular expressive requirements, often dictated by a text or programme. The fifth of his *Twelve Studies*, Op. 33 (1919), is one of a small number of works of the period which retain a key-signature and pay some respect to the conventions of major-minor harmony. The First String Quartet, Op. 37, of the same year is another example, at least in its first two movements, respectively in C major and E major. Even the fugal *finale*, the most explicit of several experiments in polytonality dating from these years (it employs four key-signatures rising in minor thirds—C, E flat, F sharp and A), cadences firmly in C major.

More characteristic are those works where a tonal structure is still discernible, articulated by emphasized pitches or triads and by pedal points, while the intervening melodic-harmonic material for the most part disregards any tonal obligations. In this sense the last of the *Métopes*, Op. 29, is centred 'on' D major and the first of the *Masques*, Op. 34, 'on' A. The third of the *Mythes*, Op. 30, composed in 1916 and entitled 'Dryades et Pan' is representative. Ex. 47 indicates how D has

Ex. 47

been established as a centre at the outset of the piece, first as a pitch and later as a triad of D major, though the major-minor triad seldom returns and the piece ends on an open fifth on D. This centre, recurring at important structural points, acts as a point of reference amidst elaborate 'Impressionistic' harmonies which include parallel structures, symmetrical accompaniment patterns and dissonant chord progressions.

In much of Szymanowski's middle-period music such an underlying tonal scheme can be traced only by forcing the point. A work such as the First Violin Concerto, Op. 35 (1916), makes use of tonal expectations at a local level but has no clear underpinning tonal structure. At those points where the music comes to rest on a plain triad, the effect is of a moment of tranquillity in the midst of constantly shifting, rhapsodic harmonies, but such moments are of local significance only and are not, as are comparable moments in Debussy, a means of establishing a tonal region. It is in a sense the converse of Bartók's middle-period music where a tonal scheme is present but the triad consistently avoided. Throughout the concerto voluptuous 'Romantic' harmonies exist side by side with static harmonic areas often based on the whole-tone or pentatonic scales. Pedal points again function as a means of holding the texture together, but for the most part the harmonies are unsystematic, similar in their wayward, rhapsodic sweep to Delius, but much more remote from an underlying tonal structure.

Shorter pieces such as the last of the *Songs of a Fairy-tale Princess*, Op. 31 and the sixth of the Op. 33 Studies cadence in a quasi-tonal manner in their final bars but give little indication in their overall harmonic language of a background tonality so that the final cadence can hardly be regarded as an outcome of a coherent tonal argument. In these works the unity of the music will depend upon contextual relationships which vary from work to work; in the study, for example, the important unifying features are the consistency of its configuration, the on-going rhythmic patterns and the use of an invariant chord colour, based on the tritone and perfect fourth.

Yet even in the most harmonically intractable of Szymanowski's middle-period works such as the Third Piano Sonata, Op. 36 (1917) and the *Four Rabindranath Tagore Songs*, Op. 41 (1918), tonal thinking exerts its influence in a subtle, indirect manner in the tendency for material to be repeated at the same pitch, in the use of melodic patterns which have a tonical basis and of dissonance/consonance relationships as a means of shaping the musical material. In fact much of this middle-period music illustrates particularly clearly Reti's concept of 'pantonality', the blending of tonical phrases where no unequivocal tonality reigns, and it may be regarded as representative of an attitude to tonality adopted in many twentieth-century works. The point is perhaps most clearly made by direct comparison between two works which eschew any single tonal centre—Szymanowski's Third Piano Sonata and the 'Prelude' from Schoenberg's *Suite*, Op. 25, his first completely serial composition. In both works there are clear pitch hierarchies. In the Schoenberg these are created by means of an 'invariant dyad' G-D flat; yet these pitches have a referential rather than a tonical function and there is no sense in which the harmonic language of the piece has been determined by this hierarchical relationship.[11] In the approach to the *adagio* of Szymanowski's sonata, on the other hand, there has been an obvious concern to create momentary tonal connections between different components of the texture. The G flat major of the right hand (bars 196–221) is contradicted by the seventh chords of the left hand while a long-range bass motion outlines a dominant formation in C (Ex. 48). The function of the C flat here is that of a pivot, eventually creating a whole-tone dominant which resolves onto

Ex. 48

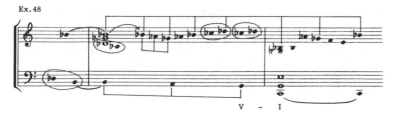

C. At the same time the beginning of the *adagio* theme preserves elements of G flat, permitting them to blend with the bass affirmations of C major.

A broader comparison with Schoenberg may throw some light on Szymanowski's attitude to tonality in his middle-period works. Both composers were exploring new worlds of sensibility which carried them beyond the formal disciplines and constraints of the traditional tonal system. Although Schoenberg allowed himself in some works to explore the most far-reaching implications of his new 'freedom', he was primarily and acutely aware of the need to *communicate* these new areas of feeling, though always on his own terms. This involved a search for constructive methods capable of organizing and giving coherent expression to the new resources made available by the loss of tonality—'Composition with twelve tones has no other aim than comprehensibility'.[12] Szymanowski, on the other hand, was less preoccupied with the search for a means of projecting the new areas of feeling than with exploring them to the limits of subjective fantasy. His musical language was to change in later years at precisely the time when, due to external circumstances, he became forcibly aware of the need to communicate, and therefore to objectify, his deepening inner vision.

TRADITIONAL FORMS AND CONSTRUCTIVE METHODS

One of tonality's closest allies was sonata-form, a formal principle which emerged from the dramatic and structural possibilities inherent in formalized classical tonality. Initially the dynamic of sonata-form was one of tonal contrast; thematic contrast, where it was present at all, remained a subsidiary aspect of the structure. As tonality declined in the nineteenth century, however, tonal dialectic was gradually replaced by thematic dialectic in many sonata structures, though the former continued to exert a significant influence. The central antithesis between 'statement' and 'development'—between stability and instability— was still achieved by tonal as well as thematic means, though the placing of 'statement' and 'development' within the tripartite struc-

ture tended to become more and more flexible. Certainly Charles
Rosen's view of sonata-form in the later nineteenth century as a
'shadowy life-in-death' is a useful corrective to misguided conceptions of
the form as external pattern, but it perhaps underestimates the extent to
which the sonata *principle* retained a vital role in the late nineteenth-
century formal process.[13]

The validity of sonata-form and other formal types developed within
the tonal era when employed in an atonal context has often been questioned, and it is significant that Schoenberg, who had been faithful to
sonata-form in his tonal music, clearly felt unable to retain it as a vehicle
for his early atonal material, though it is present as a greatly emaciated
background in some works. (Anthony Payne has pointed out with
reference to Op. 16, No. 1, that the time-scale of the classical sonata-
form exposition was dictated less by thematic considerations than by the
need to establish firmly the tonic and dominant regions. The 'exposition' of Schoenberg's piece is therefore short and concentrated, concerned only with the statement of basic motives, while the 'development', denied the opportunity of modulation, is given over to an ever
more tightly knit contrapuntal combination of these motives, a situation
which was already developing in the First String Quartet and First
Chamber Symphony.) [14] It may of course be argued that there can be
no 'exclusivity' in formal thinking, that the process of adaptation could
and did lead naturally to a view of sonata-form based on thematic
identity, in which the contrast between 'statement' and 'development'
would be achieved by means other than tonal. There can be no doubt
that Schoenberg regarded his discovery of the serial method as a means
of renovating the form; he saw the method not simply as a replacement
for, but as a logical outcome of, nineteenth-century constructive
methods, enabling him to *renew* the forms and phraseology of the
classical tradition. Webern was referring to this renewal of the old
forms when he remarked in 1933: 'The last few years have tried rather
to adhere very strictly to these forms. But in fact that has only just
become possible again.' [15] There is, indeed, a neo-classical element in
Schoenberg's early serial music which has proved distasteful to those
younger serialists who feel that there is little relationship between the
outward form and the inner unifying principle, such as that between
sonata-form and tonality.

Aaron Copland has touched upon this problem when writing about
the later sonatas of Skryabin. He described the composer's use of sonata-
form as 'one of the most extraordinary mistakes in all music', stating

that although the thematic material is 'truly individual, truly inspired', Skryabin had 'the fantastic idea of attempting to put this really new body of feeling into the strait-jacket of the old classical sonata-form, recapitulation and all'.[10] It has been remarked that in Skryabin's fifth sonata the sonata-form outlines still have meaning in relation to the work's surviving tonal structure and to the disposition and interaction of contrasting thematic and harmonic material. In that work and in the *Poem of Ecstasy*, however, there are the seeds of formal tensions which remain a problematical feature of the late sonatas. Such tensions result not only from the absence of tonal organization and harmonic contrast but from a conflict between the cumulative momentum of the music, usually achieved by textural rather than harmonic means, and the formal constraints of the tripartite mould. The *Poem of Ecstasy* had found a satisfactory compromise in that the formal elements of sonata-form have been incorporated within a progression through several climactic peaks towards the final C major apotheosis, but in the sixth and seventh sonatas Skryabin reverted to a more orthodox sonata-form structure in which the most obviously unsatisfactory feature is a full-scale, though texturally varied, recapitulation, no longer tonally or thematically indispensable.

Some of the shorter pieces of the later years, such as *Vers la Flamme*, Op. 72 (1914), with its carefully paced crescendo and gradual increase in textural complexity, achieved a much happier co-operation of 'form' and 'content'. There are, too, indications in the later sonatas, particularly the ninth, that Skryabin was moving towards a more flexible view of sonata-form, in which he retained the outlines of the form but modified it to accommodate his characteristically fragmented melodic material, using the development section to engage in intricate textural and contrapuntal devices and the abridged recapitulation for new developmental procedures which do not hold back the cumulative momentum of the music.

Szymanowski was also concerned to keep sight of traditional forms in some of his middle-period works. Sonata structures, already explored in his early 'Viennese' compositions, were retained in the First String Quartet and the Third Piano Sonata. The more characteristic extended works from this period, however, employ freely developing forms in which the capricious fancy of the composer's imagination is unhampered by any suggestion of conventional pattern. The First Violin Concerto is typically unconventional in structure. Like Skryabin's *Poem of Ecstasy* it consists of a single long progression towards the final climax (immediately following the cadenza) but unlike that work its gradually unfolding structure, revealing an unerring sense of formal balance, is achieved entirely without the support of a sonata-form background. There is no psychological break until the cadenza, for the two quick sections, although they provide necessary contrast, do not interrupt the flow of the music. In the remarkable profusion of themes, most of which never recur, a thematic unity is achieved by the close family resemblances between ideas and by the skilful preparation in the earlier sections of the work for the principal thematic groups. These enter at carefully calculated intervals in the course of the work, forming successive stages in the overall progression, and tension is built up by means of well-placed climaxes pointing the way towards the final peak. Important landmarks in the structure are the 'fantasy' sections consisting of string tremolandos, woodwind repeated notes, piano and celesta configurations and fanfares on various instruments. These sections, in which the orchestra often seems about to get out of control, to be pacified by the soloist, are the most obvious manifestations of the poetic programme behind the work.[17] The following is an attempt to indicate the main stages in the argument, though it should be stressed that these form part of a single indivisible progression:

Section 1   'Fantasy' and other themes
             First quick section leading to *Climax 1*
             'Fantasy'
Section 2   Thematic group A
             'Fantasy'
             Discussion of A leading to *Climax 2*
Section 3   Second quick section with Thematic group B
             'Fantasy'
             Discussion of A leading to *Climax 3*
Section 4   Thematic group C leading to *Climax 4*
             Discussion of B leading to
             Cadenza leading to
Section 5   *Climax 5* based on A
             'Fantasy'
             Closing reference to C

However unorthodox the structure of Szymanowski's concerto, it still depends upon the traditional techniques of thematic repetition and development which characterize more conventional formal types. These techniques are also of central importance in shaping much of the early atonal music of the 'Second Viennese School', often in a context where the residue of traditional forms is still discernible. But there are also significant premonitions in this *œuvre* of the neo-classical *renewal* of established formal types which we associate more closely with early serialism. In his 1929 lecture on *Wozzeck*, Berg referred to the musical structure of Act II, Scene 1 as a sonata-form movement, and the outlines of the form can be discerned in the background with a recapitulation beginning at bar 123. Unlike that of Skryabin and Szymanowski, however, Berg's use of the form is not so much a residue of traditional procedure as an attempt to compensate for the loss of tonality by presenting his harmonically complex material in clearly defined formal moulds. He expressed the dilemma as follows: 'When I decided to compose a full-length opera I was confronted with a new problem, at least in the harmonic sphere. How could I hope to achieve, without the well-tried resources of tonality and its possibilities of formal organization, the same compelling musical unity?' [18]

The use of closed forms for unifying purposes is seen at its most rigid in *Wozzeck* (the work also includes a fugue, scherzo and trio, passacaglia and quasi-rondo), but it plays a part in other atonal compositions, and particularly in Schoenberg's *Pierrot Lunaire*. The Waltz and barcarolle movements are two instances of Schoenberg's use of popular forms, though they are clearly much less rigorous in construction than the contrapuntal forms of *Nacht*, a passacaglia based on a three-note motive, and *Parodie*, whose strict canons are laid out as follows:

Canon by inversion	Cl. Vla. Recit.	b. 1–15
Double Canon	Picc./Cl. Recit./Vla.	b. 16–21
Double Canon	Cl./Fl. Recit./Vla.	b. 26–29
Canon by inversion	Cl. Vla.	b. 26–29
Coda	Piano	b. 29–

Most famous of all is *Mondfleck* where the double canon is strictly palindromic and is accompanied by a piano fugue.

Such contrapuntal forms go beyond the provision of a clearly defined structure, however, for they are a means of ordering the texture of the music which is systematic enough to act as substitute discipline for traditional tonal-harmonic relationships, a development which has been noted in its conceptual stages in works such as Schoenberg's First Chamber Symphony. As an alternative unifying principle to tonality, 'contrapuntal logic' will be examined in a later chapter, together with other aspects of the thematic process which assumed constructive importance in atonality. But although such thematic procedures took on an altered significance in an atonal context, they were of course firmly rooted in tradition. There is a line of succession from the contrapuntal textures of Mahler through Schoenberg's First Chamber Symphony to *Pierrot Lunaire* and from the motivic integration of Brahms through Schoenberg's First String Quartet to the first of his *Five Orchestral Pieces*, Op. 16. Indeed the retention of thematicism—the repetition and development throughout a work of recognizable thematic material—in atonality was its most fundamental link with the tonal past. Berg expressed this in 'What is "atonal"?': 'The main thing to show . . . is that the melody, the principal part, the theme, is the basis, or determined the course, of this, as of all other music.'[19]

TRADITIONAL PHRASEOLOGY

In his book *Alban Berg*, Hans Redlich has pointed out the striking resemblances in thematic material between the second movement of Berg's String Quartet, Op. 3, and the first of his *Three Orchestral Pieces*, Op. 6, and Mahler's Seventh Symphony, emphasizing the similarities in rhythmic structure and melodic contour.[20] There is always point in thus relating atonal music to its immediate nineteenth-century background, for it often betrays its tonal ancestry by revealing close analogies with the phrase and rhythmic structure, the textural patterns and the melodic/harmonic phraseology of tonal music.

The attitudes of Skryabin and Szymanowski towards phrase and rhythmic structure in their later music were diametrically opposed. Skryabin tended to retain the four-bar phrase as the basic unit of construction even when this was no longer a product of classical harmonic rhythm, though there are of course exceptions and a tendency to create more and more flexible rhythmic patterns within the phrase. This fidelity to the four-bar phrase remains a problematical feature of works which have cut themselves loose from traditionally functioning harmony, particularly when it is expressed in such obvious form as in the last of the *Four Preludes*, Op. 74 (1913):

$$8 \qquad 4 \qquad 4+4+4$$
$$[4+4] \quad [2+2]$$

The phrase structure of Szymanowski's middle-period music is altogether more flexible, his avoidance of the obvious in this respect directly analogous to the increasing sophistication of his melodic and harmonic language. None the less, just as diatonic passages alternate with chordal structures of extreme dissonance in many of these works, complex phrasing may take its place beside conventional, often symmetrical, phrases, and the implication of a latent regularity often underlies the most asymmetrical pattern. In the eighth of the *Twelve Studies*, Op. 33, for example, traditional phrase lengths act as a foil to irregular lengths:

$$2+1\tfrac{1}{2} \quad 2+1\tfrac{1}{2} \quad 4+2 \quad 2+1\tfrac{1}{2}+2$$

Schoenberg's discovery of serialism signalled a return not only to Baroque and Classical formal types in his *Suite*, Op. 25 and Wind Quintet, Op. 26, but to traditional phrase and rhythmic patterns. In *The Path to the New Music*, Webern referred to 'the development of those classical forms that found their purest expression in Beethoven; the period and the eight-bar sentence . . . everything which has happened since then can be traced back to these forms'.[21] At the same time it has been noted that the flexible phrase and rhythmic structure of the first movement of Schoenberg's second quartet was moving in a contrary direction, extending Brahms's use of asymmetrical phrase lengths and internal rhythmic subtleties within the phrase. In the atonal works which followed the quartet, phrase and rhythmic freedom of a much more radical and unprecedented type is apparent, but even this development must be viewed within a context where traditional patterns are often retained for complete pieces or at least as a foil for 'arhythmic' procedures within a single work. In the fifth song from *Das Buch der hängenden Gärten* the two and four-bar units are reinforced by melodic sequence and rhythmic repetition of a traditional type, though there are occasional overlaps between the vocal line and the accompaniment:

$$4 \qquad 4 \qquad 4 \qquad 6$$
$$[2+2] \quad [2+2] \quad [2+2] \quad [3+3]$$

The importance of such measured rhythmic stress in confirming a background of diatonic functions has already been emphasized in relation to the third song from the same cycle (Ex. 44i).

Even where the phrase structure of early atonal music is irregular and its rhythmic procedures are complex, the punctuation of the phrase frequently relies on traditional cadential phraseology. Rhythm had always played an important part in the tonal cadence and, in the absence of tonality, even more emphasis was placed upon it as a means of dissipating the music's momentum or, alternatively, of emphasizing the structural downbeat which articulates the phrase. In the first of Webern's *Five Pieces for String Quartet*, Op. 5, for example, the cadence at bars 12–13 is characterized by a rhythmic expansion of a two-note motive, descending stepwise, which relates closely to traditional procedure. The textural contrast at this point emphasizes, incidentally, the renewed importance of texture as a means of cadential articulation in an atonal context.

The opening of the second of Webern's quartet pieces draws attention to a further important link with tradition. The textural layout of the music, comprising a viola melody with chordal accompaniment on second violin and cello, is reminiscent of tonal music, although the harmonies do not function tonally. Traditional textures of this sort were often retained in early atonality and they serve to balance the frequent textural complexity which followed the decline of tonal harmony and which often makes it difficult to distinguish meaningfully between important and subsidiary material, between 'theme' and 'accompaniment'. A closer examination of Webern's Op. 5, No. 2 reveals, moreover, that the nature of the melodic line—its contour, phrasing and rhythmic structure—relates it even more specifically to the late-Romantic world of Mahler and Strauss, with their widely leaping, straining melodies and sighing appoggiaturas. The tensions and relaxations of the music have been achieved by means of an interaction of rhythmic, harmonic and melodic material which is not so remote from traditional tonal procedure. It may be examined in bars 5–6 (Ex. 49). The characteristic 'shape' of the phrase is achieved partly by the rapid

Ex. 49

rise and gradual fall of its melody and partly by its rhythmic structure. Both factors contribute to an accumulation and release of tension which centres on the F natural of bar 6, accentuating the falling 'appoggiatura' which in itself strongly suggests a tonal background. The underlying chordal movement, although rejecting traditional diatonic relationships, retains the stepwise part-movement which is a feature of tonal harmony, and strengthens the quasi-tonal feeling of the appoggiatura by creating a 'suspension' on the third beat of bar 6.

Inevitably such traditionally conceived textures reinforce those tonal implications which were discussed earlier in the chapter and which form such an important part of our aural experience of early atonality. Even in works which do not readily permit a tonal interpretation of the pitch content the phraseology may well forge strong links with tonal procedure. This is certainly the case in the final bars of Schoenberg's Op. 19, No. 1 and they may be used to summarize several of the points made in the chapter. Affinities with tonal procedure are already suggested here by the explicit textural differentiation between 'melody' and chordal 'accompaniment' (Ex. 50). They are strengthened by the

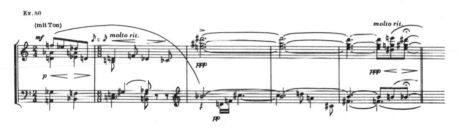

stepwise, predominantly semitonal part-movement of the harmony (by no means wholly divorced from a triadic background) and by the cadential 'appoggiaturas' in the principal melody and subsidiary voices. They are further strengthened by a regular rhythmic pulse and, for the last four bars, a stable metric pattern which is discernible despite the *ritardando*.

12

'Free' atonality

'Anything may happen; everything is possible and probable. Time and space do not exist; on an insignificant groundwork of reality imagination spins and weaves new patterns; a mixture of memories, experience, unfettered fancies, absurdities and improvisation.' Such notions, expressed by Strindberg in his preface to *The Dream Play* (1903), had a telling impact on an emerging group of German 'Expressionist' writers and painters with whom Schoenberg identified closely, particularly in the years between 1908 and 1913. Expressionism was never such a clearly defined movement as Cubism or Futurism. Its outlines were blurred and its intentions vague, but it began to take recognizable shape under the impact of new, revolutionary developments in France and Italy as they blended with a heightened expression of traditional qualities in German art, in particular its deeply serious, introspective quality, often pessimistic, occasionally cruel (the rediscovery of the intensely expressive distortion of early German painters such as Grunewald proved an important inspiration to the Expressionists). Central to the spirit of Expressionism, as articulated in *Der Blaue Reiter* and in Kandinsky's *On the Spiritual in Art* (both published in 1912), was the concept of the 'inner element' or 'inner necessity' in the shaping of a work of art, without reference to pre-existing formal types. Kandinsky remarked that 'Inner necessity is the basis of both small and great problems in painting. Today we are seeking the road which is to lead us away from the external to the internal basis.' [1]

The attempt to explore man's 'inner nature' in art was related to and assisted by Sigmund Freud's scientific inquiries into the workings of the hitherto uncharted subconscious mind (uncharted, that is, by science). Freud's researches had wide and profound repercussions on all the arts. In music his influence can be detected in the new, exploratory element of psychological realism which is found in operatic subjects such as *Erwartung*, *Bluebeard's Castle*, *Wozzeck* and *Lulu*, but his impact, and that of Expressionist thought, was felt at a deeper level in the musical language of some early atonal music by Schoenberg, Berg and Webern. Kandinsky's distinction between the 'internal condition' and the 'external condition' necessary for creative activity is in effect a distinction between the artist's inspirational experience, which has been incubating below the levels of consciousness and over which he has little control, and his conscious manipulation of that experience when it has emerged from the subconscious. While the intuitive process had always played a major part in artistic creation, it had usually been allied to a set of conventions for the realization of the artist's formal and expressive intentions; such a set of conventions is the major-minor key system of classical tonality.

The Expressionists were not of course rejecting 'form' but rather insisting that the subjective creative impulse, born of 'inner necessity', should create its own form, the 'shaping spirit of the imagination', and that at a time when the formal and linguistic conventions of eighteenth- and nineteenth-century art were beginning to break down. The impact of such ideals was particularly strong on a group of works by the 'Second Viennese School' in which tonality has been submerged without being replaced by any thorough-going alternative constructive method, the form and coherence of the music depending to a quite unprecedented degree on the composer's intuitive sense of formal balance. The concept of a 'law of feeling', an *Expressionslogik*, would seem to have particular relevance to these works, though it should not be taken to imply an untrammelled outpouring from the 'dark embryo'. Schoenberg's notion of 'liberty of expression' [2] may be tempered by Webern's description of 'constant testing' [3] and Berg's reference to 'severe aural checking by the inner ear'.[4] Such 'freedom' amounts in effect to another form of discipline, albeit one in which the 'rightness' of an event is determined to an unprecedented degree by the composer's intuition.

Certain effects of tonal collapse when it has not been met by alternative unifying methods have been noted in an analysis of the last of Berg's Op. 2 songs. Certainly there are aspects of the musical language of this song which rely heavily on traditional features. Triadic combinations and extended passages in thirds inevitably create strong tonal allusions, just as the semitonal part-movement of chord progressions, the recurrence of characteristic melodic and harmonic ideas and the 'theme and accompaniment' textures form important links with tonal procedure. Despite such features, however, the absence of an underlying constructive principle which could 'explain' the language of the complete piece ensures that the momentary association of ideas on an intuitive level plays a large part in determining the 'form' and 'content' of the work. In such a context an attempt to demonstrate a work's coherence and cohesion will involve a discussion of less tangible features than the familiar thematic and harmonic form-building techniques, and the latter have often been given disproportionate importance in analyses of early atonal music. Analytical commentators on the atonal works of Schoenberg, Berg and Webern in particular should resist the temptation to discuss momentary connections at the expense of total form, and to over-emphasize the structural significance of unifying features whose chief attraction is their familiarity.

It was perhaps inevitable that the collapse of tonal harmony, with the resulting lack of functional differentiation in melodic and harmonic material, should have led to a re-shaping of the basic elements of composition in many works of the early atonal period. A renewed importance was given to parameters of musical thought other than pitch—to rhythm, *timbre*, texture, register and dynamics—in the articulation of musical structures, creating new concepts of 'form' which vary from work to work. Even with respect to pitch content, the function of a phrase may well be determined by the general characteristics of a melodic line or a harmonic succession rather than by organized thematic or motivic relationships. This point can perhaps be clarified with reference to bars 12–16 of Berg's song Op. 2, No. 4. A pitch-duration graph of this passage would indicate that the two most important characteristics of the vocal line are its gradual ascent, with peak notes closing together as the climax is approached, and the gradually widening compass of its successive melodic phrases, again contributing to the climactic effect. The choice of pitches making up this vocal line has been dictated neither by thematic nor motivic considerations, nor by the need to make harmonic sense with the piano accompaniment. The only determining factor, apart from the general characteristics already mentioned, would seem to be a fairly consistent avoidance of octave doubling with the piano part, the influence of natural speech inflections and the persistence of a tonally derived view of intervallic quality (e.g. the particular emotive associations of such intervals as the major seventh and minor ninth).

In those works of Schoenberg, Berg and Webern where no thematic or motivic organization is apparent, the structure may depend on a complementary relationship between ascending and descending melodic ideas, between melodic material and non-melodic textural patterns, between clearly defined rhythmic patterns and rhythmically unstable material, between loud and soft, and so on. The most fruitful method of examining such works would be one which attempts to define the musical 'gesture', as we did with the vocal line of bars 12–16 of Berg's song, and then relates that gesture to its immediate and overall context.

FORM AND *GENRE*

A glance at the output of Schoenberg, Berg and Webern between the years 1908 and 1913 reveals immediately that their rejection of traditional tonal functions resulted in a similar rejection of the traditional instrumental *genres* which had been developed within the tonal era. The four-movement sonata-symphonic structures were replaced for the most part by successions of shorter pieces—the *Five Movements for String Quartet*, Op. 5 by Webern, the *Four Pieces for Clarinet and Piano*, Op. 5 by Berg and the *Five Orchestral Pieces*, Op. 16 by Schoenberg are representative. More extended structures of traditional mould returned only with the development of serialism.

The difficulty of structuring extended paragraphs of instrumental music in the absence of tonality was clearly one of the principal reasons for this and also for the preponderance of vocal music written during these years. In his analysis of his Op. 22 songs, Schoenberg pointed out that 'compositions for text are inclined to allow the poem to determine, at least outwardly, their form'.[5] The expression of a text has always acted as a means of stretching the language of music. The musical imagery which is evoked by extra-musical ideas has often been left to stand alone when the 'prop' has been removed, as in the transfer of stylistic fingerprints from eighteenth-century opera to the symphonic literature. As tonality declined, the use of a text or programme assumed considerable importance both as a formal prop and an expressive catalyst, often determining the overall shape and the detailed melodic-harmonic content of a work in the absence of a self-consistent compositional method. This is the case in Berg's song Op. 2, No. 4. The external shaping of the song, the placing of its sudden, shattering climax following an extended opening section, quiet but intense in mood, and succeeded by a short, hushed coda, is determined by Mombert's verse which sets the scene of a girl's tryst with her lover and explodes in anguish with her outburst of grief as he fails to arrive. The emotive imagery of the poem is largely responsible for the intense dissonance of the harmony and the wide, expressive leaps of the vocal line, developed to the point at which tonality has been submerged; one is reminded of

T. S. Eliot's remark in another context: 'The content of feeling is constantly bursting the receptacle.' Bars 12–16 of the song indicate how its musical language can be 'explained' by textual parallelism. The degree of dissonance perfectly mirrors the poetic content, from the warm major thirds of bar 12 when the girl is first pictured to the nine-note dissonant combination which accompanies her cry 'Er kommt noch nicht', the emotional kernel of the song. The increasing melodic and harmonic tension preceding this climax is supported by cumulative rhythmic patterns, the use of registral extremes and a crescendo from *p* to *fff*.

The early atonal works of Schoenberg (*Das Buch der hängenden Gärten*) and Webern (the Op. 3 and Op. 4 songs [6]) demonstrate a comparable dependence on poetic texts, though in the Schoenberg this is not always expressed by means of a conventional parallelism of text and music. Heinz J. Dill has drawn attention to the distinction made by Schoenberg himself between the *Oberfläche der Wortgedanken*, the 'surface layer of meaning', and the *wirklicher Inhalt*, the 'real content' of poetry, a distinction which is entirely typical of Expressionist thinking. [7] Schoenberg was largely indifferent to the former and, far from expressing textual details by means of musical literalism, often created musical structures whose relationship to the text was one of polarity, in which the very structural strength of the text was required so that the music could 'dissolve and transform' it. While this is a useful insight in connection with the George songs, Schoenberg's remarks on the use of a text as an aid to the construction of larger musical thoughts would seem to indicate a more conventional aesthetic of vocal writing, at least in some works:

> 'A little later I discovered how to construct larger forms by following a text or poem. The differences in size and shape of its parts and the change in character and mood were mirrored in the shape and size of the composition, in its dynamics and tempo, figuration and accentuation, instrumentation and orchestration. Thus the parts were differentiated as clearly as they had formerly been by the tonal and structural functions of harmony.' [8]

The attempt by W. M. Stroh to find a deeper constructive relationship between text and music based on a pointillistic treatment of key words in a series of independent units combined to produce larger units and finally the total form in Schoenberg's Op. 15, No. 14 carries little conviction even in this work and could in any case hardly form the basis for useful generalizations on Schoenberg's attitude to his texts. [9]

The most ambitious work to rely completely on a dramatic prop was

Schoenberg's monodrama *Erwartung* (1909), an extended essay in 'non structured' music which has proved singularly resistant to formal or thematic analysis.[10] *Erwartung* is an astonishing instance of sustained musical invention, untrammelled by formal pattern, thematic development or repetition, and holding together only by the cohesive force of the composer's musical imagination and formal instinct allied to a pre-existing dramatic shape. It forms the high-water mark of musical Expressionism, its 'plot' a heavily Freudian, deeply symbolic monologue—uttered in short, ejaculatory phrases—of a woman who searches for her lover at night in a forest and finds him dead near a house with closed shutters. Her nightmarish, and ultimately mis-directed (i.e. temporal rather than spiritual) search for fulfilment gave rise to a freely associative musical language of which Willi Schuh has aptly remarked: 'The only explanation of Schoenberg's sure-footedness amid the boundless immensities of his new musical realm is that he moulded this music as if obeying the compulsive dictates of his inner vision.' [11]

Erwartung is an exceptional work in that its musical 'stream of consciousness', rejecting traditional form-building methods, has been cast in an extended mould, written moreover in an incredible seventeen days. Much more typical was the trend towards ever more concise musical miniatures, especially in the field of instrumental music, where there is no text to act as a formal support. Schoenberg's unfinished orchestral pieces of 1910 were early examples of this highly concentrated, aphoristic style and they were immediately followed by a group of miniatures by Webern, all composed between 1910 and 1914 and comprising the *Three Pieces for Violin and Piano*, Op. 7, the *Bagatelles for String Quartet*, Op. 9, the *Five Orchestral Pieces*, Op. 10 and the *Three Pieces for Cello and Piano*, Op. 11. Schoenberg followed his own orchestral pieces with the *Six Little Piano Pieces*, Op. 19 (1911) while Berg's contributions were the *Altenberglieder*, Op. 4 and the *Four Pieces for Clarinet and Piano*, Op. 5, composed in 1912 and 1913 respectively. Schoenberg wrote of these works: 'One of the most important aids to comprehension is clarity of design. *Brevity* facilitates a grasp of the whole; it furthers clarity and it encourages comprehension. Unwittingly I wrote *unusually short* pieces at that time.' [12] In the absence of traditional tonal-harmonic relationships which had served 'as a means of distinguishing the features of the form', extended argument clearly became more difficult, especially in instrumental works. But the appearance of these 'unusually short' pieces was not simply a negative response to tonal decline. It has been remarked that the suppression of tonal harmony led to a renewed importance being ascribed to parameters which had previously played a less crucial constructive role than pitch content, and the extreme brevity of many works of the period is in part a function of that change. When every aspect of a work's musical language—its pitch, rhythm, *timbre*, dynamics and so on—makes an equal contribution to its overall structure, the time-scale will tend to be reduced. The 'form' of these miniatures (they eschew for the most part any obvious pattern involving repetition or audible variation) results from an interaction of parameters which is unique for each piece, making generalization impossible. To adapt T. S. Eliot: the psychic material tends to create its own form—the eventual form will be to a greater or less degree the form for that one piece and for no other. It is hoped that by examining such works *via* different parameters, something of their interaction will emerge.

Despite the absence of conventional form-building techniques in many early atonal works by the 'Second Viennese School', it is often possible to subdivide such works (including the miniatures) into complementary formal sections shaped, as in any other music, by tensions and relaxations and articulated by cadence points or 'structural downbeats'. In the third of Schoenberg's Op. 11 piano pieces, where no systematic organization of the melodic and harmonic language can be found without forcing the point, this subdivision into component sections of varying lengths, characterized by particular types of rhythmic and textural material and articulated by relatively clearly defined cadence points, is of crucial importance in an attempt to grasp the overall structure. The opening four bars of the piece make up a stable, self-contained section characterized by continuous semiquaver movement (breaking into demisemiquavers in bar 3) and by a driving rhythmic motive in the bass. The cadence, alternating sharp staccato chords with a tritone figure, is unambiguous and is reinforced by rhythmic augmentation of the two-note figure, a *ritardando*, *decrescendo* and textural simplification. Similarly the final twelve bars comprise a long but indivisible section which begins by glancing back to the opening of the first piece in a moment of rhythmic and textural simplicity, before building up to the work's main climax —a whirlwind of sound which gradually loses momentum and disintegrates into the rhythmic discontinuity of the final bars. The essential structural points here are that these sections are relatively extended and have a clear directional movement, generated in the opening section by the rhythmic momentum of the bass, and in the closing section by the accumulation and release of tension.

They are offset by a succession of short, 'static' intervening episodes, sharply contrasted in rhythm, texture and dynamics, and unstable in their combined effect. In a context of maximum contrast and variety, connections may be felt between these sections based on the most tenuous associations. Bars 4 and 7 have a similar rhythmic structure, for example, as do bars 8–9 and bars 12–13, while the sequence of dynamic levels in bars 21–3 recalls that of bars 15–18. The connections are less important than the contrasts, however, for contrast in this piece functions almost as a principle of progression; textural complexity engenders (and enhances) melodic simplicity, rhythmic definition gives way to rhythmic instability, maximal dynamic levels are succeeded by minimal dynamic levels. The thematic and tonal contrasts of the traditional sonata movement have here been replaced by extreme contrasts of texture, rhythm and dynamic levels, all concentrated within a short time-span.

The third of Berg's Op. 5 clarinet pieces similarly falls into complementary, thematically unrelated sections, though there is some intervallic integration of material. The opening section (bars 1–3) is characterized by a rapid interchange of ideas between clarinet and piano and is linked to a second, slower section where the piano has a harmonic accompaniment to the clarinet's melodic phrases. The third section, very slow, employs *ostinato* figures of varying durations while the final section is distinguished from the rest in character by rapid semiquaver movement. Despite the brevity of the piece, the effect is more of a highly compressed alternation of slow and fast sections along traditional lines than of the mosaic-like juxtaposition of fragmentary ideas which is characteristic of Schoenberg's Op. 11, No. 3.

Rather different to both is the succession of four brief statements which make up the second of Schoenberg's unfinished orchestral pieces of 1910, each statement articulated by pause markings on the bar-lines and distinguished by contrasting textures, *timbres* and types of melodic-harmonic material (the piece is just eight bars in length). The first of Webern's Op. 11 cello pieces is markedly similar in construction, its four short sections clearly separated by *rit . . . . a tempo* indications and by rests. Indeed the ubiquity of *rit . . . . a tempo* markings in the early atonal literature is itself a telling indication of the pressing need to find methods of formal articulation which might replace the tonal cadence. Each of the four sections of Webern's piece has a distinctive structure which differentiates it from the others and which is defined as much by timbral quality (many shades of tone-colour and types of articulation are used within a short time-span) and rhythm as by motivic or intervallic characteristics. One prophetic development whose implications will be discussed in a later chapter is the fact that the length of individual statements is at least partly determined by the limitation that each employs the total chromatic with a calculated economy.

PITCH CONTENT

In their exploration of all the implications of tonal collapse, Schoenberg, Berg and Webern—in at least some of their early atonal compositions—abandoned important constructive methods which had grown out of, or become associated with, tonality. The most important of these was thematicism; the use of thematic identity, as established by repetition and development, as a major form-building element. Schoenberg himself wrote that 'intoxicated by the enthusiasm of having freed music from the shackles of tonality, I had thought to find further liberty of expression. In fact . . . I believed that now music could renounce motivic features and remain coherent and comprehensible nevertheless'.[13] The avoidance of thematic repetition in several atonal works gave rise to the term 'athematic' which, like 'atonal', was first applied as a term of abuse. While some of the 'athematic' works replace thematicism with internal intervallic relationships, others appear to avoid any conscious organization involving a precise pitch content, at least in the horizontal dimension.

The absence of thematic repetition and development in the fifth of Schoenberg's Op. 19 piano pieces makes an examination of general melodic characteristics appropriate, though comprehension is aided here by intervallic connections and by the simplicity of the rhythmic structure, including audible repetition of rhythmic motives. A detailed description of the principal melodic line (Ex. 51) would indicate that there are two complementary gestural relationships which help to create a balanced overall structure—between ascending and descending melodic directions, and between melodic material which has been confined within a narrow compass over an extended time-span and

Ex. 51

material with a wide compass contained within a short time-span. A closer inspection reveals that, in addition to these general characteristics which help define the external form of the piece, internal cohesive devices, based on intervallic relationships, to some extent limit the choice of pitches (see chapter 13).

Two athematic miniatures by Webern, the first of his *Five Orchestral Pieces*, Op. 10 (1911–13) and the first of his *Three Pieces for Cello and Piano*, Op. 11, are equally susceptible to inspection from this point of view. Although there has been no apparent attempt at motivic integration of material in the orchestral piece, Ex. 52 indicates the presence of subtle cross-references and momentary connections between pitches or intervallic groups. It differs from the Schoenberg in that the melodic

Ex. 52

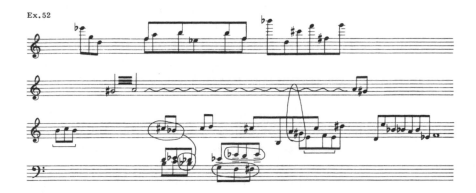

material is more fragmentary and less clearly directional, with short phrases spanning a wide compass. It is nevertheless possible for the ear to isolate and follow through a number of separate melodic strands which unfold on different planes. Ex. 52 indicates how the melodic lines may be grouped in this way. It also shows that there is an effective balance between the single melodic strands at the beginning and end of the piece and the contrapuntal interweaving of lines in the central section.

In Op. 11, No. 1 the melody has been more clearly differentiated from a supporting harmonic accompaniment, though it is more widely spanning and even more fragmented, comprising short groups of notes which never exceed four. These last two characteristics point to enduring features of Webern's style common to both early and late works—the frequent use of octave displacement (the 'appoggiatura' B natural–B flat which acts as a cadential close to the opening statement is an example of a familiar figure placed in a new light by means of double octave displacement) and the integral role of silence as an ingredient of the musical phrase, the melody continuing, as it were, through the rests. While the former may be regarded as an ultimate extension of the widely spanning melodies of the late-Romantics, the latter is innovative (unless one includes Medieval and Renaissance practice) and was to have a significant influence on later European music. As in Schoenberg's Op. 19, No. 5 there are intervallic relationships which to some extent limit the choice of pitches in Webern's miniature, while the exhaustibility of the total chromatic is a further limiting factor.

The fifth of Schoenberg's Op. 16 orchestral pieces (1909) again avoids any thorough-going motivic organization of its pitch content, though the intransigence of this is to some extent offset by a traditional rhythmic phraseology. The piece comprises a single melodic line which travels from one instrumental group to another throughout the orchestra against a background of freely related interweaving melodic strands. It has been remarked that the rejection of tonal harmony led in some works to a lack of differentiation between melodic and harmonic material, making it at times difficult to distinguish meaningfully between principal and secondary material. To help clarify the orchestral textures of Op. 16, Schoenberg introduced the terms *Hauptstimme* and *Nebenstimme* which were later to be adopted by Berg in his *Three Orchestral Pieces*, Op. 6 and other works. The principal melody of Op. 16, No. 5 has a clear overall 'shape' which is dictated mainly by register but also by varying compass and rhythmic structure. It approaches the piece's main climax by way of graded climactic peaks, whose imminence is made clear by rapid rhythmic activity, dense textures, increasing dynamic levels and widely leaping melodic phrases. The corresponding 'relaxation' sections have, predictably, more stable rhythms, sparser textures, decreasing dynamic levels and smoother melodic lines. The formal balance of the piece is unerring, depending on an intuitive balancing of such factors as the pace of climactic approaches, the length of relaxation sections and the varying intensities of the climaxes. 'Hidden' motivic connections in subsidiary voices play a minor unifying role, as does the recurring emphasis on specific pitches at climactic points in the *Hauptstimme*, for these remain subsidiary to the much broader relationships which determine the piece's overall form—the varying densities, the overall registral 'shape' and the purposeful contouring of the *Hauptstimme*, with its close link between compass and duration.

In the third of Schoenberg's Op. 11 piano pieces the co-existence of melodic ideas and non-melodic textural patterns is in itself an important structural determinant in the absence of more systematic methods of organization. Passages of melodic beauty and simplicity such as bars 8–9, 12–14 and 23–4 are balanced by, and depend for their effectiveness on, the textural and rhythmic complexity of surrounding material. In bars 1–4 and 18–22 melodic lines explode or disintegrate into non-melodic textures in a manner which suggests a parallel with the last of Berg's Op. 5 clarinet pieces, where there is again a careful balance between melodic ideas and the colouristic webs of sound into which they dissolve.

In athematic compositions, the choice of pitches will often be influenced strongly by vertical considerations and above all by the conscious avoidance of octave doublings, a feature of both Webern miniatures discussed above and of Schoenberg's Op. 19, No. 5. Indeed in the latter the one exception in bar 5 sounds almost like an error and behaves in any case rather like an inverted suspension, returning immediately to the more characteristically dissonant interval of a major seventh. Octave doubling was avoided in early atonal music partly because of its association with the tonal literature but more because it creates a dramatically contrasting harmonic colour in a context of prevailing dissonance and tends therefore to disturb seriously harmonic consistency.

In many atonal compositions by Schoenberg, Berg and Webern, this negative postulate is almost the only systematic influence on the vertical construction of the music, but there are other less formalized, though no less important, constraints. These are present even in the most refractory of Schoenberg's athematic scores such as *Erwartung*, the last of the Op. 16 pieces and the third of the Op. 11 pieces, three essays whose harmonic language has indeed a great deal in common. One constraining element is the persistence of dissonance/consonance relations as a means of shaping the music. This has an obvious emotive significance in the monodrama, but serves also as a method of creating tensions and relaxations in the instrumental works in a way which Schoenberg was noticeably to abandon in his early twelve-note compositions. Equally important is the tendency in these works towards an overall harmonic homogeneity. Certain harmonic units are especially prominent—motive (a) from Berg's early music, comprising a tritone and perfect fourth; the combination of major or minor thirds and the major seventh; the augmented triad. Such harmonic units are often employed

with a consistency which approaches at times that of the tonal literature, and they are frequently superimposed in such a way that they
preserve their identity (Ex. 53). Finally, and perhaps most important,
there is an obvious concern in these works to integrate the vertical and
horizontal dimensions of the music by means of an interpenetration of

Ex.53

both dimensions by the same intervallic patterns (Ex. 54).

Ex.54

RHYTHM

In several early atonal works, Schoenberg, Berg and Webern explored the unprecedented rhythmic flexibility which became possible only when rhythm was no longer required to support harmonic progression, though it has already been demonstrated that other works rely heavily upon a phrase and rhythmic structure which is clearly a product of tonal functions. Certainly the absence of a regular pulse in many such works, or in parts of them, is an obstacle to their communication at least as great as the undermining of the triad and the 'emancipation of the dissonance'. This is demonstrated by the readier acceptance of Bartók's essays in severe dissonance which are made more palatable by their strongly affirmed pulse. The rhythmic innovations of Bartók and Stravinsky are indeed of quite a different nature to those of the 'Second Viennese School', their displaced accents and rapidly changing metres depending for their effectiveness upon a clearly defined pulse. But the disintegration of a traditional rhythmic structure should not be viewed as a wholly negative response to tonal decline. It provided new scope for structural planning based on the unprecedented variety of rhythmic procedure which became available after Schoenberg's second quartet. In a perceptive article, Philip Friedheim has indicated how a structural relationship can be traced in several atonal works based on greater or lesser rhythmic stability.[14] The rhythmic curve on which such a relationship might be plotted would range from a clearly defined metre, through a clearly defined pulse but ambiguous metre, to an ambiguity of pulse and (therefore) metre.

Some of the most radical developments in the field of rhythm are to be found in the early works of Webern. A chart of rhythmic articulation in the first of his Op. 10 orchestral pieces (Ex. 55) shows that an underlying pulse is absent entirely, despite occasional suggestions of regular metre as in the rhythmic sequence of bars 6–7. Any such suggestion tends to be immediately cancelled by obtruding patterns in other parts, in the present instance by the triplet crotchet figure on trumpet and trombone. In such a context the slightest detail can assume structural importance, as does the recurring semiquaver figure of Op. 10, No. 1 in bars 6, 9 and 12, each appearance reinforcing the point until the idea

Ex. 55

can serve as a final cadence. A similar complexity exists in the first of the Op. 11 cello pieces. For the most part no metre can be discerned, though short rhythmically coherent phrases emerge in bars 2 and 4 of the piano part only to be obscured by the succeeding cello phrases. Even more extreme is the third of the Op. 11 pieces where the basic unit of measurement is so slow and the avoidance of rhythmic stress so complete that there is no implication of an underlying pulse at any point.

In each of these pieces Webern has consciously avoided regular pulse and metric definition. In the fourth of his Op. 4 songs, on the other hand, a pulse is established at several points by the equal durations of the vocal line. Ex. 56i shows this and illustrates also how the basic unit

Ex.56

is continuously changed from quaver to triplet quaver to dotted semi-quaver, preventing any consistent and unequivocal pulse being established for the piece as a whole. Moreover the constantly changing time-signature ensures that even where a pulse is established locally it is not supported by an underlying regular metre. Rhythmically the piano accompaniment can either support the pulse which is established by the voice as in bars 1–3 (albeit with a suggestion of a different metre), or it can undermine that pulse as in bars 6–8, so that viewed as a whole the song reveals a structural relationship between greater and lesser rhythmic stability. Ex. 56ii, a rhythmic analysis of the entire piece, makes this relationship clear. There is a progression from the relative stability of the opening to the instability of the passage ending at bar 8, the close of the first section. This progression is then repeated for the second section ending at bar 12, while the coda is unstable (though this instability is to some extent countered by the use of repeated melodic ideas in cadentially augmenting note-values).

The opening of Berg's Op. 4 songs (1912) is an intriguing example of rhythmic complexity arising not from the avoidance of a basic pulse but from the overlapping of fixed metric units of varying lengths. As the climax is approached these patterns dissolve into a rhythmically incoherent, quasi-impressionistic orchestral sonority, immediately suggesting an overall rhythmic 'shape' which balances regular and irregular rhythms. Such a relationship acts as a structural determinant in many atonal works and often provides a useful pointer to the total form where more systematic constructive methods are not employed. The third of Berg's Op. 5 clarinet pieces, for example, opens with a three-note rhythmic motive which, although metrically displaced, implies an unambiguous pulse in the ensuing bars before disintegrating into the more fragmentary ideas which lead into the slow section. In this a regular triplet quaver *ostinato* is established by the clarinet's five-note motive, but it is undermined by the piano's gradually augmenting note-values and gives way to the rhythmic discontinuity of the final bars.

Viewed in such terms the final bars of Schoenberg's Op. 19, No. 1 (Ex. 50) assume special significance in the context of the work as a whole. They achieve the rhythmic stability and simplicity for which the opening of the piece seemed to be searching, but which was obscured by the initial tied quaver (sounding like a downbeat because of the accompaniment figure) and the rhythmically disruptive chord in the first complete bar (Ex. 57). In the eleventh song from *Das Buch der hängenden Gärten* a similar relationship between stable and unstable rhythmic elements can be detected despite the slow tempo. The opening idea (Ex. 58i) presents a regular pulse whose larger grouping remains ambiguous, figures (a) and (b) each suggesting a different metric unit. The innocent ear is likely to shift the bar lines and re-interpret the note-values as in Ex. 58ii. From this point until the entry of the voice,

rhythmic regularity disintegrates and the recitative-like vocal line does little to re-establish a stable pulse. It is only with the rhythmic (and melodic) sequences of bars 13–15 that a coherent metrical pattern is established (Ex. 58iii) and when figure (b) returns in bar 20 the underlying metric unit has been clarified. The final phrase is of a traditional rhythmic simplicity with cadential repetition and a strongly emphasized final downbeat.

The opening of the first of Schoenberg's Op. 11 piano pieces illustrates in microcosm the complementary relationship between rhythmic stability and instability which is so important in Schoenberg's early atonal music, although the fundamental pulse remains stable in this

instance. There is a progression from the regular rhythm of the opening phrase towards a gradual disintegration of rhythmic coherence as the motives drift apart and the metrical grouping becomes imprecise, and back to the stability of the opening (Ex. 59). Moreover, Philip Friedheim has convincingly demonstrated the importance of rhythmic motives and of an overall progression from rhythmic clarity towards

Ex. 59

rhythmic instability in that most radical of Schoenberg's compositions, the third of the Op. 11 pieces. It should already be clear, however, that no single approach to this piece can hope to do more than untangle a single thread of what amounts to a highly complex structural fabric. One can have little grasp of the total form of the piece if one fails to relate this rhythmic 'shape' to the other 'shapes' which can be traced in relation to other parameters—melodic structure, dynamic levels, texture and sectional construction. Admittedly these often coincide, as in bars 8–9, 12–13 and 24–5 where the moments of greatest melodic and rhythmic clarification come together, but equally they may pull against the rhythmic shape. On the basis of dynamic levels and texture, for example, there is a clear progression towards a climactic point at bar 30 acting as a final peak in a series of explosive outbursts, which in no way corresponds to the descending curve based on rhythmic organization. It has already been demonstrated, moreover, that a semblance of arch shape is suggested by the varying lengths and character of the formal sub-sections of the piece again at variance with its rhythmic shape.

OTHER PARAMETERS

The rejection of tonality and of the hierarchical distinctions in melodic-harmonic language which are its defining characteristics meant that the articulation of musical structure, formerly dependent upon these distinctions, came to rely more on other parameters of sound which do not involve a precise pitch content. Rhythm was perhaps the most important of these, but others assumed new importance as structural determinants, among them *timbre*, texture, register and dynamics.

These developments had roots in the nineteenth century. Just as the increasing flexibility of rhythmic structure in the early twentieth century may be traced in different ways to such composers as Mussorgsky and Brahms, the increasing differentiation of orchestral colour and the tendency for orchestration to become a major part of the substance of a composer's musical thought in later nineteenth-century Russian and French music had already moved far beyond the decorative functions of *timbre* associated with earlier periods. To a marked degree the music of Debussy elevates *timbre* to an unprecedented structural status; already in *L'Après-midi d'un Faune* the *colour* of flute and harp functions referentially.

In the final chapter of *Harmonielehre* (original version) of 1911, Schoenberg outlined his notion of a '*timbre*-structure' in which successions of changing tone-colours might create independent formal shapes which might be organized in a manner analogous to pitch structure. Something of this concept is present in the short wisps of melody which move from one solo instrument to another in the 1910 orchestral pieces, but it is more fully explored in parts of the Op. 16 pieces. In the last of these there is a '*timbre*-structure' based on the constantly changing instrumental tone-colours of the principal melody, though the extent to which this can be heard as an independent structural dimension interacting with the pitch structure is doubtful. Much more thoroughgoing is the third of the Op. 16 pieces where the main musical material comprises a succession of sustained chords and scraps of melodic material making use of alternating whole-tone scales and a 'fixed pitch' motive. The structure of the piece depends primarily on subtle changes of tone-colour within the chords, giving rise to an overall arch shape which makes use of more rapid colour changes to form its central section. This is at once the most experimental and the least characteristic of all Schoenberg's compositions (the closest parallel is the last of the Op. 19 piano pieces).

Webern's Op. 10 orchestral pieces were in part a response to Schoenberg's Op. 16 pieces and the *Klangfarbenmelodie* concept is here an integral aspect of the construction of the music. In the first piece, for example, there are frequent changes in *timbre*, often within a single melodic phrase, establishing an independent set of relationships which interacts with the melodic groupings indicated in Ex. 52 and which contributes equally to the overall form. This is a feature, too, of the first of his Op. 11 cello pieces, despite the limitation which the medium imposes on instrumental *timbre*, for within a few bars the cello plays harmonics, *am Steg*, pizzicato, and *am Griffbrett*, creating the maximum variety of tone-colour with a minimum of notes, while the principal melody travels freely from cello to piano. *Klangfarbenmelodie* preoccupied Webern throughout his creative life, carrying through into the later serial compositions. A particularly rich example is the slow movement of the *Concerto for Nine Instruments*, Op. 24, where the melodic line is shared among the eight melodic instruments in groups of two or three notes, but his orchestration of the *ricercare* from Bach's *Musical Offering* betrays the same preoccupation.

Berg, on the other hand, despite a superb ear for orchestral sonorities, was less interested in using *timbre* as a means of creating new constructive patterns (apart from some often mentioned exceptions). The orchestral backdrops to his *Altenberglieder* and *Wozzeck* are bathed in subtly blended, evanescent sonorities which call for several innovatory instrumental devices, but they are an extension and refinement of traditional tone-painting rather than a new means of organization.

The structural deployment of contrasting textures, registers and dynamic levels was again not by any means new to music, but where these had tended to play a subsidiary role in the construction of tonal music, they assumed much greater importance when tonality declined. In the first of Berg's Op. 5 clarinet pieces, the fan-like widening of registers, reaching the extremes at the main climax before closing in again, and the opposing directions of clarinet and piano melodies (resulting in several 'intersections') are structurally important. In the fourth piece there is a careful balance between three 'static' harmonic areas and two enclosed sections in which melodic material dissolves into impressionistic textures which occupy contrasting registers. Such observations, however obvious, are often the only way we can elucidate the *overall* form of athematic compositions as opposed to finding momentary connections and relationships between their components.

The role of dynamics also assumed some importance in many early atonal works, including these pieces by Berg. In a work such as Schoenberg's Op. 11, No. 3 the use of extreme contrasts in dynamic levels plays an integral part in the articulation of the structure. Similarly the sudden 'forte' which announces the coda of his Op. 19, No. 5 is, in an overall 'piano' context, an important structural moment, as is the single bar of 'forte' in the second of his unfinished orchestral pieces of 1910. One of the most fascinating developments in this field was Webern's exploration of the varying gradations lying between *pppp* and *p* with characteristic subtlety. In his Op. 10 orchestral pieces there are only two points where the dynamic level is permitted to rise above 'piano', investing both moments with remarkable emotional and structural significance.

The 'emancipation' of parameters of sound which are not governed by a precise pitch content had the utmost importance for the future development of Western music. It was inevitable that as such parameters made an increasing contribution to musical structure, they would become susceptible to organization of a systematic nature. There are already such indications of a systematic ordering of rhythm and duration in the work of Bartók and Stravinsky, Messiaen and Blacher, while Debussy foreshadows in several works a comparable ordering of *timbre* and texture. The attempt by many composers in Europe and America following the Second World War to subject every dimension of a work to serial ordering is an ultimate extension of this development. But the desire of these composers functionally to relate pitch and duration reflects a further, more deep-seated need, a need to find a method of formal organization and progression-through-time which might replace thematicism. To this need the athematic, pre-serial works of the 'Second Viennese School' have direct relevance.

13

Rappel à l'ordre

The desire for a conscious control of the new means and forms will arise in every artist's mind.[1]

It was inevitable that the rejection of tonality, formerly the most important form-giving principle in music, should have led to a re-shuffling in many works of the existing relationships between parameters of sound, such as has been examined in the last chapter. Composers were plunged into an unfamiliar world—'as though the light had been put out'[2]—and, in exploring it, they were obliged to rely to an unprecedented extent on their intuitive sense of formal balance, resulting in new and often startling relationships.

The impulses at work during this period of transition were of a complex nature. In particular the composer's dissatisfaction with traditional methods cannot easily be separated from his desire to create new methods. The disintegration of traditional rhythmic symmetries, for instance, undermined one of the main props of tonal thinking, but at the same time it made room for new types of structural planning which could exploit the resulting rhythmic flexibility. Equally the rejection in some works of a traditional thematic process deprived the composer of an important method of construction, but cleared the path for alternative types of organization based on intervallic invariance or, more radically, on changing tone-colours. Many of the 'new' procedures which were developed in atonality were in any case new only in the sense that they threw into relief techniques which had played a less crucial constructive role in tonal music. In this respect a distinction must be drawn between those traditional features which were salvaged from the tonal past—residual tonal elements, traditional textures and phrase and rhythmic patterns—and those which were developed and intensified to become important constructive methods in their own right, without the support of tonal harmony. Chief among the latter were the contrapuntal and variation methods which formed an integral aspect of the thematic process of tonal music and the integration of material by means of closely knit motivic or intervallic relationships, again often found in the tonal literature. It will be the task of the present chapter to examine some of the ways in which composers were reaching out towards such 'new' disciplines and ultimately towards 'new' unifying principles.

NEO-TONALITY: A THEME IN SZYMANOWSKI

Before examining the organization of atonality, however, we should recognize that for several composers who had explored atonal textures the *rappel à l'ordre* took the form of a return to structures in which the tonal principle once again plays a major part. Szymanowski was one such composer, and it will be worth looking in some detail at his unequivocal return to tonal argument after the tonal evasion of many of his middle-period works. In view of the overall title of Part 3 and of the chronology of Szymanowski's later music, this discussion might best be regarded as an extended parenthesis.

The new directions in Szymanowski's music from about 1920 onwards were closely bound up with changes in his material circumstances and aesthetic intentions. Those middle-period works in which tonality was dissolved away by an intensely expressive and 'exotic' dissonance reflect to some extent a 'splendid isolation' from which he was rudely shaken when his family home in the Ukraine was razed to the ground during the Bolshevik revolution and when he returned to Poland, now free and independent, in 1920 to find an appalling gap separating his music from a Polish audience. In a letter of the greatest significance written to the musicologist Jachimecki in 1920, he remarked: 'I am a stranger to them, incomprehensible, and probably even useless to the general structure of Polish music.' [3]

His growing conviction that a 'nationalist' aesthetic, however out-moded in Western Europe, had validity in the newly independent Poland led to a spate of articles on Polish music and to a rethinking of his own musical language. The song-cycles *Slopiewnie*, Op. 46 (1922) and *Songs of Kurpie*, Op. 58 (1922) were among the first works to reveal the impact of this rethinking and of a discovery of immense importance made in the same year. Early in 1922 Szymanowski travelled to Zako-pane, a village in the southern Tatra highlands of Poland and discovered there a highland folk-music, played on two fiddles and a string bass, which has uniquely 'exotic' characteristics, highly dissonant and with fascinating heterophonic effects. He found in this music a key to his dilemma, a dilemma which he expressed as follows: 'I do feel, as regards Polish culture, that I hang in a vacuum. . . . But I cannot afford a complete abnegation, for my inner life is developed too strongly.' [4] With the aid of Goral folk music he was able to pursue a 'nationalist' path without sacrificing the exoticism which was an integral part of his 'inner life'. In his article *About Goral Music*, Szymanowski wrote: 'My discovery of the essential beauty of the Goral music, dance and architecture is a very personal one; much of this beauty I have absorbed into my innermost soul.' [5] Several of Szymanowski's later works quote directly from this body of folk music, most notably the colourful ballet *Harnasie* which makes use of wedding dances from the Tatra highlands and transforms them into a glittering and exciting score. One of the crucial influences on *Harnasie* and other works at this time was the work of Stravinsky, and in particular the Russian composer's treatment of folkloristic materials in works such as *Pribaoutki* and *Les Noces*.

Two works stand at the threshold of the late period, described by the composer himself as 'a new period in my creative life'. [6] They are the song-cycle *Slopiewnie*, in which he turned to Polish folklore to reveal, as it were, the innate creativity of the Polish people, and the *Stabat Mater*, Op. 53 of 1926 in which he returned to a triadic language designed to communicate directly to the nation. In both works Szymanowski succeeded in overcoming the essentially subjective character of earlier works while losing little of their richness and variety. The Stravinsky of *Pribaoutki* is clearly the dominant influence on the song-cycle, where the slowly moving, rhapsodic harmonies of the middle-period music have been replaced by unchanging harmonic 'areas' which succeed each other without transition, the on-going energy generated by rhythmic displacement of *ostinato* patterns. Similarly the earlier flexible chromatic melodies have been trimmed to modal patterns, often pentatonic in character, which are stated as *ostinato* phrases. The dissonant harmonic complexes of the earlier style have been retained in most of this work, but they have now lost their mystical quality by taking on a precisely defined function in the music's structure, acting as points of punctuation or as the *objets sonores* for rhythmic patterning.

An important unifying feature in the cycle as a whole is the emphasis, both melodic and harmonic, on the tritone interval. Ex. 60i indicates the prominence of the tritone in the harmonic area which opens and closes the first song (the importance of the 7/3 unit is another feature which is retained in the later style, though again with greatly altered significance) and in the vocal line's tendency to oscillate from B to F. It

Ex.60

(i) No.1

(ii) No.2

(iii) No.3

(iv) No. 4

'C' major

is intriguing that E natural should be the only pitch to be omitted from the opening section as it is strongly emphasized as a dominant when the music approaches its cadence onto A.

The recitative-like opening of the second song has a bass line in open fifths descending chromatically through the interval of a perfect fourth over a long time span. An inner voice revolves around the pitch D flat while the vocal line (again emphasizing the tritone F-B) rises through peak notes F and G to A, the whole presenting a perfectly balanced structure (Ex. 6oii).[7] The use of slowly moving, directional bass lines, often thickened into open fifths, is of course another feature which Szymanowski has retained from 'Impressionism'. The second section of the song begins in a C major-minor harmonic area and moves, after a transposition to E major-minor, to a succession of two harmonic areas, each delineated by a chord built upon a tritone. The bass line descends from E flat to C in preparation for the final section which makes use of displaced *ostinato* figures in a harmonic area of C7 while the voice has a mode on A with sharpened fourth and flattened seventh. As the voice rises from E, through F sharp and G, to A there is a final 'folk-style' vocal exclamation which sharpens the seventh to suggest A major. The final chord fuses A with C major-minor (Ex. 6oii).

Ex. 6o indicates how the purposeful juxtaposition of harmonic areas in the first four songs creates a dramatic tonal argument, albeit not of a traditional kind. The first song is built upon a centre of A, the second of C, and the fourth again of C. These tonal centres are established not by triads but by means of unchanging harmonic areas and modal *ostinati*.

The third song, 'St Francis', with its pitch structure organized over an extended time span to create a beautifully symmetrical pattern moving from B to E (Ex. 6oiii), is set in a deliberately archaic, triadic style which recalls the Church music from *King Roger* and foreshadows the *Stabat Mater*. Of the latter Szymanowski wrote: 'I have tried first of all to achieve the direct emotional effect, the general intelligibility of the text and the fusion of the emotional substance of the word with its musical equivalent.' [8] The opening of the work (bars 1–23) presents in microcosm the characteristic blend of materials which persists throughout. Bars 1–7 have a stark, linear quality which is a new feature in Szymanowski's music and which is found in other works of the later period such as the first *Berceuse*, Op. 48, the fifth of the *Kurpie Songs*, Op. 58 and several of the Mazurkas. In bars 8–10 the dissonant harmonies of his earlier style reappear, but they are now heard in relation not only to the linear writing which precedes them but to the simple triadic material which follows (bars 13–23). This reinstatement of the triad as fundamental harmonic unit was of crucial importance for Szymanowski's later music and it immediately suggests parallels with the later works of Debussy and above all Bartók. The newly discovered harmonic simplicity of the *Stabat Mater* coexists with older characteristics of his style, however, and has the effect of objectifying the latter by defining their role in the overall structure.

It is significant that in his final period Szymanowski should have turned to absolute music and to extended structures, composing in rapid succession the Second String Quartet, Op. 56, the Second Violin Concerto, Op. 61 and the *Symphonie Concertante*, Op. 60 for Piano and Orchestra (all written between 1930 and 1932). Having to some extent synthesized old and new features of his style and having returned to the triad as basic harmonic unit, he concerned himself in these works with problems of musical structure on an extended scale.

The Second Violin Concerto may be taken as representative. As in *Slopiewnie* and the *Stabat Mater*, 'exotic' materials have been severely disciplined to take their place within a lucid structure which is quite different to the rhapsodic forms of his middle-period works. The soaring cantilena of the First Violin Concerto has been replaced by a rigorous thematic economy and the layered dissonance of the harmonies, formerly static and 'mystical' in character, has been transformed by an energizing rhythmic drive and the demands of a clearly defined tonal structure. The richness of the later work lies, however, in the fact that 'exoticisms' have not been eliminated but rather pruned and disciplined. When a moment of relaxation is a structural necessity, as at fig. 17 or fig. 32, for example, the chromatically flexible melodies and rhapsodic harmonies of earlier works return.

It has already been observed that in his middle-period music Szymanowski was not concerned to find unifying methods which might replace tonality, but was content rather to extend traditional harmonic and melodic procedure to the point at which tonality was 'refined out of existence'. This may be one reason for the fact that the crisis of communication in the early twenties led him back to tonality rather than to a search for methods of organizing atonality. Another reason is clearly that his use of folkloristic materials as the basic ingredients of the later music was in itself a means of safeguarding tonality. It is hardly surprising that Bartók should have been his model for works which attempt to build extended structures from folkloristic material. In an article entitled *Béla Bartók and Folk Music*, written in 1925, Szymanowski said of Bartók: 'He hopes to establish a Hungarian *school* that will equal the great musical cultures of Germany, France and Russia. Our aim in Poland is a very similar one. . . .' [9] Bartók's influence is apparent not only in the tough, brittle writing of passages such as fig. 26 of the Second Violin Concerto (it is even more explicit in the *finale* of the *Symphonie Concertante*) but in the whole concept of a folkloristic material forging its own tonal language which remains remote from traditional diatonic thinking. As in Bartók's later music tonality is once again affirmed by triads rather than single pitches, though this by no means implies a return to major-minor keys.

Formally the Second Violin Concerto is in one movement but, unlike the first concerto, this can be clearly subdivided into four sections. The first is a ternary structure and is almost monothematic, with the principal theme constantly transformed and set against changing backgrounds until the climax at fig. 13. A more relaxed middle section leads to a shortened recapitulation and cadenza. The second section is equally concentrated, its march-like theme (with a close affinity to the theme from the first section) presented in various guises, including a 'folk-style' variant, and offset by a short middle section. The third, slow section has a background of static harmonies and a series of expressive duets between soloist and woodwind instruments, while the final section recapitulates the material of the first two in reverse order.

The opening melody of the work suggests three possible tonal backgrounds—E minor, A minor with flattened seventh and C major with sharpened fourth—and these are used to create the main tonal framework of the concerto. Tonal centres are affirmed by triad and reinforced by long pedal points. Ex. 61 summarizes the tonal structure of the first section, indicating that centres of A, C and E are employed to underline

Ex. 61

major structural points and to create dramatic tonal conflicts. The first statement of the main theme is supported by an A minor harmony, the second (fig. 1) by E major and the third by a C7 region (fig. 6). At two dramatic points (preceding fig. 8 and at the climax, fig. 23), the theme is stated in E major over a pedal C.

For Szymanowski the *rappel à l'ordre* took the form of a return to clear structural outlines and a tonal argument. It was a direction which has something in common with the 'neo-classicism' which dominated Polish music in the thirties and forties and it may be worth adding a brief postscript about Szymanowski's relationship to the next generation of Polish composers and the re-emergence of Polish music which followed political independence. Younger Polish composers were attracted less by Szymanowski's music than by the clear-cut forms and mannered charm of Parisian neo-classicism, a style owing something to Stravinsky and Prokofiev, but more to the teaching of Nadia Boulanger, who worked with an entire generation of Polish composers. These composers gave the style a specifically Polish flavour, however, making use of folk materials and characterized by bright, 'primary' instrumental colours. In attempting to fuse national characteristics with progressive European trends, they were following the principle established by Szymanowski's later music, however dissimilar the musical results. Ultimately Szymanowski's influence was of an ideological rather than a purely musical nature. As the sole champion of progressive ideas in a period of apathy and reaction, he cleared a path for younger composers, and by the high standards which he consistently set himself, he served as a challenge and an inspiration to them.

THE 'MYSTIC CHORD': A THEME IN SKRYABIN

During the years 1909–10 Skryabin was living in Brussels where the established contacts with the work of Delville's Theosophist movement and extended his acquaintance with the writings of Hélène Blavatsky. These were not productive years by Skryabin's usual standards. It was a period of gestation during which he was preoccupied with spiritual and musical questions which were to be given full expression in the tone-poem *Prometheus*, completed in 1911. Both the metaphysical 'programme' of *Prometheus* and its basic constructive method were to remain constant for all Skryabin's later music—there is indeed a sense in which the later sonatas and miniatures may be regarded as aspects of a single, composite work, a preparation for the final *Mysterium* in which sounds, colours, scents and movement would be combined in a final ecstasy. The Promethean myth, as interpreted by Skryabin, depicts man in pre-conscious state and his subsequent illumination by the Promethean spark through which he achieves human consciousness and creative power. The dualism which runs through the programmes of later works by Skryabin (the 'black' and 'white' mass sonatas) is born of the conflict between those who have rightly understood the Promethean gift and used it on the highest spiritual plane and those who have used it to create suffering and evil. The detailed programmatic content of the sonatas is to some extent illuminated by the labels attached to thematic fragments: 'la rêve prend forme', 'charmes', 'appel mystérieux', and so on.

While for Skryabin the discovery of a new technical means of expression was intimately related to such extra-musical concepts, it is the musical end-product which is of prime interest to us today. It has been demonstrated that in his music from 1903 to 1908 tonal unity was almost imperceptibly replaced by harmonic unity; already in 1908 he was close to the harmonic system which underlies his later music. That system was all but formalized in some of the shorter pieces written before the fifth sonata, pieces such as the *Poem of Languor*, Op. 52, No. 3 (1905) and *Enigma*, Op. 52, No. 2 (1907), but the miniatures composed in 1910 while Skryabin was working on *Prometheus*—the *Deux Morceaux*, Op. 57 and *Feuillet d'Album*, Op. 58—point even more clearly to the future. One of the most important steps forward—particularly apparent in Op. 58—is the much closer integration of melodic material with the underlying harmonic support. A summary of the harmonic language of Op. 58 demonstrates this and further indicates how narrow is the stylistic gap separating the works of 1908 and the later compositions (Ex. 62). The continuing importance of Type 1 harmony and especially

Ex. 62

of progression (a) in the later music has already been pointed out. Progression (b), on the other hand, could not be similarly accommodated by the later harmonic system and its presence in Op. 58 and in the *Two Pieces*, Op. 59, is a final reminder of Skryabin's earlier style.

The harmonic system of later works has much in common with serialism in that each work is based on a given set (usually comprising six notes) which acts as a source of both harmonic and melodic material and which is transposed onto different degrees of the scale, inevitably giving rise to many invariant features. The differences from orthodox serialism are that Skryabin is not concerned about a fixed note order within the set, about avoiding the repetition of pitches before the cycle is complete or about including all pitches in each transposition, so that his treatment of the set is more akin to the hexachordal 'troping' of some of Schoenberg's later compositions. A more fundamental difference is his retention of a *harmonic* quality guaranteed by his consistent distribution of the sets in dominant-quality areas closely related to Type 1 from transitional works. An understanding of the continuity of harmonic procedure underlying the transition into his system of fundamental chords would surely have prevented the sort of misconception which arises from Ellon Carpenter's remark that 'Skryabin comes so close to the twelve-note system that it seems probable he would have taken it as the next logical step'.[10] This harmonic continuity is emphasized in the interpretation of the system offered by Russian musicologist Varvara Dernova, recently published in Russia and summarized by Faubion Bowers.[11] This interpretation recognizes the importance of both the dominant quality of the fundamental chords and of the tritone link; in Dernova's terminology the components of my progression (a) are labelled 'departure dominant' and 'derived dominant' (*Da* and *Db* respectively) while the added sixth or 'accessory' note (the only one in most of Skryabin's fundamental chords which disturbs their whole-tone character) is labelled 'V' when it belongs to *Da* and 'W' when it appears in *Db*. The Promethean chord would appear in Dernova's analysis as in Ex. 63.

Ex.63

The detailed working of the system may be examined with reference to the Seventh Piano Sonata. Ex. 64 presents the fundamental chord and demonstrates how the principal thematic material has been derived from it. The method is employed with remarkable consistency, though the flattened fourth and sharpened sixth are employed as semitonal inflections throughout. In *Serial Composition and Atonality*, George Perle has drawn attention to pivotal segments other than the 7/3 unit which create links between transpositions, notably the diminished seventh and the segment superimposing two minor thirds a perfect fourth apart.[12] Undoubtedly Skryabin made use of such pivotal segments as a means of linking and even (occasionally) combining transpositions, but I have found no evidence to support Perle's claim that there is a 'closed system of transpositions' based on these segments. The choice of transpositions in the seventh sonata has been governed by the tritone link and by the work's quasi-tonal structure, not mentioned by Perle. In much the same way there would appear to be no 'system' governing the choice of successive complementary sets in Schoenberg's later serial compositions.

The evolution of Skryabin's harmonic system from incipient directions suggested by the works of 1903 to its final crystallization in 1910–11 was both an original and a consistent development—much more of an evolutionary process than Schoenberg's approach to serialism. It is all the more striking in that its underlying principle—a unity of harmony and melody—is not only closely analogous to serialism but pre-dates it by several years. As a replacement for traditional tonality, Skryabin's method was just as self-consistent as Schoenberg's. It was not, however, so widely ranging in technical and expressive potential, and the resulting weaknesses of the later sonatas have been noted. Not only is there an insensitivity to the relationship between an exploratory harmonic language and the inflexible formal and architectonic moulds into which

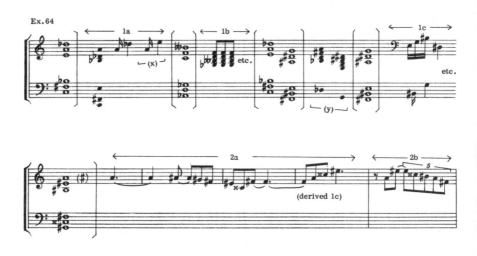

that language has been poured, but there is a serious lack of harmonic variety and contrast resulting from Skryabin's tendency to dispose his sets in dominant-quality areas. The result is a unified and highly personal harmonic language but one whose range of expression is severely restricted, so that it lends itself more happily to the miniature than to the extended work. It is indeed this narrow range of expression which most forcibly strikes one on playing through a substantial cross-section of his *œuvre*, including early and late compositions. Despite the importance of his later method not only for his own development but as a reflection of a widespread search for order following disintegration, it is at least arguable that the technical innovation was not accompanied by a parallel spiritual maturation. It is one of those ironies which are not uncommon in music history that the finest of his extended works should have been composed before the evolution of the method was complete.

TOWARDS THE TWELVE-NOTE METHOD: A THEME IN SCHOENBERG,
BERG AND WEBERN

In retrospect we may regard serialism as an outcome of several organizing directions in the pre-serial music of the 'Second Viennese School'
while recognizing that many other developments in the *œuvre* were
pulling in contrary directions. Indeed the multiplicity of technical
procedures in the pre-serial works, especially those of Schoenberg,
remains one of their enduring fascinations. Where one atonal work will
rely heavily for its coherence upon a phraseology which is clearly a
product of tonal functions, another will demonstrate a radical reshaping
of the basic elements of composition, made possible only by the rejection
of those functions. Where tonal decline will be met in one work by
rigorous compensatory disciplines and rigid structural control, another
will appear to explore fully the freedom from 'every restriction of a
bygone aesthetic'. Yet the search for a means of organizing atonality,
for a 'conscious control of the new means and forms', was clearly a
major determining factor in the development of Schoenberg and his
pupils, even if it was not the only one. It was given expression in their
exploration of several form-building methods which could replace
traditional diatonic relationships.

One of the most important methods of pitch organization found in this
music is the use of referential sonorities without diatonic function. A
line of development might be traced in this respect from the 'Tristan
chord' through the 'fate' chord from Schoenberg's *Pelleas und Melisande*
to the fixed chord of *Entrückung*. As traditional tonal functions were
abandoned, such points of reference tended to assume greater articu-
lative importance and it is intriguing that in the second of Schoenberg's
Five Orchestral Pieces, Op. 16, an area identical to the 'fate' chord from
Pelleas should act as a stable, unchanging area in the outer sections. In
addition to this chord a number of recurring themes and motives,
always stated at the same pitch, emerge from and help to stabilize the
wealth of 'freely associated' melodic ideas which are varied continuously throughout the piece. Similarly in the third song from *Das Buch
der hängenden Gärten* (whose 'suppressed' tonal structure has been
indicated in Ex. 44iii) there is some evidence of a structural use of
referential sonorities in the recurrence of fig. (x) at its original pitch
(Ex. 65). The formation is strongly characterized registrally, while the
rhythmic dislocation of its components serves to emphasize their
removal from diatonic function. The reiterated chord which opens the
last of Berg's Op. 5 clarinet pieces and returns at bar 11, and the

Ex. 65

recurring harmonic areas of Webern's Op. 4, No. 1, function similarly as harmonic points of reference in an atonal context.

Ostinato patterns are a particular expression of this dialectic of fixed and free, and they play a prominent part in several pre-serial works by the 'Second Viennese School', functioning as fixed points against which freely developing material may be presented. Their role in Schoenberg's Op. 11, No. 2, has already been discussed and they appear again in his Op. 16, No. 1, Op. 18 and the third of the unfinished orchestral pieces. They occur also in Berg's Op. 4, No. 1, and Op. 5, No. 3, and in Webern's Op. 7, No. 1, and Op. 10, No. 3.

In addition to the *ostinato* pattern of Schoenberg's Op. 11, No. 2, there are several recurring melodic motives which are always stated at the same pitch (register may be varied) and which function as referential features. Similarly in the first movement of Berg's String Quartet, Op. 3 a two-note falling motive assumes a quasi-tonal cadential function and takes its place beside other harmonic and melodic referential features. The second movement makes even greater use of such 'fixed pitch' motives as Ex. 66 indicates. In the fourth of Schoenberg's Op. 16 orchestral pieces invariant pitch formations function not simply as referential points but as a means of developing a more extended argument based on their juxtaposition and combination. Here invariant pitch formations have been more obviously divorced from residual tonal centres, assuming primary importance in the composer's concern tô *organize* atonality. The emphasis has shifted decisively from analogy with traditional procedure to its creative reinterpretation.

A more specific form of referential feature is the single pitch which can act as an unchanging point of orientation in an atonal context. There are indications that the E flat which concludes Schoenberg's Op. 11, No. 1 has a centralizing function in the piece as a whole. It is significant that it should be the only pitch-class to be omitted from the opening section of the work (bars 1–11), strengthening its impact as the bass note for the second section. It is further emphasized and repeated at the main climax of the piece (bars 49–50) and at bars 55–7 before its appearance at the final cadence. Again in 'Der Kreuze' from *Pierrot Lunaire* a single emphasized pitch 'D' forms an unchanging point of reference in a piece which suggests none of the broader relationships of tonality. One can profit from some of David Lewin's observations about pitch centricity in 'Der Kreuze' without accepting all the ramifications of his involved 'explanation' of the pitch structure.[13] Certainly Schoenberg's tendency to 'close in' on a pitch centre *via* its semitonal neighbour notes is not confined to this piece.

In the first of Berg's Op. 5 clarinet pieces the pitch 'D' again acts as a centre, asserted both by repetition and through association with its

Ex. 66

semitonal neighbour notes. Ex. 67i indicates how the three pitches have been employed dramatically in bars 3–5 and are given particular emphasis at the main climax of the piece (bars 7–8). It is intriguing, though perhaps unintentional on Berg's part, that the only pitches to be omitted from the final collection should be C sharp and E flat. Ex. 67ii demonstrates a further use of pitch centres (again making use of semitonal neighbour notes) in the third and fourth pieces, while Ex. 67iii summarizes the centres of the entire cycle. Webern was less inclined to make use of pitch centres than Schoenberg and Berg, but they can be detected in some of the early works—an 'F' in Op. 3, No. 5, an E in Op. 4, No. 1 and a C sharp in the third of his *Five Movements for String Quartet*, Op. 5. Even in the third of Schoenberg's Op. 11 pieces there are hints of a purposeful organization of pitch centres, though the influence of these should not be overemphasized.

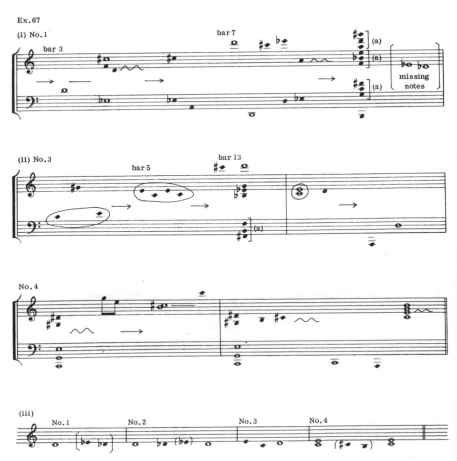

Ex. 67

The changing role of pitch centricity in Schoenberg's music is indica-
tive of a close relationship between his need to organize atonality and
his respect for tradition. Other unifying features in the atonal works are
similarly rooted in traditional procedure and similarly concerned to
avoid slavish imitation of it. The fundamental link between Op. 10 and
Op. 11, No. 1 is thematicism—the repetition and development, by
means of contrapuntal and variation techniques, of recognizable
thematic material. It has been observed that in his early tonal works the
development towards 'total thematicism', whether expressed through
contrapuntal density or elaborate motivic relationships which influence
every detail of the texture, was inseparable from the decline of traditionally functioning tonal-harmonic relationships, weakening and at the
same time replacing those relationships. Although thematicism was
threatened in a number of the atonal works, it remained the constructive basis of others. Its continuing, and ultimate, importance in Schoenberg's work is made clear in his serial music.

He regarded 'continuous variation' as the central principle to emerge
from the more progressive tendencies of an evolving nineteenth-century
thematic process, and the principle—later to be formalized by serialism
—underlies many of the subtler types of organization found in the pre-
serial music. In the First String Quartet, Op. 7, the thematic elements
have been interrelated through an intensive motive working which
affects even accompanimental detail; an extension of Brahmsian
preoccupations and techniques which significantly anticipates developments in the atonal music. In Op. 11, No. 1, for example, a continuous
process of motivic development cuts across the still discernible outlines
of a sonata-form, underlying the thematic 'surface' of the work (a
surface which does not exclude sequential repetition) and assuming
primary responsibility for unity. The total integration of thematic and
harmonic elements towards which much of this motive working
seems to be striving, clearly foreshadows the serial method.

The opening bars of Op. 11, No. 1, have proved an inexhaustible
mine for analytical speculators. There has, however, been remarkable
disagreement among them concerning the interpretation of residual
tonal characteristics and the nature of their motivic and intervallic
organization. Though often penetrating, Reinhold Brinkmann's motivic
analysis of the piece [14] suffers from the sheer all-inclusiveness of its
approach, its wealth of 'relationships' tending to confuse as much as to
clarify. George Perle's isolation of an intervallic cell which influences
both harmonic and melodic elements is, on the other hand, a useful

Ex. 68

insight, the more so as it has a wider application for atonal works.[15] Ex. 68 indicates that there is a similar integration of thematic elements in Berg's Op. 3 quartet, with the work's opening motive forming a *Grundgestalt*. (An interesting characteristic of this motive is the fact that five of its six notes belong to a single whole-tone scale. This relates it to the theme at bar 58 of the first movement of Schoenberg's Second String Quartet with which it also shares a similar rhythmic structure.) As in Schoenberg's Op. 11, No. 1, there is a close interpenetration of melody and harmony, with the basic motives saturating the texture at every level; the three-note motive introduced in bar 10, for instance, accounts for almost every detail of the ensuing section, while its inversion gives rise to a 'new' idea in bar 20. The continuation of this 'new' idea had in fact already appeared at the opening of the work.

The unifying force of intervallic invariance is clearly intensified when it has been allied to a closely argued motivic integration of material— as in Schoenberg's Op. 11, No. 1, and Berg's Op. 3—but it plays a part, too, in works where there has been no apparent attempt to establish thematic or motivic identity. Ex. 69, a partial analysis of the opening section of Schoenberg's Op. 19, No. 5, indicates some of the features which can contribute to coherence in an atonal, athematic work. The momentary connections based on pitch identity (Ex. 69i) are less significant here than the indications of an intervallic integration of material through various permutations of a three-note cell combining the intervals of a minor third and minor second (Ex. 69ii). A similar intervallic integration of otherwise differentiated material can be detected in the second of the 1910 orchestral pieces and in several movements from *Pierrot Lunaire* (in some movements such as 'Columbine' the emphasis on the third and seventh has a symbolic as well as a purely musical

Ex. 69

(i)

(ii)

meaning). From this point of view, the 'tonal' structure of Schoenberg's
Op. 19, No. 2, might be regarded as subsidiary to the piece's exploration
of a single intervallic cell.

In the third of Berg's Op. 5 clarinet pieces there is a similar intervallic
integration of material making use of the minor third and semitone
(Ex. 70), but it is above all in the pre-serial music of Webern that such

Ex. 70

cellular thinking, involving the transposition and often elaborate permu-
tation of three- and four-note cells is fully explored. George Perle has
convincingly demonstrated that the fourth of his *Five Pieces for String
Quartet*, Op. 5, may be derived from a single intervallic cell,[16] while
Ex. 71 shows that the familiar minor third and semitone cell, with
inversions and octave displacements, governs the melodic and harmonic
material of the first of the Op. 11 cello pieces.

Other constructive methods in the early atonal literature result from
an increased emphasis on counterpoint. It has been shown that in transi-

Ex. 71

tional works such as Schoenberg's First Chamber Symphony the tension between a strengthening 'contrapuntal logic' and a weakening tonal-harmonic foundation is expressed in a particularly acute form; parts of the work foreshadow the linear freedom of atonality. Yet even in *Pierrot Lunaire*, where the counterpoint is no longer subject to the constraints of tonal harmony and the part-movement tends to be clearly differentiated by rhythm and colour, the vertical result is anything but arbitrary. Close examination reveals that the counterpoint is still strongly influenced by vertical constraints—among them the persistence of dissonance/consonance relationships, the desire for harmonic homogeneity and the concern to integrate the vertical and the horizontal. None the less in works such as the first and fourth of his Op. 16 orchestral pieces, Schoenberg took advantage of the relative vertical freedom of atonality to organize his material through a rigorous contrapuntal combination of basic motives, while in exceptional (and often-cited) instances elaborate canonic devices are the primary form-giving feature. In 'Nacht' from *Pierrot Lunaire* the exhaustive deployment of a single three-note cell in prime, retrograde and retrograde inversion forms has an obvious connection with later twelve-note practice. Already one is reminded of Schoenberg's 'hat' or Webern's 'ashtray' which, seen from all sides, is always the same, and yet different.

One of the most prophetic developments in the pre-serial music of the 'Second Viennese School' was the tendency towards an ever-increasing chromatic density, with fewer and fewer note repetitions within the complete chromatic cycle. The opening melody of the second movement of Berg's Op. 3 quartet, for example, comprises ten notes of the total chromatic with only two repetitions, while the opening of *Pierrot Lunaire* rotates nine notes of the total chromatic in four cycles without repetitions, the sustained flute note providing a tenth. The two omitted pitches, the tritone F-B, form part of the important harmonic pedal (consisting of the familiar tritone and seventh formation, motive (a) from Berg's Opp. 1 and 2) which supports the dramatic cello solo in the second section of the piece, bars 28–33. A similar quasi-serial rotation is to be found in the ninth song from *Das Buch der hängenden Gärten*, where

Ex. 72

the opening material is repeated in four varied cycles to create a theme and variations structure.

Particularly interesting is the construction which opens Webern's Op. 11, No. 1, where, if we regard the two chords as constituting a single harmonic area, there is a complete twelve-note statement shared between melody and harmony, as indicated in Ex. 72i. Ex. 72ii illustrates the calculated economy with which he disposes the total chromatic in the fourth of his Op. 10 orchestral pieces; the complete cycle of twelve notes appears barely more than twice in the complete piece. Webern's own remarks in relation to his Op. 9 *Bagatelles* are significant: 'While working on them, I had the feeling that once the twelve notes had run out the piece was finished. Much later I realized that this was all part of the necessary evolution.' [17] Twelve-note aggregates of this kind also appear in the unfinished oratorio *Die Jacobsleiter* which occupied Schoenberg during the ten years which separate his Op. 22 songs of 1913 and the *Five Piano Pieces*, Op. 23.[18] In the last of these piano pieces such aggregates have been formalized into a primitive definition of the elements of serialism.[19]

The quasi-serial rotation of fixed-pitch material in Schoenberg's Op. 15, No. 9, and Op. 21, No. 1, the contrapuntal density of 'Nacht' from *Pierrot Lunaire* and the intensive motive working of his Op. 16, No. 1, all in different ways anticipate the twelve-note method. An increasing concern to interrelate melodic and harmonic material is evident in the thematic integration of Berg's Op. 3 quartet, the motivic integration of Schoenberg's Op. 11, No. 1, and the intervallic integration of Webern's Op. 5, No. 4. In each case there is a demonstrable connection with the 'unity of musical space' which is a central principle of the later method. Allen Forte has, however, proposed an analytical method for the pre-serial works based on set theory which would suggest a much clearer conceptual relationship between 'atonality' and serialism than the technical features outlined in this chapter.[20]

In *The Structure of Atonal Music* Forte submits the music of Stravinsky, Skryabin, Ives, Ruggles, Busoni and Varèse, as well as that of the 'Second Viennese School' to analysis by means of set theory. This would indicate that he is not discussing a system of composition utilized by each of these very different figures, but rather attempting to create a method for the systematic description of atonal music. At the same time, in an earlier article on Schoenberg,[21] Forte strongly suggests that the procedures were a part of the composer's conscious process. He remarks, 'It appears that Schoenberg developed his new procedures during a very short time, probably during the latter part of 1908' and again 'the very complexity of those procedures suggests an obvious reason for the fact that Schoenberg's way of composing atonal music was not success-fully adopted by anyone other than his students, Webern and Berg'. If such procedures—audible or inaudible—were indeed a part of Schoenberg's process of composition, Forte's work has some validity; the reader must judge for himself whether three movements from *Pierrot Lunaire* could have been composed in one day using these methods, or the whole of *Erwartung* in seventeen days! [22] If, on the other hand, Forte's relationships are not a part of the conscious process of composi-tion, they may equally be justified if they form, or could form, a part of our aural experience of the music. In certain works of Webern in particular, Forte may indeed have helped to make audible certain relationships between components which had formerly remained unnoticed. But the unpardonable aspect of his theory is its dismissal of those relationships—conscious or unconscious—which are already audible and significant for the listener. He rejects, for example, Roy Travis's characterization of the final bar of Schoenberg's Op. 19, No. 2, as a 'tonic sonority' on the grounds that 'the triad C-E-G is a non-set' [23] and suspects that the tonal allusions at the beginning of Op. 21, No. 21, may have been 'intended to baffle some unsuspecting critic'.[24] He rejects totally Perle's concept of the intervallic cell and (further evidence that he regards the process as a conscious one) the notion that some elements are 'independent details', regarding it as 'indeed unfor-tunate that these views have become as widely disseminated as they have'.[25]

However one reacts to the provocative and challenging theories of Allen Forte, there can be no doubt that on the most fundamental level of structure serialism was to provide for Schoenberg and his pupils a means of formalizing the concept of continuous or developing variation which lies at the root of more specific technical features of atonality. Schoenberg's need to objectify his musical experience, to relieve himself of too great a dependence on the subconscious, led him to evolve a unifying principle which would be sufficiently broadly based and self-consistent to form the basis of a *language*. Clearly many of the developments in his pre-serial music may be understood in terms of his search for such a principle, but analysis indicates that other developments were moving in a quite different direction (*pace* Allen Forte). *Pierrot Lunaire* perfectly draws together the widely diverging, even conflicting, 'linguistic' directions within the pre-serial *œuvre*. 'Enthauptung' represents an extreme expression of one such direction, the furthest Schoenberg progressed in the rejection of familiar form-giving techniques such as thematic repetition and development. At the other extreme is 'Mond-fleck' where every note has a thematic basis, rigorously pre-determined. Other movements such as 'Valse de Chopin' and 'O Alter Duft' 'explain' their atonal material by presenting it in traditional guise, with a conventional phrase and rhythmic structure and quasi-tonal part-movement. In the most characteristic works of the 'Second Viennese School' during this period these aspects co-exist and interact in a manner which is uniquely different for each piece. Nor was the momentum generated by these diverse developments totally dissipated by the discovery of the serial method. One of the fascinations (for some, one of the problems) of the serial works of Schoenberg in particular is the extent to which several of the conflicting tendencies inherent in the pre-serial music remain unreconciled.

Notes on the text

Chapter 1: The nineteenth-century background

1 Arnold Schoenberg, 'My Evolution', *Style and Idea*, ed. Leonard Stein, trans. Leo Black (London, 1975), p. 86.

2 Some clarification of terminology will be attempted in a later chapter.

3 There have been many different views of 'tonality' from Fétis to the present time. Schoenberg defined it as 'the art of combining tones in such successions and such harmonies or successions of harmonies, that the relation of all events to a fundamental tone is made possible'; *Schoenberg*, ed. Merle Armitage (New York, 1937), p. 280. Another useful definition has been suggested by Delbert M. Beswick: 'Tonality is the organized relationship of musical sounds, as perceived and interpreted with respect to some central point of reference that seems to co-ordinate the separate items and events and to lend them meaning as component parts of a unified whole'; *The Problem of Tonality in Seventeenth Century Music* (Ph.D. dissertation, University of North Carolina, 1950), p. 18.

4 These represent a vertical and horizontal expression of an acoustical phenomenon in nature. Despite its influence on subsequent theory, it is difficult to lend much credence to Rameau's natural-base 'explanation' of the subdominant in *Nouveau Système de Musique Théorique* (1726).

5 Heinrich Schenker has demonstrated the poverty of a view of tonal harmony which interprets solely in the vertical dimension.

6 Schoenberg, *Structural Functions of Harmony*, ed. Leonard Stein (London, 1969), p. 76.

7 This middle section is present in the Hedley, Ekier and Smith editions of this, Chopin's last, mazurka. For a full account of the several versions, reconstructed from the composer's near-chaotic manuscript, see Frank Dawes, 'The last mazurka', *The Musical Times*, January 1976.

8 Schoenberg, 'Composition with Twelve Tones', *Style and Idea*, p. 217.

9 The question of dissonance/consonance relations is a thorny one. Schoenberg's view of the distinction as one of degree (*Style and Idea*, pp. 216–17) is refuted by Rudolph Reti who regards it as one of kind; *Tonality—Atonality—Pantonality* (London, 1958), 38–9.

10 Both Schoenberg and Webern regarded Brahms as an 'advanced' harmonist; Schoenberg, 'Brahms the Progressive', *Style and Idea*, pp. 398–441 and Webern, *The Path to the New Music*, ed. Willi Reich, trans. Leo Black (Pennsylvania, 1963), p. 47.

11 'Harmonic rhythm' refers to the rate of change in harmonic progression. Perceptive analytical work has been undertaken in this sphere by Jan LaRue and Shelley Davis. It has been published in various articles and in LaRue's *Guidelines for Style Analysis* (New York, 1970).

12 Unless of course one subscribes to the view of Alfred Lorenz (*Das Geheimnis der Form bei Richard Wagner, 11, Tristan und Isolde*, Berlin, 1926) that *Tristan* is in E minor.

13 Such key symbolism was by no means new to the symphonic literature; it had already played an important role in Beethoven.

14 In *Tonality and Musical Structure* (London, 1970), Graham George rejects the term 'progressive tonality' as a description of tonal structure in the symphonies of Mahler and Nielsen, examining these works in the light of his theory of 'interlocking tonal structures'.

15 The dialogue is perhaps at its most intriguing in the Russian symphony where Western European prototypes could not easily be ignored.

16 'Pan-diatonic' or 'scalar' harmony refers to the quasi-indiscriminate use of all the notes of a diatonic scale without respect for classical tonal functions.

17 M. D. Calvocoressi, *Mussorgsky* (London, 1946), p. 32.

18 Schoenberg, 'Brahms the Progressive', *Style and Idea*.

19 The concept of a *Grundgestalt* from which all the thematic material of a work may be derived is explored in Hermann Scherchen's *The Nature of Music*, trans. William Mann (London, 1950), and further in Rudolph Reti's *The Thematic Process in Music* (London, 1961).

20 U. von Rauchhaupt (ed.), *Schoenberg, Berg and Webern. The String Quartets: A documentary study* (Hamburg, 1971), p. 16.

21 The technique of thematic transformation may be distinguished from thematic development in that it results in a new, self-sufficient theme, now independent of its source.

22 A more complete discussion of Liszt as an innovator would include his contribution to keyboard technique and to the development of programmatic instrumental music.

Chapter 2: The significance of Busoni

1 Busoni was one of the relatively few musicians who were familiar with Liszt's late piano pieces at the time. In 1907 he examined all the manuscripts in the Liszt-Haus, Weimar, having been commissioned to edit a centenary edition of Liszt's Collected Works.

2 Although largely self-taught as a composer, Busoni did have a year's formal training (1880–1) with Wilhelm Mayer [Rémy] at Graz.

3 Edward J. Dent, *Ferruccio Busoni—A Biography* (London, 1974), p. 230.

4 From the foreword to his edition of Liszt's Studies (Berlin, 1909). Reprinted in Ferruccio Busoni, *The Essence of Music and Other Papers*, trans. Rosamond Ley (London, 1957), p. 155.

5 Busoni, *Sketch of a New Aesthetic of Music*, trans. Th. Baker (New York, 1962), p. 89.

6 Ziehn emigrated to America in 1868 and was influential as a theorist and teacher in Chicago. He was the initial stimulus for the *Fantasia Contrappuntistica* and was the subject of an article by Busoni entitled *The Gothics of Chicago*. The influence of Ziehn's theory of symmetrical inversion (*Harmonie- und Modulationslehre*, Berlin 1888 and *Canonical Studies*, Milwaukee, 1912) on Busoni's work was considerable.

7 There exist several different versions of the *Fantasia*.

8 *The Essence of Music*, p. 20.

9 Roman Vlad, 'Busoni's Destiny', *The Score*, 7 (1952), pp. 3–10.

10 This point is discussed in detail in a penetrating paper (to which I am indebted in several respects) by John C. G. Waterhouse: 'Busoni: visionary or pasticheur?', *Proceedings of the Royal Musical Association* 92 (1965–6), pp. 79–94.

11 Such a symbol expresses vividly Busoni's interpretation of the legend in terms of man's, and specifically the artist's, duty to struggle for perfection even in the knowledge that the goal is an impossible one. Faust proclaims after the vision of Helen has eluded him, 'Man is not able to attain perfection. Then let him strive according to his measure and strew good around him, as he has received it.'

Chapter 3: New tonal languages

1 The transparent orchestral textures of *Parsifal* differ in some respects from those of *Tristan* and *The Ring* and they were to exert some influence on Debussy's orchestral style.

2 André Schaeffner, 'Debussy et ses rapports avec la musique Russe' in P. Souvtchinsky, *Musique Russe* (Paris, 1953), pp. 95–138.

3 The significance of the *Commedia dell' Arte* for Debussy's work is discussed in Wilfred Mellers, *Studies in Contemporary Music* (London, 1947), pp. 43–45.

4 Pierre Boulez has made the point admirably in his remarks on *Pelléas* which accompany his recording of the work: 'Notions of mystery and dream only acquire their real value beyond precision in perfect clarity.'

5 The sustained dominant major ninths in Debussy suggest at times striking parallels with the later music of Grieg, greatly admired by Debussy (a comparison of their quartets is instructive). Several such harmonic fingerprints in Grieg's music found their way into the music of Delius and ultimately into film music and popular *genres*.

6 In *Pagodes*, Debussy similarly highlights regions associated with the pentatonic scale which is the piece's most prominent harmonic resource.

7 In *Tonality—Atonality—Pantonality*, Reti discusses Debussy's music in relation to the 'melodic tonality' of oriental music and Gregorian chant. He refers to a marriage between this and the 'harmonic tonality' of Western traditions, a 'blending of two different tonal worlds'.

8 Igor Stravinsky and Robert Craft, *Conversations with Igor Stravinsky* (London, 1958), p. 48, and Serge Moreux, *Béla Bartók* (London, 1953), p. 92.

9 Busoni remarked on hearing the *Bagatelles*, 'At last here is something that is new'. Lajos Lesznai, *Bartók* (London, 1973), p. 70.

10 Edward T. Cone, 'Stravinsky: The Progress of a Method', *Perspectives on Schoenberg and Stravinsky*, ed. Benjamin Boretz and Edward T. Cone (Princeton, 1968), pp. 156–64.

11 Indeed the term 'bitonal' might be regarded as self-contradictory, if by 'tonal' we mean pertaining to a central point of reference.

12 G. W. Hopkins, 'Stravinsky's Chords (1)', *Tempo* 76 (Spring, 1966), pp. 6–12.

13 For further analytical comment on this movement see Edward T. Cone, 'Stravinsky: The Progress of a Method' in *Perspectives on Schoenberg and Stravinsky*, ed. Benjamin Boretz and Edward T. Cone (Princeton, 1968), pp. 156–64.

14 According to the fascinating and provocative theories of Erno Lendvai (*Béla Bartók: An Analysis of his Music*, London, 1971), this construction would be built upon both the tonic and dominant 'axes'. The C/F sharp relationship in the work would represent the 'principal branch'—the 'pole' and 'counterpole'—of its overall structure, while the violin's E/B flat relationship would represent a 'secondary branch'.

Chapter 4: 'A pull within the art'

1 Egon Wellesz has described how he found Schoenberg analysing the harmonies of *Salomé* during the period when he was composing the First Chamber Symphony: *The Origins of Schönberg's twelve-tone system*, a lecture delivered in the Library of Congress (Washington, 1958), p. 3. Indeed the opening cello theme from the chamber symphony may well have been modelled on the opening theme of Strauss's *Don Juan*. Later Schoenberg was to acknowledge a debt to Strauss, albeit grudgingly: 'Whatever I may have learnt from him, I am thankful to say I misunderstood.' Erwin Stein, ed., *Arnold Schoenberg: Letters* (London, 1964), p. 51.

2 For detailed comment see Gosta Neuwirth, *Die Harmonik in der Oper 'Der Ferne Klang'* (Regensburg, 1972).

3 Nicholas Chadwick, 'Franz Schreker's Instrumental Style and its Influence on Alban Berg', *Music Review* 35 (1974), pp. 29–46.

4 Wellesz, op. cit., pp. 4–5.

5 Patrick Gowers, 'Satie's Rose Croix Music (1891–1895)', *Proceedings of the Royal Musical Association* 92 (1965–6), pp. 1–26.

6 Wilfred Mellers discusses Koechlin's relationship to Satie in 'A Plea for Koechlin', *Music Review* 3 (1942), pp. 190–202.

7 Schmitt's harmonic and rhythmic innovations at times anticipate and may even have influenced the Stravinsky of *The Rite of Spring*. Martin Cooper, *French Music* (London, 1951), pp. 149–50.

8 Hans Hollander, *Janáček* (London, 1963), p. 119.

9 For Ives, integration would ideally be achieved on a 'transcendental' rather than a purely musical level. In this connection it is interesting to compare him with Mahler, who was similarly concerned to include many different stylistic worlds within his music but who achieved at the same time a tonal and thematic integration of his diverse materials. Beyond

this, Mahler's 'counterpoint of styles' very often has an ironic intention which is wholly absent from Ives.

10 It is intriguing to read of Elliott Carter's reaction to new styles and techniques in the twenties: 'Obviously it was easy even in the twenties to distinguish between Schoenberg, Stravinsky, Bartók and Varèse, but it was very hard to put your finger on what it was that made each so different. . . .' Allen Edwards, *Flawed Words and Stubborn Sounds: A Conversation with Elliott Carter* (New York, 1971), p. 44.

11 Schoenberg paid tribute to Zemlinsky's deep understanding of Brahms at a time when that composer was out of favour in 'progressive' circles: 'My Evolution', *Style and Idea*, p. 80.

12 Van Dieren's interest in a complex contrapuntal technique may well have been stimulated by his close friend Busoni. I am indebted to Mr Leslie East, however, for the provocative suggestion that certain harmonic procedures in Van Dieren's early pieces and sketches may in turn have influenced Busoni's more 'advanced' style. There is further discussion of the relationship between both composers in Wilfred Mellers, 'Bernard van Dieren 1884–1936: Musical Intelligence and "The New Language"', *Scrutiny* (December, 1936), pp. 263–76.

13 However daring and novel Rebikov's piano miniatures and 'musico-psychological dramas' may have seemed at the time, they appear somewhat inconsequential today, though there have been apologists (e.g. Alex Rowley, 'Rebikoff', *Music Review* 4 (1943), pp. 112–15).

14 According to H. Eimert the Russian composer Golyscheff also developed an independent twelve-note technique during the second decade; *Lehrbuch der Zwölftontechnik* (Wiesbaden, 1952), pp. 57–8.

15 Massimo Mila uses this designation in 'Itinerario Stilistico' from the symposium *Alfredo Casella*, ed. by Fedele d'Amico and Guido M. Gatti (Milan, 1958), p. 39.

16 Alfredo Casella, *The Evolution of Music* (London, 1924), xxi.

17 Casella, *21+26* (Milan, Rome, 1931), p. 18. (My translation.)

18 At Busoni's suggestion, Casella later made a version for piano and orchestra.

Chapter 5; Skryabin

1 Martin Cooper, 'Scriabin and the Russian Renaissance', *Ideas and Music* (London, 1965), pp. 127–34.

2 The descending minor ninth represented for Skryabin the 'descent of spirit into matter', the alternating whole-tone step up and down suggested the breathing of Brahma, creator of the world, and so on.

3 M. D. Calvocoressi and A. Eaglefield Hull, *Mussorgsky and Scriabin* (London, 1916) Part 2, p. 134.

4 Hugh Macdonald, 'Words and Music by A. Scriabin', *The Musical Times* 1547 (January, 1972), pp. 22–7.

5 The initial statement of the theme is built on an 'enhanced dominant' C sharp, with the F sharp added on a second statement at bar 68.

Chapter 6: Schoenberg

1 Willi Reich, *Schoenberg: A Critical Biography*, trans. by Leo Black (Edinburgh, 1971), p. 7.
2 Schoenberg, 'Heart and Brain in Music', *Style and Idea*, p. 53.
3 Alban Berg, 'Why is Schoenberg's music so difficult to understand?', printed in Rauchhaupt, op. cit., pp. 20–30.
4 Ibid., p. 16.
5 Webern, op. cit., p. 53.
6 Rauchhaupt, op. cit., p. 42.
7 Several passages in early Schoenberg suggest Beethoven as a conscious model. In his analysis of the D minor quartet (Rauchhaupt, p. 39), Schoenberg himself referred to the influence of the 'Eroica' Symphony on the structure of the work, and theme 3 suggests a conscious homage to the earlier composer. The Trio section from the Scherzo of the second quartet also begins with an idea strongly reminiscent of the Allegro from the first movement of Beethoven's Op. 132.
8 Cf. Op. 10, bars 31–5 and Op. 37, first movement, bars 160–4; also Op. 10, bars 80–3 and Op. 37, first movement, bars 57–60.
9 Rauchhaupt, p. 47.
10 Ibid., p. 17.
11 Theodor W. Adorno, *Philosophy of Modern Music*, trans. Anne G. Mitchell and Wesley V. Bloomster (London, 1973), p. 81.
12 Rauchhaupt, op. cit., p. 49.

Chapter 7: Berg and Webern

1 Rauchhaupt, op. cit., p. 122.
2 Chadwick, 'Berg's Unpublished Songs in the Österreichische Nationalbibliothek', *Music & Letters*, Vol. 52, No. 2 (April 1971), 123–40.
3 The interval structure (though not the spelling) of the chord is that of the 'French sixth', though of course it does not function tonally. It is worth mentioning that the 'French sixth' has an entirely different character to the other varieties of augmented sixth. Its whole-tone and symmetrical qualities render it tonally ambiguous—akin to Schoenberg's 'vagrant' harmonies—and it was popular with many composers of the late nineteenth and early twentieth centuries. Skryabin's progression (a), for example, has the interval structure of the 'French sixth'.
4 Schoenberg, 'Composition with Twelve Tones', *Style and Idea*, p. 128.
5 For further discussion of these works see Edward T. Cone, 'Webern's Apprenticeship', *The Musical Quarterly* LIII No. 1 (January 1967), pp. 39–72 and W. Wilsen, *Equitonality as a Measure of the Evolution towards Atonality in the Pre-Opus Songs of Anton Webern* (Ph.D. dissertation, Florida State University, 1975).
6 Walter Kolneder, *Anton Webern*, trans. Humphrey Searle (London, 1968), pp. 31–2.

Chapter 8: Szymanowski

1 Bogusław Maciejewski and Felix Aprahamian (eds.), *Karol Szymanowski and Jan Smeterlin: Correspondence and Essays* (London), pp. 85–92.

2 This was published in the Cracow literary magazine *Życie* in 1899. The Warsaw *Życie* (ed. Przesmycki) in which translations of Baudelaire, Rimbaud and Verlaine regularly appeared, was founded in 1887. Its Cracow counterpart, controlled by Przybeszewski, appeared a decade later.

3 Witold Rozycki, 'Reminiscences about Szymanowski', in Maciejewski, *Karol Szymanowski: His Life and Music* (London, 1967), p. 27.

4 Wagner's shadow falls unhappily on parts of the early works. notably the last of the *Four Studies*, Op. 4 (1900–2).

5 Szymanowski became acquainted with Russian music early in life when the Russian opera made its twice-yearly visits to Elisavetgrad, near the Szymanowski estate.

6 One is reminded of Schoenberg's use of symmetrical structures for similar expressive purposes in the *finale* of Op. 10.

7 Five new Hafiz songs were composed in 1914 and added to Nos. 1, 4 and 5 of Op. 24 to make a new cycle for voice and orchestra.

Chapter 9: Cross-currents

1 Busoni actually made a 'performing version' of Schoenberg's Op. 11, No. 2. The links between both composers are discussed in some detail in H. H. Stuckenschmidt, *Schönberg: Leben, Umwelt, Welt* (Zürich, 1974), pp. 200–12.

2 Schoenberg felt able to return to a tonal idiom intermittently during his later years in America, but only after the twelve-note technique had been consolidated.

3 Reich, op. cit., p. 23.

4 Stylistic affinities between Skryabin and Szymanowski go much further than this. They are discussed at length in Jozef M. Chominski, 'Szymanowski a Skriabin', *Studia nad Tworczoscia Karola Szymanowskiego* (PWM, 1969), pp. 37–112.

Chapter 10: Concept and terminology

1 Fétis was the first theorist to use the term in something like its present sense. See Bryan Simms, 'Choron, Fétis and the Theory of Tonality', *Journal of Music Theory* 19 (Spring, 1975), pp. 112–39.

2 Beswick, op. cit., pp. 1–29.

3 Matthew Shirlaw, *Theory of Harmony* (Illinois, 1955).

4 Lloyd Hibberd has suggested the term 'tonicality' (also used by Reti) to distinguish the broader meaning of tonality in 'Tonality and related Problems in Terminology', *The Music Review* 22 (1961), pp. 13–20.

5 Andres Biner, 'A New Comment on Tonality by Paul Hindemith', *Journal of Music Theory* 5 (1961), pp. 109–12.

6 Schoenberg objected to the term 'atonal'—'I have nothing to do with anything "atonal"'—in *Harmonielehre* (3rd ed. Vienna, 1921), footnote to pp. 487–8. See also Berg, 'What is "atonal"?' in Reich, op. cit., pp. 32–4 and Webern, op. cit., pp. 42.
7 Reti, *Tonality—Atonality—Pantonality*, pp. 60–1.
8 Ibid., p. 65.

Chapter 11: Atonality and tradition
1 Webern, op. cit., p. 36.
2 Reich, op. cit., p. 32.
3 Ibid., p. 32.
4 At least two commentators have referred to a centre of F for this movement. I am unable to see or hear this.
5 Webern's suggestion of an underlying G major tonality for Op. 15, No. 2 lends support to this type of investigation.
6 Reinhold Brinkmann, *Arnold Schoenberg: Drei Klavierstucke, Op. 11* (Wiesbaden, 1969).
7 Roy Travis, 'Directed Motion in Schoenberg and Webern', *Perspectives of New Music* (Spring–Summer 1966). Others have interpreted the C-E in the final bar of Op. 19, No. 2 as a subdominant rather than a tonic sonority.
8 Reich, op. cit., p. 34.
9 Hans Redlich, *Alban Berg: The Man and his Music* (London, 1957), p. 53.
10 Brinkmann, op. cit., and Hopkins, 'Schoenberg and the "logic" of atonality', *Tempo* 94 (Autumn, 1970), p. 15.
11 The only exception is in bars 18–19 where dyads have been grouped symmetrically around the pitches G and D flat.
12 Schoenberg, 'Composition with Twelve Tones', *Style and Idea*, p. 215.
13 Charles Rosen, *The Classical Style* (London, 1971), p. 460.
14 Anthony Payne, *Schoenberg* (London, 1968), pp. 21–5.
15 Webern, op. cit., p. 34.
16 Aaron Copland, *Our New Music* (New York and London, 1941), pp. 37–8.
17 The work was inspired by a poem 'May Night' written by Szymanowski's favourite poet, Micinski.
18 Redlich, op. cit., p. 94.
19 Reich, op. cit., p. 32.
20 Redlich, op. cit., pp. 69–70.
21 Webern, op. cit., p. 33.

Chapter 12: 'Free' atonality
1 Kandinsky, *Concerning the Spiritual in Art* (New York, 1947), p. 54. This edition is based on the first English translation by Michael Sadleir, though with some re-translations.
2 Schoenberg, 'My Evolution', *Style and Idea*, p. 88.
3 Webern, op. cit., p. 51.
4 Reich, op. cit., p. 33.

5 *Perspectives on Schoenberg and Stravinsky*, p. 27.
6 For detailed comment, see Elmar Budde, *Anton Weberns Lieder Op. 3* (Wiesbaden, 1971).
7 Heinz J. Dill, 'Schoenberg's George-lieder: The Relationship between the Text and the Music in light of some Expressionist Tendencies', *Current Musicology* 17 (1974), 91–5.
8 Schoenberg, 'Composition with Twelve Tones', *Style and Idea*, pp. 217–18.
9 Wolfgang Martin Stroh, 'Schoenberg's Use of Text: The Text as a Musical Control in the 14th *Georgelied*, Op. 15', *Perspectives of New Music* (Spring–Summer, 1966), pp. 35–44.
10 Unconvincing attempts have been made by Philip Friedheim to indicate the structural importance of rhythm, and by Walter and Alexander Goehr of melodic contour, in the work's overall form. An interesting insight is provided by Herbert H. Buchanan in 'A Key to Schoenberg's *Erwartung*, Op. 17', *Journal of the American Musicological Society* XX (Fall, 1967), pp. 434–49. He refers to the structural importance of a substantial quotation from Schoenberg's earlier song Op. 6, No. 6, together with an anticipatory section.
11 Reich, op. cit., p. 54.
12 In his analysis of Op. 22, *Perspectives on Schoenberg and Stravinsky*, p. 26.
13 Schoenberg, 'My Evolution', *Style and Idea*, p. 88.
14 Philip Friedheim, 'Rhythmic Structure in Schoenberg's Atonal compositions', *Journal of the American Musicological Society* XIX (Spring, 1966), pp. 59–72. For a rhythmic analysis of the fourth of Schoenberg's Op. 19 piano pieces see Grosvenor Cooper and Leonard B. Meyer, *The Rhythmic Structure of Music* (Chicago, 1960), pp. 174–7.

Chapter 13: Rappel à l'ordre
1 Schoenberg, 'Composition with Twelve Tones', *Style and Idea*, p. 219.
2 Webern, op. cit., p. 54.
3 Maciejewski, *Karol Szymanowsky: His Life and Music*, p. 68.
4 Ibid., p. 68.
5 *Correspondence and Essays*, p. 97.
6 Ibid., p. 102.
7 H. H. Stuckenschmidt, 'Karol Szymanowsky', *Music & Letters* (January, 1938), pp. 36–47.
8 Maciejewski, *Karol Szymanowsky: His Life and Music*, p. 81.
9 *Correspondence and Essays*, p. 98.
10 Faubion Bowers, *The New Scriabin* (London, 1974), p. 171.
11 Ibid., pp. 146–71.
12 George Perle, *Serial Composition and Atonality* (London, 1968), pp. 41–3.
13 David Lewin, 'Inversional Balance as an Organizing Force in Schoenberg's Music and Thought', *Perspectives of New Music* (Spring–Summer, 1968), pp. 1–21.
14 Brinkmann, op. cit.
15 Perle, op. cit., pp. 10–15.

16 Ibid., pp. 16–18.

17 Rauchhaupt, op. cit., p. 124.

18 Elaine Barkin comments interestingly on the quasi-serial exhaustivity of register in the first of these pieces in 'Registral Procedures in Schoenberg's Op. 23, No. 1', *Music Review* (May 1973), pp. 141–5.

19 Quite independently of Schoenberg, the Austrian composer Josef Mathias Hauer developed a twelve-note method in 1919 in his *Nomos*, Op. 19. Wellesz (op. cit.) considers Hauer's 'tropes' to have been an important influence on Schoenberg's formulation of the method.

20 In several articles and *The Structure of Atonal Music* (New Haven and London, 1974). Note also Jan Maegaard's statistical method of identifying different chord types in the pre-serial music of Schoenberg in *Studien zur Entwicklung des dodekaphonen Satzes bei Arnold Schönberg* (Kobenhavn, 1972).

21 Allen Forte, 'Sets and Nonsets in Schoenberg's Atonal Music', *Perspectives of New Music* (Fall–Winter, 1972), pp. 43–64.

22 Schoenberg assures us that the 'laws' governing the harmony of his pre-serial music became clear to him only after the process of composition, a process which he once described as 'trusting his hand'.

23 Forte, 'Sets and Nonsets in Schoenberg's Atonal Music', p. 52.

24 Ibid., p. 54.

25 Ibid., p. 44.

Appendix

1915   Szymanowski, *Songs of a Fairy-tale Princess*, Op. 31
1916   Szymanowski, First Violin Concerto, Op. 35
1917   Szymanowski, Third Piano Sonata, Op. 36
1922   Szymanowski, *Slopwienie*, Op. 46
         Bartók, Second Violin Sonata
1923   Stravinsky, Serenade in A
1924   Busoni, *Doktor Faust*
1932   Szymanowski, Second Violin Concerto, Op. 61

Bibliographical note

Much of the detailed analytical comment on twentieth-century music is to be found in periodical literature rather than books, and I have made frequent reference to this literature in the Notes. In addition to the full-length studies used extensively in the preparation of the book, I cite here a select number of relevant books which have appeared since its first edition.

Antokoletz, Elliott, *The Music of Béla Bartók* (Berkeley, Los Angeles and London, 1984)

Baker, James, *The Music of Alexander Scriabin* (New Haven, 1986)

Beaumont, Antony, *Busoni the Composer* (London, 1985)

Blaukopf, Kurt, *Mahler*, trans. Inge Goodwin (London, 1973)

Boretz, Benjamin, and Cone, Edward T. (eds.), *Perspectives on Schoenberg and Stravinsky* (Princeton, 1968)

Bowers, Faubion, *The New Scriabin* (London, 1974)

Brinkmann, Reinhold, *Arnold Schoenberg. Drei Klavierstücke Op. 11. Studien zur frühen Atonalität bei Schoenberg* (Wiesbaden, 1969)

Bujic, Bojan (ed.), *Music in European Thought 1851–1912* (Cambridge, 1988)

Busoni, Ferrucio Benvenuto, *Sketch of a New Aesthetic of Music*, trans. Rosamund Ley (London, 1957)

Cone, Edward T. *Music: A View from Delft*, ed. Robert P. Morgan (Chicago and London, 1989)

Cowell, Henry and Sidney, *Charles Ives and his Music* (London, 1955)

Dahlhaus, Carl, *Schoenberg and the New Music*, trans. Derrick Puffett and Alfred Clayton (Cambridge, 1987)

Dahlhaus, Carl, *Between Romanticism and Modernism: four studies in the music of the later nineteenth century*, trans. Mary Whittall (Berkeley, *c.* 1980)

Dent, Edward, *Ferrucio Busoni: A Biography* (London, 1974)

Dunsby, Jonathan, *Schoenberg: Pierrot Lunaire* (Cambridge, 1992)

Forte, Allen, *The Structure of Atonal Music* (New Haven and London, 1974)

Forte, Allen, *The Harmonic Organization of 'The Rite of Spring'* (New Haven, 1978)

Gable, David and Morgan, Robert (eds.), *Alban Berg: Historical and Theoretical Perspectives* (Oxford, 1991)

George, Graham, *Tonality and Musical Structure* (London, 1970)

Gilliam, Bryan, *Richard Strauss's Elektra* (Oxford, 1991)

Griffiths, Paul, *Bartók* (London, 1984)

Griffiths, Paul, *Stravinsky* (London, 1992)

Haimo, Ethan, *Schoenberg's Serial Odyssey: The Evolution of his 12-note Method* (Oxford, 1990)

Howat, Roy, *Debussy in Proportion: A Musical Analysis* (Cambridge, 1983)

Jarman, Doublas, *Alban Berg: Wozzeck* (Cambridge, 1989)

Jarman, Douglas, *The Music of Alban Berg* (London, 1979)

Kárpáti, János, *Bartók's String Quartets*, trans. Fred Macnicol (Budapest, 1967)

Kerman, Joseph (ed.), *Music at the Turn of the Century* (Berkeley and Los Angeles, 1990)
Kolneder, Walter, *Anton Webern: An Introduction to his Works*, trans. Humphrey Searle (London, 1968)
Lendvai, Ernö, *The Workshop of Bartók and Kodály* (Budapest, 1983)
Lester, Joel, *Analytic Approaches to Twentieth-Century Music* (London and New York, 1989)
Lewis, Christopher Orlo, *Tonal Coherence in Mahler's Ninth Symphony* (Michigan, 1984)
MacDonald, Malcolm, *Schoenberg* (London, 1976)
Moldenhauer, Hans, *Anton von Webern* (London, 1978)
Nichols, Roger, *Debussy* (London, 1972)
Nichols, Roger and Langham Smith, Richard, *Claude Debussy: Pelleas et Melisande* (Cambridge, 1989)
Parks, Richard, *The Music of Claude Debussy* (New Haven, 1989)
Pasler, Jann (ed.), *Confronting Stravinsky* (Berkeley, 1986)
Payne, Anthony, *Schoenberg* (London, 1968)
Perle, George, *Serial Composition and Atonality: An Introduction to the Music of Schoenberg, Berg and Webern* (London, 1968)
Pople, Anthony, *Skryabin and Stravinsky, 1908–14: Studies in Theory and Analysis* (New York, 1989)
Pople, Anthony, *Berg Violin Concerto* (Cambridge, 1991)
Puffett, Derrick, *Richard Strauss's Salome* (Cambridge, 1989)
Puffett, Derrick, *Richard Strauss's Elektra* (Cambridge, 1989)
Rauchhaupt, U. von (ed.), *Schoenberg, Berg, Webern: The String Quartets. A Documentary Study*, trans. Eugene Hartzel (Hamburg, 1971)
Redlich, Hans, *Alban Berg: The Man and his Music* (London, 1957)
Reich, Willi, *Schoenberg: A Critical Biography*, trans. Leo Black (Edinburgh, 1971)
Reti, Rudolph. *Tonality—Atonality—Pantonality* (London, 1958)
Rosen, Charles, *Schoenberg* (London, 1976)
Samson, Jim, *The Music of Szymanowski* (London and New York, 1980)
Samson, Jim (ed.), *The Late Romantic Era: Man & Music Vol. 7* (London, 1992)
Schmalfeldt, Janet, *Berg's 'Wozzeck': Harmonic Language and Design* (New Haven, 1983)
Schoenberg, Arnold, *Style and Idea* (ed.), Leonard Stein, trans. Leo Black (London, 1969)
Schoenberg, Arnold, *Structural Functions in Music*, ed. Leonard Stein (London, 1969)
Straus, Joseph N., *Remaking the Past: Musical Modernism and the Tonal Tradition* (Cambridge, Mass., 1990)
Straus, Joseph N., *Introduction to Post-Tonal Theory* (New Jersey, 1990)
Tallián, Tibor, *Béla Bartók: the Man and his Work*, trans. Gyula Gulyás (Budapest, 1981)
Tyrrell, John, *Leos Janácek: Kát'a Kabanová* (Cambridge, 1982)
Ujfalussy, Jozsef, *Béla Bartók*, trans. Ruth Pataki (Budapest, 1971)
Van den Toorn, Pieter C., *The Music of Igor Stravinsky* (New Haven, 1983)
Van den Toorn, Pieter C., *Stravinsky and the Rite of Spring: The Beginnings of a Musical Language* (Oxford, 1987)
Walsh, Stephen, *The Music of Stravinsky* (London, 1988)
Webern, Anton, *The Path to the New Music*, ed. Willi Reich, trans. Leo Black (Pennsylvania, 1963)
Whittall, Arnold, *Schoenberg Chamber Music* (London, 1972)
Wilson, Paul, *The Music of Bartók* (New Haven, 1992)

Index of names and titles

Index

Index

Van Gogh, Vincent, 121
Varèse, Edgard, 22, 227
Vaughan Williams, Ralph, 41, 66, 72
Verdi, Giuseppe, 20, 27
Verlaine, Paul, 63, 229
Vlad, Roman, 28, 225
Vomacka, Boleslaw, 73

Wagner, Richard, 3, 4–6, 8, 9, 10, 14, 15, 17, 19, 20, 33, 34, 35, 41, 61, 79, 81, 93, 94, 100, 110, 126, 143, 229
Waterhouse, J. C. G., 225
Watts, G. F., 79
Webern, Anton von, 14, 19, 100, 109, 115–16, 126–8, 137, 144, 148, 162, 164, 168, 174, 177–97, 211–21, 223, 228, 230; Concerto for Nine Instruments, Op. 24, 196; *Entflieht auf leichten Kahnen*, Op. 2, 127–8; Five Canons, Op. 16, 127; Five Movements for String Quartet, Op. 5, 164, 174, 180, 214, 219; Five Orchestral Pieces, Op. 10, 182, 186, 190, 195, 197, 212, 219; Five Songs, Op. 3, 128, 181, 214; Five Songs, Op. 4, 181, 191, 212; *Gefunden*, 126; *Im Sommerwind*, 126; *Heimgang in der Fruhe*, 126; *Helle Nacht*, 126; *Nachtgebet der Braut*, 126; Passacaglia, Op. 1, 126, 127, 128; *Path to the New Music, The*, 100, 173; Piano Quintet, 127; Six Bagatelles, Op. 9, 116, 182, 219; 'Slow Movement' for String Quartet, 126; String Quartet, 126–7; Three Pieces for Cello and Piano, Op. 11, 182, 184, 186, 191, 196, 217, 219; Three Pieces for Violin and Piano, Op. 7, 182, 212; *Vorfruhling*, 126
Wedekind, Frank, 59
Wellesz, Egon, 62, 70–1, 144, 226, 232
Wilsen, W., 228
Wolf, Hugo, 7, 61, 93

Yasser, Joseph, 151
Yeats, W. B., 79
Young Poland, 130

Zelenski, Wladyslaw, 129
Zemlinsky, Alexander von, 70, 93, 144, 227
Ziehn, Bernhard, 26, 225